Ma... ...ent... ...om... ...e
for the Hospitality, Tourism
and Leisure Industries

Management Accounting
for the Hospitality, Tourism and Leisure Industries
A Strategic Approach

second edition

Debra Adams

THOMSON™

Australia • Canada • Mexico • Singapore • Spain • United Kingdom • United States

Management Accounting for the Hospitality, Tourism and Leisure Industries:
A Strategic Approach, Second Edition
Debra Adams

Publishing Director John Yates	**Publisher** Jennifer Pegg	**Editorial Assistant** Natalie Aguilera
Production Editor Alissa Chappell	**Manufacturing Manager** Helen Mason	**Marketing Manager** Leo Stanley
Typesetter Gray Publishing, Tunbridge Wells	**Production Controller** Maeve Healy	**Cover Design** Ian Youngs
Text Design Design Deluxe, Bath, UK	**Printer** Zrinski dd., Croatia	

Contents

Part I: Introduction 1

An introduction to the concept of strategic management and the application of finance and accounting information to the decision-making process in a business operation.

Part II: External analysis 69

To analyse the business, economic, structural and competitive forces that shape organizational strategies and industry positioning.

Part III: Internal appraisal 123

To examine strategic frameworks for portfolio, operations and resource analysis.

Part IV: Strategic options 201

To examine the methods used to generate and evaluate strategic options, strategies for change and the issues associated with planning for change.

Part V: Strategic implementation and evaluation 273

To examine ways of monitoring business strategy, achieving structure and strategy alignment and sustaining strategic focus.

Preface

In today's world the business organization is operating in an environment that is in a continual state of change owing to increasing advances in technology, fluctuating economic climates and changing workforce and customer expectations. To navigate a successful passage through these turbulent conditions, business managers must possess the skills and competences to enable them to make effective decisions and control business performance.

This second edition of this textbook has been written and updated with the purpose of providing the manager working in the hospitality, tourism and leisure industries with a practical understanding of the key financial aspects of business management and control to improve the level of effective decision making in the strategic management process. The emphasis is on how financial management theories and techniques can be used in practice to support the decision-making process with examples based on the business sector.

The process of strategic management is normally regarded as an integrated approach to the processes of planning, implementing and evaluating business strategy to maximize the ability of the organization to meet its objectives. The first step in the process is to define clearly the long-term goals and objectives of the organization. These usually include maintaining a balance between maximizing shareholder value and ensuring the long-term sustainability of the organization. Strategic analysis includes a review of the external environment in which the business operates to establish the current positioning of the organization and also where it is likely to be operating in the future. This external analysis includes a review of competitors, suppliers, customers, the economy, governmental influences, and legal and other regulatory changes. Increasingly, the role of technology for enhancing distribution channels as well as improving product delivery and evaluation of results is essential for ensuring competitive advantage in a crowded marketplace. The external analysis should be combined with a rigorous internal analysis of all resources and internal operations. Consequently, having established where the organization is currently positioned and where it wants to go, it is possible to develop a range of business strategies for implementation.

Modern strategic management theory suggests that the speed of change is such that the strategic management process can no longer be implemented as a linear step-by-step process, but that an ongoing integrated approach is required. As a result, the requirement for strategic management accounting information to support the strategic decision-making and control process has never been more vital.

Frequently, the finance function in organizations is now regarded as a service activity with both internal and external customers. Key activities include the provision of accurate record-keeping while meeting the statutory requirements and recommendations for corporate governance. In addition to this, the internal users of accounting data require information that will enable them to monitor past performance and to forecast and plan future performance effectively.

Traditionally, the role of management accounting has been heavily biased towards the comparison of costs with revenues, focusing on the internal operations of the business. Accounts are, by definition, historical and inward-looking, and the process of accounting is governed by the underlying concept of prudence. However, there is a need in most organizations for accounting information to be produced with a strategic perspective in mind. This involves considering not just the internal operations but also the external environment and the impact of the competition.

If used effectively, the process of strategic financial management can provide the financial information required to monitor existing business strategies and provide support for strategy formulation. Consequently, this book has been written to follow the chronology of the strategic decision-making process with the aim of placing management accounting in the context of strategic decision making, to enable managers to use accounting information to support them in the decision-making process.

The chapters in Part 1 start with a review of the basic principles and practices of financial management and strategic management. They include an introduction to the strategic management process and an overview of rudimentary accounting practices and techniques. These chapters are intended for those who have limited knowledge of financial accounting. The chapters in Parts 2 and 3 are designed to provide a range of tools and techniques to support the processes of internal and external audit. The aim of Part 2 is to address the role of financial information in a strategic review of the environment. It examines the role of competitor accounting, strategic cost analysis and pricing. Part 3 covers the strategic process of internal appraisal, focusing on budgetary control, working capital control and performance measurement. Part 4 focuses on the determination of corporate strategy, providing chapters on financing, investment appraisal, risk assessment and cost of capital measurement. Part 5 concludes by considering the future of the hospitality, tourism and leisure industry and the impact, in particular, of globalization and information technology.

In general, the approach adopted throughout the text is to demonstrate the financial technique under discussion with appropriate examples drawn from the sector. Some financial techniques have been given greater prominence than might be normally expected because of their particular relevance to the sector. Chapter 13, on business valuations, is such an example. Where possible, the financial theories have been illustrated with practical insights based on research drawn from the industry sector and the author's own experience based on over 15 years of being associated with the UK hospitality and tourism industry.

Every effort has been made to quote the sources of material and to seek permission to reproduce tables and diagrams from other sources. I am particularly grateful to the British Association of Hospitality Accountants who have kindly given permission for a range of materials and examples to be used in this textbook.

This book is intended for final-year undergraduate programmes and postgraduate courses in hospitality, tourism and leisure management and related disciplines. This book will also be useful for middle to senior managers working in the sector, particularly those engaged in management development programmes. A range of additional resources is available for facilitators and tutors.

Finally, I am delighted that this book has been used for a number of years for both non-financial students and accounting students requiring more knowledge about the hospitality, tourism and leisure industries. I hope that you enjoy this new second edition.

Debra J. Adams
April 2006

The second edition

My thanks to those users of the first edition of this text who have put forward their suggestions for the improvement of this new edition.

This new edition includes:

- learning objectives for every chapter
- additional case-study material with questions provided
- additional questions and answers on the key topic areas
- in Part I, an update on international accounting standards and the regulations associated with corporate governance
- in Part II, an update on strategic management processes
- in Part III, an update on performance measurement techniques including an overview of the balanced scorecard methodology
- in Part IV, an update on the alternative techniques available for funding expansion in the hospitality, tourism and leisure industries
- in Part V, an update on internationalization and global issues.

Acknowledgements

This book could not have been written without the support of a number of people who provided me with support and advice.

I would like to thank the following companies for permission to extract information from their annual reports and accounts including: InterContinental Hotels, Radisson Hotels and Resorts, Walt Disney Company, Hilton Hotel Group, Thomas Cook, easyJet, Four Seasons and British Airways.

My thanks are due to the editors of the *Financial Times*, *The Times* Online and the *Leisure Property Report*.

I would also like to thank my editors, Natalie Aguilera and Jennifer Pegg, for their long-suffering patience awaiting the revisions to this edition.

Finally, I must include a huge thank you to my family for their continuing support throughout.

The companion website

Visit the companion website at: www.thomsonlearning.co.uk/adams2
to find a range of teaching and learning materials for facilitators, including the
following:

For students:

- multiple-choice questions
- links to relevant sites on the World Wide Web
- glossary explaining key terms mentioned in the text

For tutors:

- downloadable lecturer's guide
- downloadable PowerPoint slides
- additional questions and answers
- extra case studies and guidelines.

Walk through tour

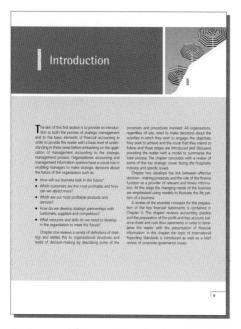

Part opener An overview of each section of the book, detailing how the chapters link together.

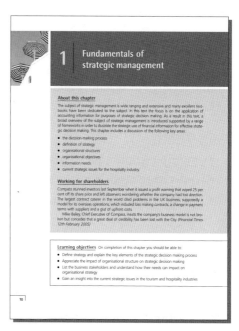

Chapter opener Bullet points highlight the main topics covered, and the learning objectives for each chapter.

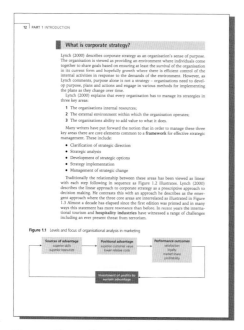

Figures Figures illustrate key points in the text in a clear and accessible manner.

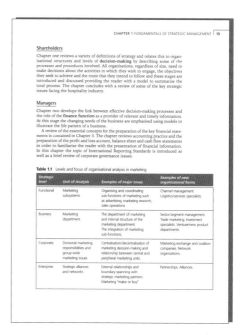

Tables Tables provide a useful range of relevant data relating to each chapter's content.

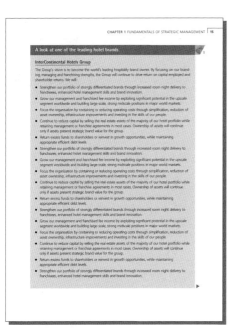

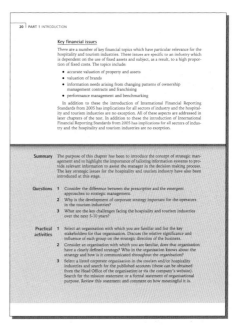

Case studies Real-life case studies demonstrate the practical implications of management accounting in tourism, hospitality and leisure industries.

End-of-chapter features Each chapter ends with a set of questions covering the core content, a summary of the chapter, a list of further reading, and a list of websites for further reading.

Introduction

The aim of this first section is to provide an introduction to both the process of strategic management and the basic elements of financial management accounting. This approach assumes that the reader has little prior knowledge of these aspects and aims to provide a basic level of understanding before embarking on the application of management accounting to the strategic management process. Organizational accounting and management information systems have a crucial role in enabling managers to make strategic decisions about the future of the organization, such as:

- How will our business look in the future?
- Which customers are the most profitable and how can we attract more?
- Which are our most profitable products and services?
- How do we develop strategic partnerships with customers, suppliers and competitors?
- What resources and skills do we need to develop in the organization to meet the demands of the future?

Chapter 1 reviews a variety of definitions of strategy and relates this to organizational structures and levels of decision making by describing some of the processes and procedures involved. All organizations, regardless of size, need to make decisions about the activities in which they wish to engage, the objectives they seek to achieve and the route that they intend to follow, and these stages are introduced and discussed, providing the reader with a model to summarize the total process. The chapter concludes with a review of some of the key strategic issues facing the hospitality, tourism and leisure industries and specific issues relating to financial management.

Chapter 2 develops the link between effective decision-making processes and the role of the finance function as a provider of relevant and timely information. At this stage the changing needs of the business are emphasized using models to illustrate the life pattern of a business.

A review of the essential concepts for the preparation of the key financial statements is contained in Chapter 3. The chapter reviews accounting practice and the preparation of the profit and loss account, balance sheet and cash-flow statements to familiarize the reader with the presentation of financial information. In this chapter the topic of International Reporting Standards is introduced, along with a brief review of corporate governance issues.

1 | Introducing strategic management

About this chapter

The subject of strategic management is wide ranging and extensive and many excellent textbooks have been dedicated to the subject. In this text the focus is on the application of accounting information for purposes of strategic decision making. As a result, in this text a broad overview of the subject of strategic management is introduced, supported by a range of frameworks to illustrate the strategic use of financial information for effective strategic decision making. This chapter includes a discussion of the following key areas:

- the decision-making process
- definition of strategy
- organizational structures
- organizational objectives
- information needs
- current strategic issues for the hospitality industry.

Case study: Working for shareholders

Compass stunned investors last September when it issued a profit warning that wiped 25% off its share price and left observers wondering whether the company had lost direction. The largest contract caterer in the world cited problems in the UK business, supposedly a model for its overseas operations, which included loss-making contracts, a change in payment terms with suppliers and a glut of upfront costs.

Mike Bailey, Chief Executive of Compass, insists the company's business model is not broken but concedes that a great deal of credibility has been lost with the City.

Source: *Financial Times*, 12 February 2005

Questions relating to this news story may be found on page 19.

Learning objectives On completion of this chapter you should be able to:

- define strategy and explain the key elements of the strategic decision-making process
- appreciate the impact of organizational structure on strategic decision making
- list the business stakeholders and understand how their needs can impact on organizational strategy
- gain an insight into the current strategic issues in the tourism and hospitality industries.

Introduction

In the first edition of this text this chapter opened with the statement:

For the modern hospitality business faced with the challenge of operating in increasingly diverse markets it is essential, therefore, that the processes of strategic management are as effective as possible. All organizations need to make decisions about the nature of their business activities to ensure that the resources are put to the best possible uses whilst ensuring that customer needs remain satisfied.

Almost a decade has elapsed since the first edition was printed and in many ways this statement has more resonance than before. In recent years the international tourism and hospitality industries have witnessed a range of challenges including an ever-present threat from terrorism, the growth of the spread of pandemic diseases, as well as increasing globalization and changing consumer preferences and lifestyles.

Strategic management as defined by Ward (1992) is regarded to be 'the integrated management approach to combining the individual processes required for planning, implementing and controlling a business strategy'. He suggests that it is important for every organization to continually review its activities in order to bridge the gap between where it is now and where it would like to be. This 'ideal position' is unique to each organization and is dependent on the long-term organizational goals and objectives that have been set over a period during which the external environment will continue to change. As a result, one can no longer assume that a strategy will lead to a fixed conclusion. Instead, the organization needs continually to monitor, control and adapt the business strategy, and this process is reliant on the provision of accurate and relevant accounting-based information.

The hospitality and tourism sector is a large and diverse sector with the overall purpose of providing food, drink, accommodation and leisure activities. The Sector Skills Council (SSC) for the hospitality, leisure, travel and tourism sector includes 14 industries in its definition of the sector:

- hotels
- restaurants
- pubs, bars and nightclubs
- contract food service providers
- membership clubs
- events
- gambling
- travel services
- tourist services
- visitor attractions
- youth hostels
- holiday parks
- self-catering accommodation
- hospitality services.

This text attempts to demonstrate a range of accounting tools and techniques to assist managers in the decision-making process with examples specifically based on the needs of the sector, where meeting expectations for customer service and quality of visitor experience is central to the business purpose.

The decision-making process

Drury (2005) describes the decision-making process as comprising five stages which represent the decision-making or planning process, followed by a final two stages which represent the control process. This approach is summarised in Figure 1.1.

This approach assumes that corporate decision making is a linear, rational approach where the corporate objectives have been defined in advance. In practice, the definition of corporate objectives can be a complex process. It is widely assumed that the main objective of a business is to maximize profits. However, this objective has to be balanced with the objectives of the key business stakeholders and the implications of this are described in more detail later. Drury (2005) suggests that, broadly speaking, firms seek to maximize the value of future net cash inflows, which is equivalent to maximizing shareholder value.

Figure 1.1 The decision-making, planning and control process

Source: Reproduced with permission from Drury (2005) *Management Accounting for Business,* p. 9.

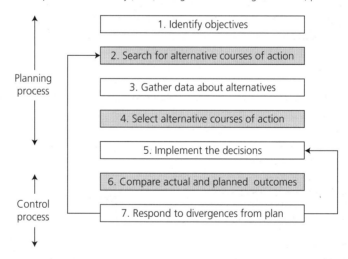

What is corporate strategy?

Lynch (2000) describes corporate strategy as an organization's sense of purpose. The organization is viewed as providing an environment where individuals come together to share goals based on ensuring at least the survival of the organization in its current form and hopefully growth where there is efficient control of the internal activities in response to the demands of the environment. However, as

Lynch comments, purpose alone is not a strategy: organizations need to develop purpose, plans and actions and engage in various methods for implementing the plans as they change over time.

Lynch (2000) explains that every organization has to manage its strategies in three key areas:

- The organization's internal resources
- The external environment within which the organization operates
- The organization's ability to add value to what it does.

Many writers have put forward the notion that to manage these three key areas there are core elements common to a framework for effective strategic management. These include:

- clarification of strategic direction
- strategic analysis
- development of strategic options
- strategy implementation
- management of strategic change.

Traditionally, the relationship between these areas has been viewed as linear, with each step following in sequence as Figure 1.2 illustrates. Lynch (2000) describes the linear approach to corporate strategy as a prescriptive approach to decision making. He contrasts this with an approach that he describes as the emergent approach, where the three core areas are interrelated, as illustrated in Figure 1.3. The differences between these two approaches for developing strategy are summarized in Table 1.1.

Figure 1.2 Linear approach to strategy development and implementation

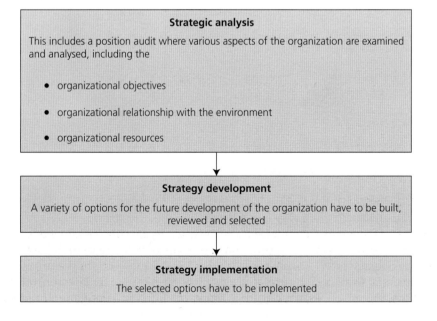

Figure 1.3 Emergent approach for developing strategy

Source: Adapted from Lynch (2000) *Corporate Strategy*, p. 61.

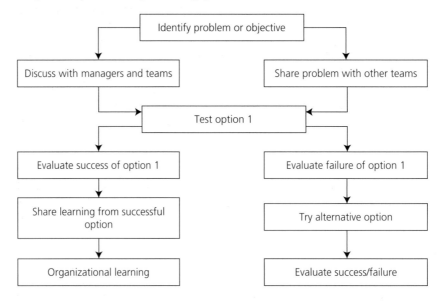

Table 1.1 Prescriptive and emergent approaches to corporate strategy

Prescriptive approaches	Emergent approaches
Top–down approach to strategic management	A responsive approach based on a shared understanding across the business
Reliant on the use of analytical tools such as SWOT and PESTLE, and matrices such as the Boston Consulting Group Matrix	Based on organizational learning
	Most effective in conditions of economic and environmental uncertainty
Most effective approach when the business environment is stable	
Planned approach based on a linear step process for implementation	

Organizational structure

The way in which an organization approaches corporate decision making and strategy management will very much depend on the organizational structure. The term structure used in the organizational sense refers to the way in which capital and human resources are arranged, and has a considerable effect on the operation of the business.

A review of texts on the subject of organizational change will demonstrate that organizations can be structured in a range of different configurations. Organizational structures can be classified according to a number of characteristic features.

The classical style is characterised by a strict hierarchy and clearly defined roles for each level. Such structures operate like a machine that is most effective under stable market conditions. However, such a structure is lacking in flexibility and is unable to react effectively in changing market conditions. The behavioural style places greater emphasis on personal responsibility and participation in decision making and, as a result, tends to stimulate greater commitment to organizational goals. In a small business decision making is highly centralized and there is often little need for formal procedures and policies. The organizational structure tends to be much simpler and, therefore, it should be easier to develop the vision statement into a set of relevant goals on which the business objectives can then be set. However, as the business grows a decision-making hierarchy needs to be employed and the challenge is to create a structure that combines flexibility and responsiveness with the controls and procedures required to deliver the business objectives.

Often, as the organization becomes larger and more structurally complex it becomes increasingly difficult to align business objectives because organizations rarely function as total entities. Instead, there are various functional activities such as operations, marketing, finance and personnel which make up the whole, and the long-term corporate objectives need to be broken down into separate but integrated strategies for each functional activity.

As the organization becomes even larger it will tend to subdivide into much smaller areas of responsibility. This can be achieved by splitting the organization into separate divisions. Each separate division may then have its own set of functional activities. Where managers have a considerable level of discretion these divisions are known as strategic business units (SBUs). Each SBU will normally have its own customers and market segment and the vast majority of strategic planning may be undertaken at this level.

Organizations are tending to move away from hierarchical structures favoured by the classical approach and are instead moving toward flatter structures achieved by 'delayering' the organization.

Mission statements

Every organization should have a clear vision for the future and this is usually summarized in the mission statement or its vision and values statement. Articulating the business mission is one way to ensure that employees are aware of the business vision. Some mission statements are several pages in length, while other companies choose to summarize in one sentence.

Case study: A look at one of the leading hotel brands: InterContinental Hotels Group

The Group's vision is to become the world's leading hospitality brand owner. By focusing on our branding, managing and franchising strengths, the Group will continue to drive return on capital employed and shareholder returns. We will:

- Strengthen our portfolio of strongly differentiated brands through increased room night delivery to franchisees, enhanced hotel management skills and brand innovation.

▶

- Grow our management and franchised fee income by exploiting significant potential in the upscale segment worldwide and building large-scale, strong mid-scale positions in major world markets.
- Focus the organization by containing or reducing operating costs through simplification, reduction of asset ownership, infrastructure improvements and investing in the skills of our people.
- Continue to reduce capital by selling the real estate assets of the majority of our hotel portfolio while retaining management or franchise agreements in most cases. Ownership of assets will continue only if assets present strategic brand value for the group.
- Return excess funds to shareholders or reinvest in growth opportunities, while maintaining appropriate efficient debt levels.

Source: InterContinental website (www.ichotelsgroup.com)

Nowadays many organizations prefer a short, concise statement to communicate the organization's aims. The following statement summarizes the vision for Radisson Hotels and Resorts:

Radisson Hotels & Resorts, a leading, global hotel company, operates, manages and franchises full-service hotels and resorts worldwide. From its franchise partners and strategic allies, to every manager and employee at every hotel, the Radisson organization is committed to providing personalized, professional guest service and 'Genuine Hospitality' at every point of guest contact in 435 hotels, representing more than 102,000 guest rooms in 61 countries.

Radisson is pursuing a vision supported by strategies and structures that defines the company as a global leader distinguished by:

- Great Places in Great Places – Having the right hotels in the right markets with a dedicated new division to develop owned and managed hotels, supplementing growth through high quality franchise locations.
- Building a Recognized and Trusted Brand
- Building Valued Relationships with the Guests it Serves
- Achieving Superior Returns for Owners and Investors.

Source: Radisson website (www.radisson.com/aboutus/story.jsp)

Organizational objectives

In the majority of organizations in the tourism and hospitality industry the setting of goals and objectives will be influenced by the people who control and work in the organization. The primary purpose of all profit-making organizations is to add value over and above the goods and services bought in or created by the organization.

However, this fundamental objective is often complicated by the actions of stakeholders both internal and external to the organization, with the result that actual activities pursued may be in conflict with the fundamental purpose of the organization. Increasingly, the time-frame over which objectives are considered is also important, often resulting in a conflict between short-term returns and long-term investment.

Case study: Walt Disney

The Walt Disney Company's objective is to be one of the world's leading producers and providers of entertainment and information, using its portfolio of brands to differentiate its content, services and consumer products. The company's primary financial goals are to maximize earnings and cash flow, and to allocate capital profitability toward growth initiatives that will drive long-term shareholder value.

Source: Walt Disney website (http://corporate.disney.go.com/investors/index.html)

The profit motive

Adding value requires making a profit on goods and services by selling these at a price in excess of the total cost of delivering the product to the customer. While most organizations aim to maximize profit growth and return on investment, the reality is that the profit maximization motive is undermined by the objectives of those stakeholders who are able to influence the organization the most. Economists argue that the pursuit of profit maximization in a competitive environment leads to economic efficiency. However, although the concept of economic efficiency is clearly desirable it is also difficult to measure in practice. Therefore, the performance of a business is typically measured quantitatively using ratios such as return on capital employed where profit is compared to the capital investment. The practical measurement of efficiency and effectiveness is much more difficult and is often a matter of subjective judgement. Each stakeholder group will seek to gain influence over a different aspect of business performance and the extent of their influence will depend on the relative strength of that stakeholder group. These stakeholder groups will now be considered in more detail.

Stakeholders

The typical range of business stakeholders or interested parties is illustrated in Figure 1.4. The power of each of these groups in relation to the other is very relevant and may change over time.

Conflict can arise between the stakeholder groups, resulting in a range of business strategies chosen to meet the demands of the most dominant groups. This means that the resulting objectives of the organization are varied and certainly are

Figure 1.4 Business stakeholders

Shareholders		Managers
Society	Company	Employees
Lenders		Customers
	Suppliers	

influenced by factors other than profit maximization because each stakeholder is deriving a different reward from the existence of the business. Each of the stakeholders will now be considered in turn.

Shareholders

Shareholders are investors who have purchased a stake in the organization. In the UK the vast majority of investors purchasing shares via the capital markets are institutional investors rather than individuals. The nature of the investor will impact on their target levels of risk and return, but typically investors in a large, international, well-diversified organization are essentially concerned with a competitive return on capital employed from their investment in the form of dividends and capital growth, which is the growth in the traded share price. These are obviously both functions of the profitability of the business and will therefore influence future business strategy. The need to pay out a reasonable dividend in relation to the investor's capital investment means that the business needs to make a level of profit sufficient to fund the dividend while allowing sufficient funds to remain within the business, in the form of retained profits, to finance growth. Failure to do this leads to shareholder dissatisfaction, with a possible fall in share price as investors disinvest, undermining the market confidence in the company. The power of the shareholder group intent on pursuing the profit maximization objective has led some business operators to review their dependence on the equities market, with the result that previously listed companies have returned to private ownership.

Managers

The management of the company have been engaged by the shareholders to maximize the profitability of the organization and are rewarded with a salary and terms and conditions in return for achieving this. In practice, this concept can be undermined by the interests of the individuals in the management team and this is commonly known as the 'agency problem'. Consequently, managers pursue a profit level that they perceive to be in excess of the minimum level acceptable to shareholders, but which also allows them to achieve their own personal goals. The managerial theorist O. E. Williamson (1990) lists these personal goals as being not only salary, but also security, status, power, prestige and professional excellence. As a result, the pursuit of profit maximization through cost reduction is undermined because expenditure contributes to gaining power, status and prestige. Many of the non-monetary rewards have the benefit of being hidden from others within the business and external shareholders, and are not subject to taxation. The structure of the organization is also relevant as this determines the level of influence exerted by the management group, emphasising the effect of ownership separate from control.

Employees

The strength of the employee group will depend on the nature of the workforce. Highly skilled permanent staff have increased power compared with a poorly skilled part-time workforce. A powerful group will pursue objectives which include increased salaries, improved working conditions and effective lines of communication. Highly unionized industry sectors are subject to extensive employee influence on corporate strategy. The levels of unionization in tourism and hospitality industries have traditionally been very low and the sector employs large numbers of part-time workers. However, increasing skill shortages in key areas such as food preparation and service have provided the workforce with the lever to demand improved working conditions and opportunities for professional development and training.

Customers

The power of the customer centres on the products and services being offered and the perceived value for money. That is the relationship between the benefits of purchasing the goods and services and the price of acquiring them. The strength of the consumer group will depend on the market conditions in which the purchase is to be made. Customers may also pay particular attention to any strategic threats that could arise from the company becoming involved in their own existing areas of trading.

Suppliers

This group of stakeholders is essentially interested in guaranteed long-term custom from the organization. At a practical level suppliers are able to exert pressure for quick payment of outstanding invoices, thereby influencing business decisions relating to the management of working capital. In return, the organization will press for improved terms and conditions with regard to product quality and delivery patterns. The level of influence of this stakeholder group will depend on the reliance of the organization on a supplier and the availability of the product required.

Lenders

This group will require that the returns of the organization are sufficient to service the cost of the debt invested with the provision for capital repayments to be made in the future. The debt holder may also form part of the decision-making team to oversee the management of the debt, thereby influencing business strategy.

Society

The power of this group will be depend on the strength of opinion of the collective and the ability of the group to have a significant effect on the business. In recent times environmental issues have become more significant and organizations have been forced to adapt their policies and procedures accordingly. This has been the result of increasing public demand for change coupled with the desire to avoid negative publicity.

Governmental influence in the form of legislation may affect the operation of the business. In the hospitality industry a recent example of governmental intervention affecting business operations is the requirements of the Food Hygiene Regulations, where investment in equipment and training has been required to meet government standards.

Incentives in the form of tax allowances or grants may serve to encourage investment in certain industries and locations. Local or even national government may show an interest and attempt to influence business decisions where strategy calls for large investment or the scaling down of operations resulting in widespread redundancies.

Goal congruence

It is possible for different stakeholder groups to have varied and possibly conflicting areas of interest in the organization and each group will try to influence business strategy accordingly. In an ideal world managers in the organization should aim to reflect the objectives of the shareholders and to a certain extent this does happen, as managers who forget their responsibilities to shareholders are likely to lose their position in an efficient financial market. Where the personal goals of managers reflect the shareholder objectives, the implementation of business strategies to further these objectives is likely to be more successful. However, difficulties arise when manager and shareholder objectives are clearly in conflict. A situation may arise where shareholders wish managers to adopt a high-risk, high-growth strategy to produce additional profits. If the strategy fails and the business collapses the shareholders may be able to offset those losses elsewhere with little personal risk. However, the managers in the business face high personal risk if the business fails and may therefore be reticent about pursuing such a strategy. Goal congruence becomes even more difficult to achieve as the business grows in size, as conflict may arise within the management group itself. Bowman and Asch (1987) believe that all businesses have to make a profit to survive, but not all businesses typically 'profit maximize'. The separation of ownership from control weakens the shareholders' influence over the organizational managers, creating a situation where managerial objectives can be pursued. This relationship is illustrated in Figure 1.5.

Figure 1.5 Business objectives

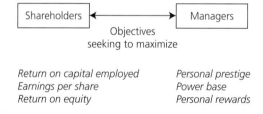

Information needs

Strategic management accounting should be a decision-support system providing relevant information to the appropriate decision maker. These decision makers are situated not only at the very top of the organization, but at various levels in the organization depending on the organizational structure. The business strategy has to be implemented all the way down through the organization and may result in several substrategies. The monitoring of the business strategy will take place at all levels in the organization, having been delegated to various managers at different levels. Therefore, the strategic management accounting system needs to provide information relevant to the needs of the user rather than raw data, and the information needs to be presented in an intelligible form in sufficient time to be of assistance in the decision-making process. Essentially, it is a balance between the cost of providing this information and the benefit to be accrued to the organization from taking a better financial decision. The increasing potential from computer power and new approaches to data transfer at lower cost mean that many organizations are able to achieve this objective.

Current strategic issues in the hospitality and tourism industries

The early years of the twenty-first century have been difficult for operators in the hospitality and tourism industries, who have been faced with the persistent threats from global terrorism as well as tragic events arising from natural disasters, all of which have resulted in the loss of consumer markets and the cost-cutting strategic activity that follows. However, in early 2005 the prospects for the UK industry were cautiously optimistic with tourist numbers increasing, hotel revenue per available room (RevPAR) slowly rising and the prospect of hosting the Olympics in London in 2012, supported by a stable economy with low inflation and low interest rates.

However, in terms of managing future strategies several factors will affect the strategic development of the international hospitality and tourism industries over the next decade. These include:

- changing patterns of ownership
- environmental issues
- information technology (IT)
- changing consumer demands.

Changing patterns of ownership

Traditionally, ownership in the hotel and catering sector within the hospitality industry has been very dispersed, resulting in an industry that was dominated by independent owners and operators. This pattern has been changing rapidly with the development of a range of approaches for achieving growth. These include:

- mergers and acquisitions
- franchising
- management contracts
- joint ventures.

The first international hotel companies were formed in the late 1940s with the growth of American companies such as Hilton International, InterContinental and Sheraton. Large multinational companies have continued to grow and to expand throughout the world, posing a constant threat to the independent operator who cannot compete in the key functional areas of marketing, information technology, purchasing power and financing. Organizational growth can be achieved through the traditional path of acquisitions, but also through other means such as franchising, management contracts and joint ventures.

Recent trends have indicated that patterns of hotel ownership are changing. There is increasing evidence from the UK and US markets to demonstrate a trend towards the separation of ownership of hotel and resort assets and their management. This in turn has resulted in the growth of the phenomenon of the hotel management contract, where the property is owned by investment companies and the property is managed by a hotel operator in return for a fee and possibly a share of the profits. Several of the major hotel operators now include managed hotels in their portfolio of properties. The nature of these arrangements means that the accounting information emphasis is focused on revenue and operating profit maximization, as these are normally the two figures on which the management fee figure is calculated. Traditional figures such as return on capital employed are of less importance to the company managing the operation.

Organizational development in the UK hotel and restaurant industry has been typified by the use of branding. Hilton International was among the first to create branded segments, but many other groups have followed this example on a worldwide basis, including Ramada, Holiday Inn and Mariott. The term franchising is used to describe a business format which involves (DTI, 1998, p. 2):

> The granting of rights by a company (the franchisor) for a third party (the franchisee) to operate their business system using a common brand and common format for promoting, managing and administering the business.

Examples include Holiday Inn, McDonald's, Burger King and Kentucky Fried Chicken. In general, franchises represent a small percentage of the total sector, but within the hotel and catering sectors there has been significant growth (Lashley and Morrison, 2000). There has been an increasing number of potential franchisees willing to pay a share of the revenue received for the right to operate under brand names, and some of them have grown into considerable hotel companies in their own right.

Environmental issues

Many hotels and resorts have become much more focused on social responsibility, including managing and monitoring their impact on the environment. As a result there has been a surge in the numbers of organizations that are out there to help a hotel become more sustainable, such as Green Hotels, Business in the Environment and Benchmark Hotel. Leaders in the hotel industry include Hilton and Inter-Continental Hotels.

Information technology

The past has already proven that the tourism and hospitality companies cannot afford to overlook the opportunities offered by the ever-increasing potential derived from the use of information technology. The most exciting development in recent times must be the marketing and distribution opportunities offered by the World Wide Web. It is estimated that 10% of the world's population already have access to the internet and this figure is rapidly increasing, providing access to markets in a way that has never been witnessed before.

It is already clear that the impact of the internet and other multimedia technologies is likely to have far-reaching effects and possibly change the structure of

Case study: Hilton Hotel Group

Hilton Hotels state that:

We recognise that our activities impact on the countries in which we operate. We are committed to protecting the environment through continual improvement of our environmental performance and prevention of pollution. All our businesses take into account the effects their activities have on the environment.

In delivering our commitment we will:

- understand the environmental issues associated with all our operations
- incorporate environmental management into everyday business practice
- comply with the relevant environmental legislation and codes of practice in the countries in which we operate
- measure performance and set improvement targets
- work with our employees, suppliers, contractors and partners to minimise our impacts
- encourage environmentally-friendly, and where possible, local sourcing of products and services
- encourage engagement of our businesses with local communities
- communicate regularly with our stakeholders on environmental issues and publicly report on our progress.

Source: Hilton International website (**www.hilton.co.uk**)

the tourism industry in particular. The most significant changes have been in the way that tourism organizations communicate with clients and how they manage the distribution channels. There is a growing mass of literature on the use of e-commerce in the tourism industries and there have been several research studies on the subject. Marcussen (2005), senior researcher at the Centre for Regional and Tourism Research in Denmark, suggests that online travel sales increased by as much as 40% from 2003 to 2004 and reached €17.6 billion in the European market in 2004, or 7.3% of the market. The rapid increase is set to continue and Marcussen predicts that a further increase of about 26% during 2005 to about €22.2 billion may be expected (9.1% of the market). He estimates that the European online travel market could reach €26.9 billion or 10.8% of the market by 2006.

Case study: Thomas Cook plc

Thomascook.com has become the UK's first true online holiday retailer with the launch of its new website. Enabling customers to build their own holiday, search and book thousands of packages from holiday companies, buy holiday money, flights, insurance and more, the UK travel company is once again leading the market.

Source: Thomas Cook website, 20 January 2005 (**www.thomascook.com/corporate/press.asp?page=pressreleases**)

Commentators originally assumed that the internet communication technologies would result in less business travel, reducing the demand for business flights, accommodation and meeting rooms. However, in many cases the reverse has been the case, with business travellers free to travel more widely while continuously keeping in touch with the parent organization and colleagues via e-mail and hand-held communication devices.

Developments in information technology have also impacted on the systems used to control businesses in the hospitality and tourism sectors. In the past 5 years we have witnessed the arrival of real-time accounting systems. This means that financial controllers now have the opportunity to create their own business templates through their accounting systems, with the flexibility to create a new chart of accounts to suit the business need and take advantage of a variety of additional features for planning and control. Increased integration of these systems across the business with links to a common database means that typically data entry comes from other parts of the business operation, entered by operational staff. These systems mean that the business unit can move from having accounting information that is accurate but out of date to a set of accounts that is more or less up to date but contains a small number of inaccuracies. In practice, this means that increasingly more time is spent checking that data have been input correctly. With this increased flexibility comes the requirement for financial controllers to have a much more detailed understanding of the accounting policies and regulations that govern the preparation of accounts. Although in the accounts department physical book-keeping at unit level is now highly automated in many ways, traditional book-keeping skills are required more than ever to understand how these systems work.

Information technology has also created a range of opportunities with regard to procurement. In particular, information technology facilitates centralized purchasing, allowing larger chains across the sector to leverage their size and purchasing power to achieve significant cost savings.

This section would not be complete without reference to the significant use of computerised Yield Management systems currently known as revenue maximization systems. This import from the airline industry is tailored to carry out an activity that has always been performed by hotels, which is to maximize both revenue and occupancy. However, computerized systems replace the intuitive feel and allow for more complex computations of room rate and the effects on demand. As hotel groups make more confident use of this management tool it is likely that published tariffs will disappear and there will be a whole range of specific prices that will vary daily and will carry with them not only the class of room but also check-in and check-out restrictions, as well restrictions on access to service and facilities.

Changing consumer demands

The early years of the new millennium witnessed several challenges for the hospitality and tourism sectors. The aftermath of 11 September 2001 meant that visitor numbers to the UK dropped and hotel occupancy levels and average room rates fell as a result. The start of 2005 witnessed a strengthening of the hospitality and tourism sectors, with increasing visitor numbers and an underlying trend in growth in occupancy and revenue statistics in the hospitality industry. Despite the drop in travel and tourism following 2001, the overall trends for the sector are buoyant. Dr Lalia Rach, Dean of the Preston R. Tisch Center for Hospitality, Tourism and Travel Administration at New York University, comments that, 'Today change is the dominant feature of the affluent travel market. With the rise of the new economy, the Wall Street "whiz kids" and the internet revolutionaries have created a new generation of young entrepreneurs who have taken their ideas and skills and become millionaires seemingly overnight. The most dramatic change in the affluent traveller's profile is the decrease in the average age and their different mindset toward travel.' Dr Rach continues to profile the new affluent traveller as follows:

> *They are exceedingly absorbed by their work providing a true example of a 24 hours a day and 7 days a week lifestyle. They work exceedingly hard and expect their relaxation to be as challenging and demanding. When they do take time to relax and enjoy themselves, they want to do so in an atmosphere that reflects their earning status, provides a reward, and is fun and unusual. Exclusivity is but one aspect that interests them while on vacation. They are looking for products and services that allow them to define themselves and to celebrate their success, but in a manner that is not traditionally defined and in many cases is not understated.*
> (http://www.hospitalitynet.org/news/4011068.html)

Critical success factors for the hospitality and tourism industries

In 2003 the Best Practice Forum published an overview of best practice in tourism, hospitality and leisure which was based on research undertaken by the Centre for Hospitality Industry Performance at Surrey University. The research identified seven core elements of best practice:

- setting goals based around a customer focus
- planning and controlling the operation
- partnering and networking
- having clear internal and external communications
- setting and achieving consistent standards
- managing the workforce effectively
- performance management and benchmarking.

(Source: Raising Your Game – Best Practice Forum Research Report 1)

Chapter 8 will consider some of the performance measurement tools used in the tourism and hospitality industries to monitor performance in these key areas.

Changing role of the finance function

In the past few years it has been clear that, across all sectors of business, the role of the finance function is changing. The continuing introduction of automated processes for the collection of data, book-keeping and maintenance of records releases the unit financial controller from the 'bean counter'-type role of the past. Increasingly, finance directors and controllers are required to make the leap to respond more directly to the imperatives of the business agenda and provide support to the business operators. In the hospitality and tourism industries they are key members of the management team and act as architects in the planning process. The finance specialists in the hospitality industry in particular have in the past been more likely to be qualified by experience than through formal examination. This pattern is now changing and qualified accountants increasingly are required to support businesses in the sector.

Key financial issues

Several key financial topics have particular relevance to the hospitality and tourism industries. These issues are specific to an industry that is dependent on the use of fixed assets and subject, as a result, to a high proportion of fixed costs. The topics include:

- accurate valuation of property and assets
- valuation of brands
- information needs arising from changing patterns of ownership management contracts and franchising
- performance management and benchmarking.

In addition to these, the introduction of International Financial Reporting Standards from 2005 has implications for all sectors of industry, and listed companies in the hospitality and tourism industries are no exception. All of these aspects are addressed in later chapters of the text.

Summary   The purpose of this chapter has been to introduce the concept of strategic management and to highlight the importance of tailoring information systems to provide relevant information to assist the manager in the decision-making process. The key strategic issues for the hospitality and tourism industry have also been introduced at this stage.

Questions   1   Consider the difference between the prescriptive and the emergent approaches to strategic management.

2   Why is the development of corporate strategy important for operators in the tourism industries?

3   What are the key challenges facing the hospitality and tourism industries over the next 5–10 years?

Practical activities

1   Select an organization with which you are familiar and list the key stakeholders for that organization. Discuss the relative significance and influence of each group on the strategic direction of the business.

2   Consider an organization with which you are familiar. Does that organization have a clearly defined strategy? Who in the organization knows about the strategy and how is it communicated throughout the organization?

3   Select a listed corporate organization in the tourism and/or hospitality industries and search for the published accounts (these can be obtained from the head office of the organization or via the company's website). Search for the mission statement or a formal statement of organizational purpose. Review this statement and comment on how meaningful it is.

4   **News story questions**

Do you recall the news story at the beginning of this chapter? Now return to that story and reread it before answering the following questions.

(a) What impact do you think this profit warning will have on future strategy planning at Compass Group?

(b) To what extent do you think business strategy is determined by the business shareholders?

(c) List the business stakeholders likely to have the most significant impact on business strategy at Compass Group. Comment on their interest in terms of a long-term or a short-term perspective.

Further reading

Brotherton, B. (ed.) (2003) *The International Hospitality Industry: Structure, Characteristics and Issues*, Oxford: Butterworth Heinemann.

Grundy, T. and Scholes, K. (1998) *Exploring Strategic Financial Management*, Harlow: Prentice Hall Europe.

O'Connor, P. (2004) *Using Computers in Hospitality*, London: Thomson.

Shaw, H. (1993) *Strategic Financial Management*, Huntingdon: Elm Publications.

Useful websites

www.basspressoffice.com/files/EnvironmentalPressPack2003-11.doc   This document provides an interesting insight into intercontinental environmental strategies

www.bized.ac.uk   This site provides some good information about some of the financial aspects of strategy and has some useful details about performance ratios

www.businessballs.com   A general management site which covers an immense array of general material

www.quickmba.com   If you are going to visit one website, this has got to be the one. Easy to navigate, with good-quality, easy-to-read information and an appropriate level of academic rigour

www.tutor2u.net   This is an excellent site which has a range of appropriate tools and aspects of strategy

www.netmba.com   Quite a comprehensive American site covering a range of business management-related topics, including finance, accounting, economics, operations and strategy www.themanager.com   There is a wealth of good information on this site, as well as a range of good and relevant articles, examples and PowerPoint presentations.

http://www.strategy-business.com/enewsarticle/   Online journal: registration needed

http://wps.prenhall.com/ema_uk_he_lynch_corpstrat_3   The companion website to *Corporate Strategy* by Richard Lynch

http://www.bitc.org.uk/index.html   The CEO and strategy home page for Business in the Community. Here you will find those news items, case studies and features that will be most useful to those taking an overview of how businesses respond to the emerging agenda of corporate social responsibility

http://www.tomorrowscompany.com/   The Centre for Tomorrow's Company is a think-tank and catalyst, researching and stimulating the development of a new agenda for business

http://www.bscol.com/   Site for information on the balanced scorecard and other toolkits

http://www.themanager.org/Knowledgebase/   A range of online resources in a number of management disciplines, including strategy

http://www.valuebasedmanagement.net/methods_strategy_maps_strategic_communication.html   Site dedicated to the development of strategy maps

http://www.cio.com/archive/110103/strategy.html?printversion=yes   A different view on the strategy maps concept as proposed by Kaplan and Norton

References

Bowman, C. and Asch, D. (1987) *Strategic Management*, London: Macmillan.

Department of Trade and Industry (DTI) (1998) *Small Firms: Introduction to Franchising*. London: DTI

Drury, C. (2005) *Management Accounting for Business*, London: Thomson Learning.

Gore, C., Murray, K. and Richardson, B. (1992) *Strategic Decision Making*, London: Cassell.

Higgins, J. (1982) Management information systems for corporate planning, in B. Taylor and J. Sparkes (eds) *Corporate Strategy and Planning*, pp. 299–310, London: Heinemann.

Lashley, C. and Morrison, A. (2000) *Franchising Hospitality Services*, Oxford: Butterworth Heinemann.

Lynch, R. (2000) *Corporate Strategy*, p. 8, London: FT Prentice Hall.

Marcussen, C. (2005) 'Trends in European Internet distribution of travel and tourism services', www.crt.dk/uk/staff/chm/trends.htm, accessed 11 May 2005.

Ward, K. (1992) *Strategic Management Accounting*, pp. 3–11, Oxford: Butterworth Heinemann.

Williamson, O. E. (1990) *Organisation Theory: From Chester Barnard to the Present and Beyond*, Oxford: Oxford University Press.

2 | Introducing strategic financial management

About this chapter

This chapter will consider the tools available to the manager to assist in the strategic management process and will examine the role of management accounting systems in supporting this process. The stages within the strategic management process have already been described as forming part of a continual process of analysis based on planning and control. Successful strategic decision making requires the support of an efficient information system which should be designed to meet the needs of the individual organization and will be required to change as the strategy develops. This chapter will consider in particular:

- the nature of management accounting
- tools for strategic analysis
- traditional accounting versus strategic accounting
- strategic management accounting in the hospitality industry.

Case study: Noble House Leisure

Restaurant firm gains £9 m prior to listing

Noble House Leisure (NHL), the restaurant company run by Robert Breare, the leisure entrepreneur, has secured £9 million of new development funding as a precursor to an expected AIM listing later this year.

The company, which owns the Jim Thompson's and Yellow River Café chains and several eateries in the City of London, is believed to be close to appointing advisers to a flotation valuing the business at up to £30 million, including debt of £12 million.

NHL will today announce that it has secured £9 million from Royal Bank of Scotland to fund the development of at least 12 restaurants over three years, the initial focus being on expanding Yellow River.

The group, which was founded in 2000, has 35 eateries, including City restaurants such as Sri Siam, Pacific Oriental and Sri Thai. It also operates three units owned by the separate Noble House Pub Company but is tipped to buy them later this year.

Mr Breare, who four years ago tried to buy Wolverhampton & Dudley Breweries, recently sold the bulk of Noble House Pub Company to Mill House Inns for about £50 million.

▶

◀

NHL's main shareholders are management, the private equity firm Botts & Company and Royal Bank. It has estimated annual turnover of £20 million and earnings before interest, tax, depreciation and amortization of almost £4 million.

Source: *The Times Online*, 5 May 2005

Questions relating to this news story may be found on page 37.

Learning objectives On completion of this chapter you should be able to:

- distinguish between management accounting and financial accounting
- apply a range of strategic tools for business analysis
- understand how to apply a range of strategic models to determine the strategic positioning of the business
- understand the concept of strategic management accounting.

Introduction

Virtually all business enterprises are required to monitor their financial activities and produce accurate audited accounts for external inspection. Admittedly, the disclosure requirements for small businesses are fairly limited, whereas at the other end of the spectrum, the published accounts of the larger listed companies are required to be somewhat more detailed. It is this information that provides the potential investor with a limited insight into the strengths and weaknesses of the business and will affect the decision whether to invest or not. The published accounts are of little value, however, to the managers operating within the business because the key operating information such as material and wage costs is not clearly visible and separate entities are hidden through the process of consolidation. Instead, the manager is reliant on a series of internal reports generated via the process called management accounting, where detailed, regular reports are produced containing information tailored to meet the needs of that particular sector of the business.

In a modern business the finance function has an important role to play both in ensuring that financial reporting is true and accurate to meet statutory requirements and in providing appropriate information for management decision-making purposes, as illustrated in Figure 2.1.

In Chapter 1 a range of business stakeholders was identified and each of these groups has an interest in business performance. These are summarized in Figure 2.2.

Figure 2.1 Role of the finance function in organizational decision-making

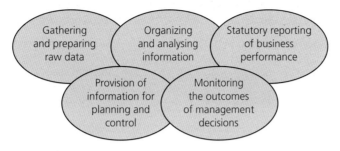

Figure 2.2 Business stakeholders

The nature of management accounting

The decision-making process centres on choosing the best alternative from a possible range of different courses of action. It is possible, of course, that the alternatives may not all be known and the best decision is normally the choice with the highest overall benefit in relation to cost. Management accounting is the process of analysing, planning and controlling the business with the purpose of supporting the financial decision-making process. Financial accounting involves the actual recording of every financial transaction and, therefore, operates in a historical framework. The end result is a set of published statements prepared to meet the demands of a legal framework, which in the UK is provided by the Companies Act. The wide availability of the published statements means that companies will wish to keep to a minimum the information that they present in order to maintain a degree of competitive advantage. The emphasis in management accounting is to provide as much information as is possible to assist the manager in controlling the business. Consequently, there are several differences between financial accounting and management accounting and these are summarized in Table 2.1.

The aim in management accounting is to help the manager to run the business and consequently an effective management accounting system segments the business into key operating areas and the manager receives individually tailored reports containing the appropriate level of detailed information. The way in which the business is segmented is discussed further in Chapter 6.

Table 2.1 Financial accounting versus management accounting

	Financial accounting	*Management accounting*
Legal requirements	Company law	Subject to the needs of managers
Users	External users	Internal users
Time dimension	Past and present	Present and future
Report frequency	Published accounts annually	Daily, weekly, monthly
Scope	Whole company or group	Divisions and departments
Emphasis	Accuracy	Speed
Criteria	Objective and verifiable	Relevant, useful, understandable
Nature of information	Prepared to generally accepted accounting principles	For use by non-accountants

Source: Reproduced with permission from Allen and Myddelton (1992) *Essential Management Accounting*, p. 7.

Tools for strategic analysis

In Chapter 1 a key part of the strategic management process was identified as the strategic analysis of the business to establish what is happening and why. Having established this it is possible to develop strategic options for moving forward. Strategic management information about the business enables these tools to be used effectively to enable decisions to be made about where the business is currently positioned now and the strategic decisions it should take in the future. There are many approaches to strategic analysis and various tools are available for analysing the internal capabilities and resources of the business. This section aims to consider those most widely discussed, including:

- SWOT analysis
- product life cycles
- portfolio analysis.

SWOT analysis

A simple approach for analysing the internal and external aspects of an organization is contained in the form of a SWOT analysis. SWOT stands for strengths, weaknesses, opportunities and threats, and is often displayed in 2 × 2 matrix as shown in Figure 2.3.

The strengths and weaknesses refer to the internal capabilities of the organization compared to the competition and the general expectations of the marketplace.

Figure 2.3 The component parts of a SWOT analysis

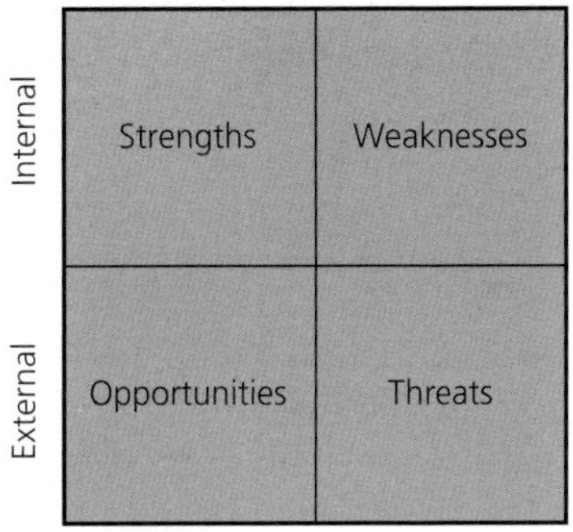

Strengths are special attributes or distinctive characteristics that can be attributed to the organization. Weaknesses are aspects that make the organization less effective than other similar operations. The analysis should be performed honestly and the results compared to the aims of the organization as set out in the mission statement and goals. Techniques for performing the analysis, such as resource audits and performance measurement, are considered in detail later in this chapter and in Part 3. An analysis of the opportunity and threats should take account of all the external environmental factors and the relationships among them. An opportunity is any chance to follow a new or revised strategy that could be of benefit to the organization. Opportunities may simply exist, but more usually need to be created. Threats are possible events that have the potential to harm seriously the organization's ability to achieve its goals and objectives.

A good SWOT analysis should highlight the critical success factors for a business and hence highlight those areas where a change in strategy is likely to have the most beneficial effect. However, a SWOT analysis is only an aid to strategic planning and the process should be carried out with considerable management judgement. Other models can also be used to provide a detailed analysis of the current position.

Michael Porter (1985) suggests a model that analyses the competitive environment facing an organization. This model categorizes competitive forces into five groups and the results can be linked with his later technique, a development of the added value concept, the value chain. The concept of value added refers to the contribution made by the organization to convert raw components into the final product. The objective of the analysis is to highlight those areas that contribute most to the total value added and subsequently develop strategies to improve or develop these areas. The techniques are explained in Chapter 4 in Part 2 in the context of competitor accounting.

Product life cycles

It is generally believed that products and services follow a 'life cycle' which is based on the current market and has significant implications for the future strategic direction of the business. The concept has faced some criticism in recent times, but the theory can still be usefully applied where common sense prevails.

Drawing on the work of Ward (1992) the theory separates the economic life of the product or service into a number of life-cycle stages:

- introduction or birth
- growth
- shake-out
- maturity
- decline.

These stages are illustrated in Figure 2.4.

Stage 1 is the initial development and launch of the product and the initial sales growth will be slow. This is a period of high risk as it is quite feasible that the product or idea will fail completely.

If the product is accepted by the market, there follows a period of rapid sales growth. This is *stage 2*. Normally the potential level of sales is not infinite and eventually the rate of growth will slow. It is quite possible that other companies will enter the market at this point and will benefit from the experiences of the pioneering company who have carried the high risk through the development stage. This point is particularly true in the hospitality and catering industry where the new product is available to all by simply purchasing the product or service and new ideas can quickly be copied without the need to go through the development stage. A number of new companies may quickly enter the market, rapidly increasing the volumes of the product available.

Stage 3 is defined as the period of shake-out which occurs when rapid growth coincides with the start of a fall in market growth. During this period there may be a period of rationalization in the market place when several competitors leave the industry or are taken over and the total capacity is stabilized.

Once a more stable position has been established with sales demand approximately meeting product provision a period of maturity ensues (*stage 4*). This period may last for several years, but eventually the demand for the product will start to fall as customer tastes change and other products have been introduced. It is possible to attempt to sustain the maturity period by making changes to the product or by seeking out new markets. The McDonalds concept is a good example of a company in the maturity stage of the product life cycle in Europe and the USA,

Figure 2.4 The product life cycle

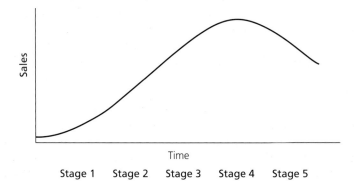

Stage 1   Stage 2   Stage 3   Stage 4   Stage 5

where additional products have been added to the menu to account for changing consumer tastes but the basic concept has remained the same. However, by seeking out new markets in former Eastern bloc countries, the product can be seen to be still in the growth sales stage in those regions.

Stage 5 is defined as the decline stage, when sales are falling in a declining market.

McDonalds Corporation

1948   McDonald brothers open first restaurant

1954   Ray Kroc persuades the brothers to franchise the operation, giving him sole rights

1955   First franchise operation opened

1961   McDonald brothers sell the trademarks, copyright and formulae to Kroc for $2.7 million

1965   Chain goes public, floated on the Stock Exchange

1971   Expansion overseas

1974   3000 units in operations at home and abroad

1984   Death of Ray Kroc, Fred Turner becomes Senior Chairman

1987   Michael Quinlan takes over as Chief Executive

1990s Company experiences problems with intensifying interest in food and health issues

2000s Launches new 'healthy eating' products such as salads and lower fat items

---

Risk and the product life cycle

The overall level of risk facing an organization when it decides to launch a new idea is a combination of two types of risk. **Financial risk** is derived from the nature of the financing of the project and the cost structure of the business. Financing risk occurs when the project is funded by debt capital rather than equity capital, with the risk arising from the fixed interest payments and the eventual need to repay the capital. Cost structure refers to the nature of the costs experienced by the business. Costs that have to be paid regardless of the level of trading are known as fixed costs and a high proportion of these render a business as high risk.

Business risk arises from the inherent nature of the product. A business will try to achieve a balance by rejecting those projects with both high financial risk and high business risk. However, the combination of low business risk and high financial risk could provide very favourable returns for shareholders.

The stages of the product life cycle have different intrinsic levels of risk over which the business has little control as these are created by the outside environment. The launch stage is the stage carrying greatest risk, but the risk is also high in the development stage when the potential size of the market is still not known. As the market matures the risk reduces and is concentrated on the length of the maturity stage. The final stage is low risk as the demand for the product dies and

Figure 2.5 Relationship between risk and return

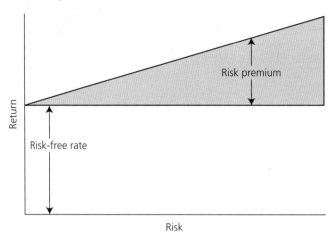

the company's strategy is tailored accordingly. Risk and return are invariably linked with a positive correlation, in that if risk increases so must the return. This basic economic principle is illustrated in Figure 2.5.

During the growth stage the cost per unit may be high, but this can be compensated for by charging a premium for the product. The selling price is forced to stabilize or even fall in the maturity stage once the competition increases. During the maturity stage emphasis falls on improving quality to justify a premium price or, where products are homogeneous, reducing operating costs while maintaining quality at the same level. Strategic methods for reducing costs in the maturity stage are considered in Chapter 4.

The product life cycle and management accounting

The various stages of the product life cycle raise a number of issues for the provision of strategic management accounting information. The type of information required for strategic decision making will vary depending on the stage at which the company is on the product life cycle. A key part of the management accounting function should be to attempt to establish where the company is actually positioned and whether it is about to enter a new phase. The difficulty in pinpointing the current position is normally the most commonly cited criticism of the product life-cycle theory and although there will always been an element of uncertainty, accounting information can be used to improve monitoring of the company's position. Table 2.2 illustrates the change in emphasis required at each stage of the product life cycle.

Each stage of the life cycle is now considered in detail in terms of:

- cash flows
- level of operating expenses
- performance measures.

Table 2.2 Separate stages of the product life cycle (PLC)

PLC stage	Launch	Growth	Maturity
Product	Unsophisticated	Range widening	Proliferation
Market	Narrow segment	Wider growth	Mass market
Competition	Low	Intensifying	High-cost producers exit
Price	High	Lower	Low
Profit	High/medium	Medium	Lower
Cash	Negative	Positive	Cash rich

Launch stage

A critical feature of the launch stage is that the cash flow of the business will be negative because funds are being used to develop, test and launch the new idea. If the concept is perceived to be successful more cash will be needed for fixed assets, working capital and launch marketing. Discounted cash-flow techniques are normally used with new concept launches, with the potential cash flows being projected well into the future and a discount rate used for the analysis which should reflect the perceived risk associated with the project particularly in the early stages. However, at this stage the forecast information cannot be sufficiently accurate to be of use for monitoring and controlling the project. Even if the initial evaluation of the project has proven to be positive the business needs to consider how an appropriate set of financial control measures might attempt to monitor performance at this stage given the level of uncertainty. Using the discounted cash-flow technique probabilities can be assigned to likely outcomes and the weighted average calculated. This approach is covered in more detail in Chapter 10, illustrating the advantages and disadvantages of such a technique.

Marketing expenditure will be crucial at this stage to establish the potential for the concept and, above all, the business should not be tempted to reduce marketing and research costs at this stage to earn short-term profits, as this will undermine the business's long-term competitive position. It is likely at this stage that the operating costs will be fairly high and will remain so until the business is able to achieve cost reduction through improved operational techniques, the benefit of experience and sales volumes.

Traditional measures such as return on investment are wholly inappropriate at this stage. One of the primary objectives of a system for monitoring should be to collect information, which reduces the risk associated with the project due to lack of knowledge. As a result the project should be controlled using milestones based on the achievement of overall objectives. This depends on the project being broken down into visible stages and each stage being assessed for likely expenditure. If this can be achieved the project can be assessed at each stage to check that it is worth continuing. To achieve this, accounting systems need to be designed to be able to cope with an ever-changing environment and as a consequence need to be flexible, informal and capable of rapid response.

Growth stage

Increasing marketing expenditure is still likely to be the key activity to create market growth as quickly as possible and to increase market share. At this stage it is common for the business to focus on product differentiation by emphasizing the particular product attributes. The marketing expenditure associated with this should be financially evaluated as a long-term investment by the business and the financial justification carried out using discounted cash-flow techniques much in the same way as it was performed for the launch stage. At some point the law of diminishing returns sets in and any further increases in marketing will not be worthwhile.

Once the product is successfully launched and the market begins to grow financial measures become more important. Forecasting should now be considerably more accurate and the accounting measures should be able to pinpoint the optimum expenditure level to avoid wasted expenditure. As the market for the product expands the business needs to grow its own sales more quickly than the market to increase market share. Therefore, the management accounting system should be producing information to analyse the competitors' existing marketing strategies and potential responses to changes in the organizational strategy. Sales revenues will now have increased rapidly from those produced during the launch stage, but the overall cash flow of the business may not yet be positive as extensive investment is required to sustain the growth of the business. Profits should not be the main focus at this stage as the company should be reinvesting in marketing and research expenditure to maximize the opportunities in the market.

Maturity stage

Once the maturity stage has been established the management style should focus on control. It is at this stage that the overall profits can be maximized and cash flows turn positive. A typical feature of this stage is overcapacity in the market as the level of competitors increases. As a result, an extremely competitive environment is created and some operators will be forced out of business or will fall victim to takeovers and mergers. Further investment is now no longer necessary and marketing should be aimed at maintaining market share rather than attempting to increase it. The financial control process should focus on the shorter term performance of the business emphasizing profitability and cash-flow generation. This is the most cash-positive stage of the business and the business should aim to maximize the benefit of these cash returns. Consequently, the control of costs at this stage is crucial and should be principally aimed at strategically reducing unit costs in relation to the competitors. Price competition will become more important at this stage, particularly if overcapacity exists and the product is well understood by the customer. An alternative is to focus on a particular aspect such as levels of service or unique selling qualities of the product.

At this stage it is appropriate to use a profit measure to control the business, and return on investment is usually considered to be the most appropriate. To ensure that this ratio is used effectively the profit margins should be monitored carefully and the manager will need information on cost structures in terms of fixed and variable costs and also, where possible, similar information for the competition. The strategic thrust at this stage is to maximize cost efficiencies and achieve maximum profitability.

A business needs to monitor the market carefully to predict accurately when the business is entering the maturity stage as a different strategic approach is required at this point. The maturity stage can be identified by reviewing the total market size and the market share held by the business. Care needs to be taken to ensure that the market really has matured and that it is not simply a temporary drop in market growth. Techniques for establishing market size and share are discussed in Chapter 5.

Decline stage

The decline stage of a particular concept will inevitably be reached as a result of changing customer needs. At this stage all costs that are no longer necessary should be removed, with no further investment being needed as the existing assets are worked until the end of their life. Financial measures such as return on capital and profitability are no longer valid as appropriate methods of financial control. The short-term measure of free cash flow is regarded as the best measure at this stage and the preparation of short-term cash flows is crucial. Cash flows may exceed profits owing to declining requirements for working capital. In the hospitality industry the decline stage can be avoided by changing the nature of the business concept to match consumer needs. This is often achieved through the use of brands that are for many organizations transferable between products and concepts, so it may be necessary to remove the branding image from a declining concept and apply it to a more growth-orientated area.

Boston Consulting Group matrix

The Boston matrix is a general strategic planning concept that can be used with the product life cycle. The simplest version of this matrix is the one produced by the Boston Consulting Group (BCG). Other more complex models have followed, but most are based on the principles demonstrated in the BCG matrix. It should be noted that all of these models require managerial judgement and common sense to make them workable in a practical situation. The matrix illustrated in Figure 2.6 enables a business to plot the position of each of its products or brands in terms of relative market share and total rate of market growth.

The rate of market growth is an attempt to measure the level of attractiveness of the industry in terms of the rate of growth of the total market available for a product. Relative market share is a guide to the competitive strength of the business in the marketplace because companies with a dominant market share tend to produce higher financial returns. However, other factors such as service quality and operational efficiency are also influential in determining the relative financial performance. The Boston matrix can be used as a strategic planning device if the position of the company can be identified. There may be some relationship between the stages of the BCG matrix and the product life cycle, although this is not always definitely the case as they are based on different parameters (Table 2.3).

Like the product life cycle, it is more successfully used for charting past performance than for predicting future performance. The characteristics for each stage are illustrated in Figure 2.7.

The use of the Boston matrix leads to a focus on diversification strategies. The analysis tends to encourage the use of positive cash flows from business activities in the mature stage to fund new ventures and concepts. The positive aspect of this is that diversification reduces risk, but in practice such a policy can lead to a lack of focus and increasing corporate costs arising from managing a diverse portfolio of activities.

Figure 2.6 The Boston Matrix

		Relative market share	
		High	Low
Market growth	High	Star	Question mark
	Low	Cash cow	Dog

Table 2.3 Relationship between the Boston Consulting Group (BCG) matrix and the product life cycle

Product life cycle	BCG matrix
Launch	Question marks
Growth	Star
Maturity	Cash cow
Decline	Dog

Figure 2.7 Boston matrix characteristics

Star	**Question marks**
Cash user	Cash user
Lower prices	High prices
Intensifying competition	Low competition
Wider market	Narrow market
Developing product	Unsophisticated product
Cash cow	**Dog**
Cash generator	Cash generator
Low prices	Low prices
Mass market	Market declining
Intense rivalry	Competitors exit
Proliferation of product	Withdraw product

General Electric matrix

This model replaces market growth with market attractiveness, and competitive strength replaces market share as the dimension by which the competitive position of each SBU is assessed. Illustrated in Figure 2.8, this model is sometimes known as the directional policy matrix. Market attractiveness on the vertical axis is the weighted average of a range of factors, including size of industry, profitability,

Figure 2.8 General Electric matrix
Source: Adapted from Bowman and Asch (1987) *Strategic Management*.

		Market attractiveness		
		High	Medium	Low
Competitive strength	High			
	Medium			
	Low			

growth rate, nature of competition, business cycle and the ability to gain economies of scale.

This is compared to competitive strength on the horizontal axis, which is the weighted average of a range of factors, including market share, profit levels, management ability, production capability and technological strength. The aim is to plot each aspect of the business to illustrate how each relates to the others in terms of competitiveness and attractiveness.

Designing strategic management accounting systems

The Chartered Institute of Management Accountants (CIMA) in the UK defines strategic management accounting as: 'A form of management accounting in which emphasis is placed on information that relates to factors external to the firm, as well as non-financial information and internally generated information' (CIMA Official Terminology, 2000, p. 50).

The majority of management accounting systems is designed to process large volumes of data on a routine daily basis. This approach is certainly adequate where historical information is known to be a sound basis for future decisions. However, strategic decisions that are designed to change the direction of the business cannot be supported by information that has simply been produced by extrapolating past performance to represent the future. Traditional accounting systems tend to focus on the past and financial planning is limited to an extension of the budgetary process. Shaw (1994) highlighted the key areas for financial planning and control, identifying the differences between a traditional and a strategic approach. Table 2.4 is adapted from his recommendations.

Some strategic decisions require one-off evaluation, for example, a decision to open a new unit or revenue-generating area within an existing business. The financial evaluation requires assessment of the net incremental effect impact on the business. Similarly, the cost of closing a business requires an evaluation of the opportunity costs of such an action. It may be necessary to consider the cost of or benefit from continuing, closing down or selling to another party. To support these types of decision the management accounting system needs to consider future incremental cash flows. This can present a problem to traditional management accounting systems, which tend to focus on historical costs based on direct costs and indirect costs that have been apportioned across the organization. Consequently, the aims and objectives of each strategic decision need to be clearly stated and information produced based on incremental costs only to monitor whether the targets are being met.

A range of financial performance measures should be used which measure both the economic performance of the business and managerial performance. The measures should be tailored to the particular strategies and may need to change in focus over time.

Economic performance focuses on the performance of the business in relation to the external environment in order to monitor the effect of all economic factors that are likely to affect the business, regardless of management performance. Managerial performance can be assessed through the use of responsibility centres, where an individual is monitored by evaluating only those revenues and costs that are controllable. The aim is to provide a system that motivates managers and clearly highlights good performance. The accounting system should produce information for internal use that is user friendly in presentation and relevant to the needs of the user. It is essential that the information produced by accountants is understandable by the managers who need to use it. Therefore, reports should be tailored to meet the requirements of the user, and this could include the use of graphs, pie charts and histograms to aid the less numerate manager.

The process of standard costing can be a useful element of a strategic management accounting system. A standard cost is an estimate of the cost of one unit of production such as a bed night or a meal, and these costs can be used effectively for forecasting and for making comparisons to actual performance, which form the basis of budgetary control.

Table 2.4 Differences between a traditional and strategic approach to accounting

Activity	Strategic approach	Traditional approach
Corporate strategy	Financial planning consistent with strategic aims based on internal capabilities and resource availability	Generally financial planning concentrates on the operational aspects of budgetary control
Capital structure	Capital structure intended to reduce cost of capital and minimize shareholder risk	Capital raised as and when it is needed leading to a possible increase in cost of capital
Dividend policy	Dividends paid only once all other possible more profitable uses of retained funds have been explored	Dividend payment level set to maximize shareholder wealth and raise share price in the short term
Investment decisions	Management only invest in projects that provide positive discounted cash flows (net present value)	Reliance on profit-based capital investment appraisal methods where profit is compared to investment
Profitability	Management seek to improve the long-term profitability of the business and return on capital employed	General emphasis on short profit maximization to improve earnings per share (EPS)
Working capital	Focus on internal cash flows	Focus on profit flows
Pricing policy	Pricing focuses on product and market considerations	Pricing based on cost and profit per unit expectations
Performance measures	Tend to be on a historical period-by-period basis emphasizing internal operations	To include a range of measures based on internal and external factors including financial and non-financial values

There remains no consensus on a precise definition of what should be included in a system for strategic management accounting, but Drury (2005) identifies three key strands:

- the extension of traditional management accounting's internal focus to include external information about competitors
- the relationship between the strategic position chosen by a business and the expected emphasis on management accounting
- gaining competitive advantage by analysing ways to decrease costs and/ or enhance the differentiation of a firm's product, through exploiting linkages in the value chain and optimising cost drivers.

The following chapters of this text consider the traditional topics associated with financial and management accounting and in each case the processes described are illustrated with examples and recommendations for a strategic approach.

Summary Many businesses use traditional management accounting systems which focus on the internal aspects of the business and the regular production of routine data. A strategic approach to management accounting includes having an external focus to monitor changes in the environment while providing information that enables strategic decisions to be evaluated. The power of information technology can be harnessed to produce reports that not only are timely and relevant, but also enable sensitivity analysis and prediction modelling to take place. The remainder of this text will consider some of the modern approaches available to the hospitality industry to improve the decision-making process and the subsequent monitoring and control of those decisions.

Questions

1 Many decisions in financial management in a large organization are made in an environment of conflicting stakeholder viewpoints. Identify the key stakeholders and give examples of possible sources of conflict.

2 Explain the difference between operational and strategic decisions in the hospitality industry.

3 Give a definition of strategic management accounting and explain how this can be used in the hospitality and tourism industries.

4 The various stages of the product life cycle raise a number of issues for the provision of management accounting information. Describe each stage of the cycle and consider how each of the following differs at each stage:

   (a) cash flows

   (b) level of operating expenses

   (c) performance measures

5 News story questions

Do you recall the news story at the beginning of this chapter? Now return to that story and reread it before answering the following questions.

(a) Describe some of the strategy tools that could be used by Noble House to evaluate their current position in the marketplace.

(b) Select one tool and with further research attempt to analyse the Noble House Group.

(c) Prepare a set of recommendations based on your analysis for presentation to the Chairman.

Further reading

Collier, P. and Gregory, A. (1994) Strategic management accounting: a UK hotel sector case study, *International Journal of Contemporary Hospitality Management* 7(1): 18–23.

Evans, N., Campbell, D. and Stonehouse, G. (2003) *Strategic Management for Travel and Tourism*, Oxford: Butterworth-Heinemann.

Harrison, J.S. and Enz, C.A. (2004) *Hospitality Strategic Management: Concepts and Cases*, John Wiley, Chichester.

Johnson, G. and Scholes, K. (2002) British Airways and the vocabulary of strategy. In G. Johnson and K. Scholes (eds) *Exploring Corporate Strategy* (6th edn), London: Prentice Hall.

Tribe, J. (1997) *Corporate Strategy for Tourism*, London: Thomson.

Ward, K. (1992) *Strategic Management Accounting*, pp. 3–11, Oxford: Butterworth Heinemann.

Useful websites

www.bized.ac.uk   This site provides some good information about some of the financial aspects of strategy and has some useful details about performance ratios

www.businessballs.com   A general management site which covers an immense array of general material

www.quickmba.com   A useful range of applications

www.tutor2u.net   An excellent site which has a range of appropriate tools and aspects of strategy

www.netmba.com   A comprehensive site covering a range of business management-related topics including finance, accounting, economics, operations and strategy

www.themanager.com   There is a wealth of good information on this site, as well as a range of relevant articles, examples and PowerPoint presentations

http://www.strategy-business.com/enewsarticle/   Online journal: registration needed

http://wps.prenhall.com/ema_uk_he_lynch_corpstrat_3   The companion website to *Corporate Strategy* by Richard Lynch

http://www.bitc.org.uk/index.html   The CEO and strategy home page for Business in the Community. Here you will find those news items, case studies and features that will be most useful to those taking an overview of how businesses respond to the emerging agenda of corporate social responsibility

http://www.tomorrowscompany.com/   The Centre for Tomorrow's Company is a think-tank and catalyst, researching and stimulating the development of a new agenda for business

http://www.bscol.com/   Site for information on the balanced scorecard and other toolkits

http://www.themanager.org/Knowledgebase/   A range of online resources in a number of management disciplines including strategy

http://www.valuebasedmanagement.net/methods_strategy_maps_strategic_ communication.html   Site dedicated to the development of strategy maps

http://www.valuebasedmanagement.net/methods_bcgmatrix.html   Information on the Boston Consulting Group Matrix

http://www.cio.com/archive/110103/strategy.html?printversion=yes   A different view on the strategy maps concept as proposed by Kaplan and Norton

References   Allen, M. and Myddelton, D. (1992) *Essential Management Accounting*, p. 7, New York: Prentice Hall International (UK).

Bowman, C. and Asch, D. (1987) *Strategic Management*, London: Macmillan.

CIMA Official Terminology (2000) London: CIMA.

Drury, C. (2005) *Management Accounting for Business*, London: Thomson Learning.

Porter, M. (1985) *Competitive Advantage*, New York: Free Press.

Shaw, H. (1994) *Strategic Financial Management*, Oxford: Butterworth Heinemann.

Ward, K. (1993) *Strategic Management Accounting*, Oxford: Butterworth Heinemann.

3 | Understanding financial statements

About this chapter

The vast majority of business managers working in the hospitality, tourism and leisure industries will need at some point in their professional lives to be able to interpret and act upon financial information. The results of any commercial business are usually summarized in three key statements, the profit and loss account, the balance sheet and the cash flow, and these are prepared at a minimum at least once per year in the form of audited, publicly available statements (for public companies) and internally within the business several times per year (management accounts). The aim of this chapter is to provide guidance for understanding how these statements are prepared and the importance of the information contained within them. There will be no attempt in the text to illustrate and teach the principles of double-entry book-keeping as this aspect is covered in a multitude of texts on the subject. However, this chapter is very much concerned with the accounting principles and concepts that support the preparation of the financial statements. This includes a detailed review of each of the financial statements and an explanation of the relationship between the statements. A more detailed review of the techniques for interpreting statements using a variety of forms of ratio analysis is given in Chapter 8.

Learning objectives On completion of this chapter you should be able to:

- appreciate the roles of the regulatory framework in accounting
- understand the principles for adjusting fixed asset accounts with regard to depreciation
- understand the concepts of accruals and prepayments
- appreciate the methodologies for the adjustment of the stock records to incorporate the current valuation
- recognize the structures for the profit and loss account, cash flow and balance sheet.

Introduction

The function of financial accounting is to record clearly every single financial transaction that the business has been involved in, both in the selling and in the production of goods and services, and to classify and summarize these transactions for presentation in a series of published reports produced on an annual basis. These reports are then used by a range of external users who have access to very little information other than that which is published. These external users include shareholders, banks and other lenders, government and the tax authorities, and customers and competitors.

Accounting principles

The statements contained in the published reports are required to give a fair and true representation of the business and, to assist in the preparation of the statements to this standard, there is a series of rules and regulations to be adhered to. In the UK the Companies Act 1985 imposes several and these, with the voluntary concepts, are backed up by the recommendations of a group of the professional accounting associations, acting as the Accounting Standards Board, suggesting how they should be put into practice. These are the *Financial Reporting Standards (FRS)*, which are gradually superseding the *Statements of Standard Accounting Practice (SSAP)*. Further amendments to the Companies Act added a further requirement that large companies should prepare their accounts in accordance with applicable accounting standards. Therefore, limited companies in the UK are required to meet the demands of the regulations imposed from four main sources:

- company law
- SSAPs and FRSs
- international accounting standards
- the requirements of the Stock Exchange.

Non-statutory regulation is based on recommendations issued by the professional accounting bodies. The six accountancy bodies in the UK are:

- the Chartered Institute of Management Accountants (CIMA)
- the Institute of Chartered Accountants in England and Wales (ICAEW)
- the Institute of Chartered Accountants of Scotland (ICAS)
- the Institute of Chartered Accountants of Ireland (ICAI)
- the Association of Chartered Certified Accountants (ACCA)
- the Chartered Institute of Public Finance and Accountancy (CIPFA).

The Accounting Standards Committee (ASC) was formed in 1970 with the purpose of publishing accounting standards that provide guidelines for the treatment of various items in the accounting process. The statutory framework for these rules and regulations is provided in the UK by the Companies Act. The accounting principles that underpin the preparation of the financial statements in the UK were originally embodied in the SSAP and their guidelines provide the framework by which UK financial statements are prepared. In total there were 25 of these statements covering a range of issues, with the aim of providing guidance on the most appropriate technique for the preparation of the entries in the financial statements. The range of these statements is illustrated in Table 3.1.

Every major developed country has its own version of accounting standards. Originally the accounting standards in the UK and Ireland were established by the councils of what were then six major accountancy bodies. The ASC was set up by the Council of the Institute of Chartered Accountants in England and Wales with the objective of developing definitive standards on financial reporting, resulting in a set of standard accounting policies.

The ASC has since been superseded by the Accounting Standards Board (ASB), in 1990, with the aim of starting a new era in accounting standard setting because the original ASC had lost much of its credibility. The SSAPs were perceived to be weak and in many cases ambiguous because they allowed for more than one treatment of a particular activity. As a result there were ample opportunities for managers to indulge in creative accounting practices which helped to meet short-term profit and return on investment targets while undermining the long-term health of the business. The new body was set up with the aim of producing a new set of accounting guidelines to improve on the policies that had gone before. At the time of printing the new FRSs shown in Table 3.2 have been produced.

The introduction of FRS 15 in particular has had implications for the hospitality industry. In response to the recommendation to introduce this FRS, the British Association of Hospitality Accountants (BAHA) has prepared and published Guidance Notes for the industry which can be purchased from the Association. Following the publication of the ASB's proposals for the initial measurement, valuation and depreciation of tangible fixed assets in its October 1996 Discussion Paper, followed by Financial Reporting Exposure Draft (FRED) 17 in October 1997, a committee of accountants was formed under the auspices of BAHA representing a broad cross-section of owners and operators of hotels, hotel accountants and independent auditors. Subsequently, discussions were held with some of the leading valuers of hotels.

The objective of the committee was to review accounting standards and practices, formulate a set of guidance notes which will facilitate a uniform framework, and ensure that there is more consistency in accounting for fixed assets within the industry. These guidance notes are not intended to be prescriptive, but to set out an approach generally accepted by the industry and provide guidance for preparers of hotel company accounts. The notes are intended to be indicative of best practice.

The preparation of financial statements is also clarified by the acceptance of accounting principles that should be uniformly applied. In practice, however, there is a considerable degree of user interpretation. The following notes provide a summary of the basic principles in statement preparation.

- **Consistency:** the accounting treatment of particular items should be the same from period to period. If this is not the case then the difference should be revealed.
- **Going concern:** an organization is assumed to continue in operational existence for the foreseeable future.
- **Matching:** the costs for the period should be matched with the appropriate revenue.

Table 3.1 Statements of Standard Accounting Practice

	Title
SSAP 1	Accounting for Associated Companies
SSAP 2	Disclosure of Accounting Policies
SSAP 3	Earnings per Share
SSAP 4	The Accounting Treatment of Government Grants
SSAP 5	Accounting for Value Added Tax
SSAP 6	Extraordinary Items and Prior Year Adjustments
SSAP 7	Withdrawn 1978
SSAP 8	The Treatment of Taxation Under the Imputation System in the Accounts of Companies
SSAP 9	Stocks and Long Term Contracts
SSAP 10	Statements of Source and Application of Funds
SSAP 11	Withdrawn 1978
SSAP 12	Accounting for Depreciation
SSAP 13	Accounting for Research and Development
SSAP 14	Group Accounts
SSAP 15	Accounting for Deferred Taxation
SSAP 16	Current Cost Accounting
SSAP 17	Accounting for Post Balance Sheet Events
SSAP 18	Accounting for Contingencies
SSAP 19	Accounting for Investment Properties
SSAP 20	Foreign Currency Translation
SSAP 21	Accounting for Leases and Hire Purchase Contracts
SSAP 22	Accounting for Goodwill
SSAP 23	Accounting for Acquisitions and Mergers
SSAP 24	Accounting for Pension Costs
SSAP 25	Segmental Reporting

Table 3.2 Financial Reporting Standards

	Title
FRS 1	Cashflow Statements
FRS 2	Accounting for Subsidiary Undertakings
FRS 3	Reporting Financial Performance
FRS 4	Capital Instruments
FRS 5	Reporting the Substance of Transactions
FRS 6	Acquisitions and Mergers
FRS 7	Fair Values in Acquisition Accounting
FRS 8	Related Party Disclosures
FRS 9	Associates and Joint Ventures
FRS 10	Goodwill and Intangible Assets
FRS 11	Impairment of Fixed Assets and Goodwill
FRS 12	Provisions and Contingent Liabilities
FRS 13	Derivatives and Other Financial Instruments
FRS 14	Earnings per Share
FRS 15	Tangible Fixed Assets
FRS 16	Current Tax
FRS 17	Retirement Benefits
FRS 18	Accounting Policies
FRS 19	Deferred Tax

- **Materiality:** changes in accounting practice are only permissible if the effect is not material.
- **Stated values:** accounting records are kept for those events measured in monetary terms.
- **Prudence:** provision should be made for all likely costs, whereas profits should not be accounted for until realized.
- **Separate entity:** a business is considered to have a separate entity to its owners, which means that personal transactions are excluded from business accounts.

The effect of the accounting policies mentioned above is effectively illustrated by comparing the cash flow and the profit and loss account of a business. The cash flow shows simply all revenues actually received and all costs actually paid. The profit and loss account recognizes both debtors and creditors. Debtors are those sales not yet received although the transaction for the sale has taken place and goods and services have been exchanged. Creditors are expenses that have been used in the accounting period but have not yet paid for. As an example, many businesses plan to pay suppliers in around 45 days from the invoice point. This means that in the monthly profit and loss account the cost of these supplies must be accounted for although the invoice has not actually been paid.

This is called the accrual concept, which forms the basis of many accounting systems around the world, whereby the non-cash effects of transactions and other events should be reflected, as far as possible, in the financial statements for the accounting period in which they occur, and not, for example, in the period in which any cash involved is received or paid. Similarly, a business may pay in advance for products and services that it has not yet used, such as annual charges for rent paid in advance. The profit and loss account must be adjusted to include only the cost of what has been used and the remainder of the payment is shown as a current asset in the balance sheet.

Profit is calculated by considering all the sales for both cash and credit and matching these with all the costs of production. As a consequence the operating cash flow can be quite different to the operating profit over similar periods. The following sections will consider the accounting treatment of specific items and activities relevant to the hospitality industry.

A second item that does not appear in the cash flow is depreciation. The depreciation of a fixed asset is a measure of the wearing out of the asset through use and this cost should be set against the profit for the period. There are different methods available for calculating the depreciation charge and profits will vary depending on which method is used. The following section provides guidelines for the more common approaches.

What is depreciation?

Depreciation is a charge made to the profits of the business to write off part of the value of a fixed asset. The more common forms of fixed asset for asset intensive businesses are land and buildings, equipment and machinery and motor vehicles. The first of these, land and buildings, may remain unchanged in value over time but in reality is likely to increase. In the UK a new FRED (17) was issued, effective from 1998, which for the first time required hotel buildings to be depreciated. In the past, UK generally accepted accounting principles had not required the depreciation of buildings if the level of maintenance on hotel buildings prevented an actual reduction in market value of the asset. With the issuance of this FRED, depreciation charges for UK hotel companies are now required.

Equipment and machinery can take a variety of forms, but include fixtures and furnishing, computer equipment, motor vehicles and specialist technology. Each category of item should be depreciated using an estimate of the useful life of the asset, resulting in a nil value or simply a scrap value at the end of its life. For example, motor vehicles tend to depreciate more quickly in the early part of their life and it may be appropriate to depreciate the asset more heavily in the early years of its life to reflect this.

Straight–line method versus reducing balance

The total depreciation to be charged over the life of the asset is calculated by measuring the difference between the original cost and the residual value, which is the value of the asset at the end of its life or period that is being considered. The straight-line method for calculating the annual depreciation charge is then simply to divide this figure by the estimated life in years. This results in an equal charge each year. An alternative approach is the 'reducing balance' method which involves depreciating the asset by a fixed percentage each year based on the year-end value of the asset. This results in higher levels of depreciation being charged in the early years of the life of the asset. The difference between the two methods is illustrated by the following example.

Kitchen equipment is purchased at a value of £10,000. The estimated life of the equipment is 5 years, when it is then considered to be worth zero. The end value of the item is also known as the residual value. The depreciation charge can be calculated using methodologies known as straight-line depreciation and reducing balance depreciation. The straight-line method simply calculates the total depreciation experienced over the life of the asset and divides this figure by the life of the asset in years. This approach always results in an equal depreciation charge each year. In contrast, the reducing balance method is based on depreciating the net value of the asset by a factor resulting in reducing depreciation charges each year. In the example shown in Table 3.3, the reducing balance depreciation has been calculated using a factor of 50%.

There is some flexibility available when choosing a depreciation rate in terms of both the method and the period over which the asset is to be depreciated. This discretion can lead to the possibility where identical businesses could declare different profit levels as a result of adopting alternative depreciation methods. A business that chooses to change its depreciation method from one accounting period to the next must declare in the published accounts that this has occurred, as the profits may then be materially affected.

Table 3.3 Comparison between straight-line charges and reducing balance charges

Year	Straight-line annual charge (£)	Year-end value (£)	Reducing balance annual charge (£)	Year-end value (£)
1	2,000	8,000	5,000	5,000
2	2,000	6,000	2,500	2,500
3	2,000	4,000	1,250	1,250
4	2,000	2,000	625	625
5	2,000	Zero	313	312

Revaluing fixed assets

Fixed assets such as land and buildings can experience both sharp rises in value during boom periods and falls in value during recession. As a result the accounts of the company can become seriously out of line with the market value. The issue of asset revaluations is certainly a tricky one for the hotel and resort industry in particular, where there is significant asset ownership. The discrepancies between actual current asset value and balance sheet book values can be considerable. The approach for estimating asset revaluations is dealt with in Chapter 13.

Accounting for inflation

The problem of trying to show a true and fair view during periods of inflation has caused accountants to enter into fierce debate and the problem has never been clearly solved. SSAP 16: Current Cost Accounting was issued in 1980 but was withdrawn in 1988 following widespread disapproval. The problem with inflation occurs when valuing assets, as the book value will always fall short of the true value. This can distort performance measures such as return on capital employed where current profits are compared with out-of-date asset values. In periods of high inflation the relationship between sales and cost of sales is also distorted as the bought-in price of materials becomes out of date. The valuation of stock in particular can cause difficulty and this matter is now considered in detail.

Stock valuations

There are four approaches to assessing what cost means when used for stock valuation purposes. The method used will affect the calculation of the cost of sales figure in the profit and loss account and will also affect the stock held value in the balance sheet. The methods are:

- **First in, first out (FIFO)**, where the cost of the most recently purchased items will be reflected in the valuation. During periods of inflation the earliest items with the lowest price will appear to be issued first, leading to a lower cost of sales calculation.
- **Last in, first out (LIFO)**, where the latest and highest prices are charged to the profit and loss account, resulting in a higher cost of sales figure and lower profits, as well as a lower stock valuation.
- **Average cost**, where the value of stock at any one time is the average of all items of cost.
- **Replacement cost**, which is the present cost to replace the asset or stock item.

The following example illustrates the effect of each method on profitability.

The information in Table 3.4 provides a summary of the inflows and outflows of a typical commodity, recording the date of receipt, the purchase price and the date of issue. This information is then summarized in a second table (Table 3.5) to illustrate the differences in closing stock value depending on the method used.

Table 3.4 Summary of the inflows and outflows of a typical commodity

Date	Units received	Purchase price (£)	Units used	Market price (£)
1/1	600	10.00		10.00
5/1	200	12.00		12.00
10/1			300	12.00
15/1			400	13.00
20/1	100	14.00		14.00
30/1			50	15.00

Table 3.5 Data to summarize calculation for the closing stock valuation

Method	Date	Received/issued Quantity	Price (£)	Value (£)	Balance Quantity	Value (£)
FIFO	1/1	600	10.00	6,000	600	6,000
	5/1	200	12.00	2,400	800	8,400
	10/1	(300)	10.00	(3,000)	500	5,400
	15/1	(300)	10.00	(3,000)	200	2,400
		(100)	12.00	(1,200)	100	1,200
	20/1	100	14.00	1,400	200	2,600
	30/1	(50)	12.00	600	150	**2,000**
LIFO	1/1	600	10.00	6,000	600	6,000
	5/1	200	12.00	2,400	800	8,400
	10/1	(200)	12.00	(2,400)	600	6,000
		(100)	10.00	(1,000)	500	5,000
	15/1	(400)	10.00	(4,000)	100	1,000
	20/1	100	14.00	1,400	200	2,400
	30/1	(50)	14.00	700	150	**1,700**
Average £	1/1	600	10.00	6,000	600	6,000
	5/1	200	12.00	2,400	800	8,400
	10/1	(300)	10.50	(3,150)	500	5,250
	15/1	(400)	10.50	(4,200)	100	1,050
	20/1	100	14.00	1,400	200	2,450
	30/1	(50)	12.25	612.50	150	**1,838**[a]

[a]Rounded.
FIFO: first in, first out; LIFO: last in, first out.

The FIFO method produces the highest closing stock valuation at £2000, and this serves to reduce the value of cost of sales and therefore increases profitability. The LIFO method produces the lowest stock valuation at £1700, thereby increasing the cost of sales and reducing profitability. As a result, for many businesses the average value or the replacement value provides the most consistent result. The management and control of stock levels is considered in detail in Chapter 7.

International Accounting Standards

The systematic recording of financial data is universally based on double-entry book-keeping principles, which have been in use by businesses for many centuries. However, differing regional practices have resulted in the presentation of results by companies with significant differences in profits reported owing to the national differences in accounting procedures. As a consequence there has been a growing movement to harmonize the accounting regulatory frameworks.

The International Accounting Standards Board (IASB) has a conceptual framework underlying its financial reporting standards and interpretations, the *Framework for the Preparation and Presentation of Financial Statements* (the Framework). The Framework sets out the concepts that underlie the preparation and presentation of financial statements for external users. IASB publishes its Standards in a series of pronouncements called International Financial Reporting Standards (IFRS). It has also adopted the body of Standards issued by the Board of the International Accounting Standards Committee (IASC). Those pronouncements continue to be designated 'International Accounting Standards' (IAS) (Table 3.6). From 2005 listed companies throughout the European Union (EU) are obliged to follow IAS rather than national standards.

The accounting statements explained

The accounting statements are produced to convey the financial performance of the business. There are three in total and the aim of this chapter is to provide the manager with an understanding of the basic principles underlying each statement. This understanding will enable the manager to interpret the financial position of any organization. The following chapters will develop this understanding further by providing additional tools for analysis such as ratio calculations using figures drawn from the financial statements.

The balance sheet

The balance sheet can be described as a snapshot of the business at a particular moment in time. It is based on the simple equation that the total value of what the company owns will equal the financial claims on the business, that is, the total liabilities.

$$\text{Assets} = \text{Total liabilities}$$

Table 3.6 International Accounting Standards

	Title
IAS 1	Presentation of Financial Statements
IAS 2	Inventories
IAS 7	Cash Flow Statements
IAS 8	Net Profit or Loss for the Period, Fundamental Errors and Changes in Accounting Policies
IAS 10	Events After the Balance Sheet Date
IAS 11	Construction Contracts
IAS 12	Income Taxes
IAS 14	Segment Reporting
IAS 15	Information Reflecting the Effects of Changing Prices
IAS 16	Property, Plant and Equipment
IAS 17	Leases
IAS 18	Revenue
IAS 19	Employee Benefits
IAS 20	Accounting for Government Grants and Disclosure of Government Assistance
IAS 21	The Effects of Changes in Foreign Exchange Rates
IAS 22	Business Combinations
IAS 23	Borrowing Costs
IAS 24	Related Party Disclosures
IAS 26	Accounting and Reporting by Retirement Benefit Plans
IAS 27	Consolidated Financial Statements
IAS 28	Investments in Associates
IAS 29	Financial Reporting in Hyperinflationary Economies
IAS 30	Disclosures in the Financial Statements of Banks and Similar Financial Institutions
IAS 31	Financial Reporting of Interests in Joint Ventures
IAS 32	Financial Instruments: Disclosure and Presentation
IAS 33	Earnings per Share
IAS 34	Interim Financial Reporting
IAS 35	Discontinuing Operations
IAS 36	Impairment of Assets
IAS 37	Provisions, Contingent Liabilities and Contingent Assets
IAS 38	Intangible Assets
IAS 39	Financial Instruments: Recognition and Measurement
IAS 40	Investment Property
IAS 41	Agriculture

It should be remembered that the balance sheet is always out of date, it does not refer to the present position or the future, and it should always balance. The items that the company owns are referred to as assets and these can be subdivided into those that are long term or fixed in nature and those that are current.

Fixed assets are typically items such as land, buildings, equipment, machinery, computers and motor vehicles. These are all assets that are normally introduced into the business with the purpose of enabling the business to function to make a profit. They are described as being 'tangible' assets because they can be seen and touched. Fixed assets that cannot be physically accounted for are called 'intangible' and the most common of these is called goodwill. This arises when a business is purchased for a value that exceeds the net value of the physical assets. Purchases of fixed assets are called 'capital expenditure' items, and this area will be discussed further in Chapters 10 and 11.

Current assets include stock, which may be subdivided into raw materials, work in progress and finished goods, as well as outstanding sales known as debtors and cash balances. The current assets normally have a short life and are used up in the operation of the business.

There are several types of liability, classified in terms of long term and short term. Long-term liabilities include loans from external parties who have simply lent to the business and who receive interest in return. Owner's capital or equity is also a type of liability in that it remains the property of the owner and technically could be repaid, although in practice this is unlikely to occur. Returns are paid in the form of dividends and are related to the performance of the business. Alternatively, the profits made could be reinvested in the company and are known as retained profits or reserves.

Short-term or current liabilities include bank overdrafts, taxation and outstanding balances owed to suppliers. It is now possible to expand the initial equation to read:

$$\text{Fixed assets} + \text{Current assets} = \text{Long-term} + \text{Short-term liabilities}$$

The balance sheet is produced as a result of a process known as double-entry bookkeeping. This forms of the basis of accounting procedures and works on the basis that for every transaction there are two equal entries. All of the business entries are recorded during the period using this method and at the end of the period the entries are checked using a trial balance to ensure that both sides are still equal.

The layout of the balance sheet can vary and the level of detail will depend on whether the statement is for internal or external reporting. Published balance sheets are subject to legal constraints to standardize the layout. The most usual format for UK companies is the vertical format, where the two balancing sections lie above and below each other rather than side by side.

The vertical format is based on the equation

$$\text{(Fixed assets} + \text{Current assets)} - \text{(Long-term and Current liabilities)} = \text{Capital} + \text{Reserves}$$

In the example from the easyJet accounts shown in Figure 3.1 the vertical format has been used.

Capital and reserves are known as owner's equity. This may be made up of share capital, which may be issued solely to the owners or to the public at large. There are various types of shares in issue, the most popular of which are ordinary shares. The types of shares available for issue are discussed in more detail in Chapter 9.

Reserves are funds accumulated from internally produced profits. Profits may be paid out as dividends or they may be retained to further expansion, when they become known as reserves or retained profit. Reserves may stay in the form of cash, but it is much more likely that they will be used to purchase fixed assets.

Figure 3.1 Balance sheet (easyJet)

Source: easyJet website (www.easyjet.com).

Consolidated balance sheet
as at 30 September

	Notes	2004 (£million)	2004 (£million)	2003 (restated) (£million)	2003 (restated) (£million)
Fixed assets					
Intangible assets	9		309.6		329.8
Tangible assets	10		330.4		320.8
Investments	11		–		–
Joint venture arrangements:					
Share of gross assets		0.6		–	
Share of gross liabilities		(0.4)		–	
			0.2		–
			640.2		650.6
Current assets					
Debtors	12	174.4		141.2	
Cash at bank and in hand		510.3		335.4	
		684.7		476.6	
Creditors: amounts falling due within one year	13	(314.7)		(260.9)	
Net current assets			370.0		215.7
Total assets less current liabilities			1,010.2		866.3
Creditors: amounts falling due after more than one year	14		(157.7)		(65.3)
Provisions for liabilities and charges	16		(63.1)		(42.9)
Net assets			789.4		758.1
Capital and reserves					
Called up share capital	17		99.8		98.5
Share premium account	18		554.2		539.6
Profit and loss account	18		135.4		120.0
Shareholders' funds – equity			789.4		758.1

These financial statements were approved by the Board of Directors on 22 November 2004 and were signed on its behalf by:

R Webster
Director

C Walton
Director

Other types of reserve are generated by certain activities. As an example, a revaluation reserve is created when fixed assets are revalued either above or below their book value. If there is a change in the fixed asset value in the balance sheet then the reserve provides the balancing entry.

The share premium account is also a type of reserve and is created when ordinary shares are sold to the public for more than their nominal or original value. The following example illustrates how this reserve is created.

Example

XYZ Ltd is to raise additional capital through the sale of unissued ordinary shares which have a nominal value of £1.00 each. The issue price is to be 10% below the market price of £2.20. Before the sale the extract from the balance sheet looked like this:

		£ million
Assets		3
Less Long-term loans		1
		2

Share capital	Authorized (£ million)	Issued (£ million)
Ordinary shares (£1 each)	2	1
Reserves		1
		2

After the sale of the remaining shares the balance sheet will show an increase in assets due to the cash being received for the sale and a change in the share capital layout.

		(£ million)
Assets		5
Less Long-term loans		1
		4

Share capital	Authorized (£ million)	Issued (£ million)
Ordinary shares	2	2
Share premium		1
Reserves		1
		4

One million shares have been sold for £2 each, which represents £1 nominal value and £1 share premium per share.

Working capital

Most businesses require funds to be available on a daily basis to allow the business to operate. These funds may be used to purchase stock in advance of trading and to pay staff. Consequently, at any moment in time a business will have money tied up in stocks and in debtors, which is those customers who have received the product or service but who have not yet paid. Too much cash tied up in these areas may deprive the business of funds for profit-generating expenditure on fixed assets. In addition, large volumes of stocks and debtors may result in losses through inefficient management. Therefore, it is essential to keep current assets as low as possible. The definition of working capital is:

$$\text{Working capital} = \text{Current assets} - \text{Current liabilities}$$

This term provides a measure of the balance between short-term funds and short-term assets. There are various approaches to monitoring working capital, ranging from measures that focus on the total amount in relation to sales, to individual measures for the components of working capital. These are considered in more detail in Chapter 7.

Investments

A company may consider investing in activities outside the scope of the existing business. Cash surpluses may be used to invest for both the short term and the long term. A short-term investment will provide a lower return, but can be converted quickly back into cash should the need arise. Long-term investments should provide the highest possible return available while suiting the long-term plans of the company. The business may consider making long-term loans to other operations in return for interest, buying shares in other companies in return for dividends or purchasing other companies in total.

The profit and loss account

The balance sheet has already been described as a useful summary of the business position frozen at a moment in time. However, this does not reveal what the business has achieved over a given period. The profit and loss account provides a summary of revenues and costs occurring over a certain time span. Published accounts produce the statement on an annual basis, but the statement may be produced as frequently as is desirable. There is generally no single layout used for the statement and published accounts aim to produce the minimum of information required to meet statutory guidelines. A sample statement taken from the published accounts for easyJet is shown in Figure 3.2.

The statement starts with the net sales (gross sales less VAT) figure for the period, which includes all sales transactions for both cash and credit. This is matched with the costs and charges for the period to reveal different levels of profit. These levels of profit are now described in detail:

- **gross profit:** the difference between net sales and the cost of the materials for producing the sales (some companies may include wage costs at this point, but in the hospitality and related sectors the cost of sales is the opening stock plus purchases less closing stocks)
- **operating profit:** gross profit less all other costs associated with trading, such as labour costs and operating expenses
- **net profit before tax:** operating profit less interest payable
- **net profit after tax:** net profit before tax less corporation tax

- **retained profit:** net profit after tax less dividends to be paid to shareholders.

Each of these profit levels can be used as a measure of profitability depending on the user's needs. However, it should be remembered that the statement is prepared based on the interpretation of the accounting standards and therefore the profit figure could vary for two identical companies depending on the methods used. An abbreviated format is used for external reporting under the Companies Act.

Figure 3.2 Profit and loss account (easyJet)

Source: easyJet website (www.easyjet.com).

Consolidated profit and loss account
for the year ended 30 September

	Notes	2004 (£million)	2003 (£million)
Turnover: Group and share of joint ventures	1,2	**1,092.4**	931.8
Less: share of turnover of joint ventures		**(1.4)**	–
Group turnover		**1,091.0**	931.8
Cost of sales		**(929.3)**	(775.0)
Gross profit		**161.7**	156.8
Distribution and marketing expenses		**(55.7)**	(61.0)
Administrative expenses	3	**(55.5)**	(47.4)
Group operating profit		**50.5**	48.4
Share of operating profit of joint venture		**0.2**	–
Loss from interest in associated undertaking:			
– committed contribution to Deutsche BA		**–**	(1.3)
Total operating profit: Group and share of joint ventures and associates		**50.7**	47.1
Interest receivable and similar income	5	**14.2**	13.7
Amounts written off investments	11	**–**	(7.8)
Interest payable	6	**(2.7)**	(1.5)
Profit on ordinary activities before taxation	3	**62.2**	51.5
Tax on profit on ordinary activities	7	**(21.1)**	(19.1)
Retained profit for the financial year	18	**41.1**	32.4
		Pence	Pence
Earnings per share			
Basic	8	**10.34**	8.24
Diluted	8	**10.11**	8.04
Basic, before goodwill amortisation	8	**14.64**	12.72
Diluted, before goodwill amortisation	8	**14.33**	12.40
Basic, before goodwill amortisation, accelerated depreciation of certain owned aircraft, committed contribution to Deutsche BA, amounts written-off investments and costs of integrating the businesses of easyJet and Go Fly	8	**15.71**	18.01
Diluted, before goodwill amortisation, accelerated depreciation of certain owned aircraft, committed contribution to Deutsche BA, amounts written-off investments and costs of integrating the businesses of easyJet and Go Fly	8	**15.38**	17.56

All activities relate to continuing operations in the current and previous year.

Internal accounts will be considerably more detailed and should be tailored to suit the needs of the business and area of responsibility. The Uniform System of Accounts for Hotels provides guidelines in a format suitable for hotel operations, and variations on this are widely used in the industry.

Uniform System of Accounts for Hotels

The UK version of the Uniform Accounting System was developed by the Hotel and Catering Economic Development Council in 1969. However, the US system, the Uniform System for Accounts in Hotels, is more widely used and this was first published by the Hotel Association of New York City in 1926. The last revision to the Uniform System of Accounts took place in 1996 and constituted a major change to the previous versions. A new revised tenth version is currently in the process of being devised in the USA.

The ninth version of the Uniform System of Accounts includes a completely revised and updated expense dictionary and chart of accounts. In addition, a new section, on ratios and statistics, has been added. All of the information about various departmental statistics has been brought together in this section, which also includes formulae and explanations for ratios not previously provided. Further guidelines for budgeting and a new section on breakeven analysis have been added.

The basic financial statements recommended by the system for external users are:

- balance sheet
- statement of income
- statement of owner's equity
- statement of cash flow.

The Uniform System offers a standardized format for internal users in the form of departmental statements that can be applied to full-service lodging properties with food and beverage operations, as well as a variety of other services and amenities. The Departmental Statement of Income is illustrated in Figure 3.3.

In addition to the Departmental Statement of Income, there are 30 supporting schedules. The Uniform System may be defined as a manual of instructions for preparing standard financial statements and schedules for the various operating and productive units that make up a hotel. The purpose of the manual is to provide a simple formula for the classification of accounts that can be adopted by any hotel, regardless of size or type. The basic aim of the system is to enable users within the industry to manage their properties more effectively with the information provided, and to enable users from outside the industry to understand the industry more readily as all the statements they are reading are similar and comparable. The benefits of using the system can be defined as follows:

- The system is simple, easy to understand and, therefore, of particular benefit to all non-accountants in the hotel industry.
- As all hotels use the same concepts and terminology the Uniform System enables the compilation of hotel statistics, both nationally and internationally.
- The presentation and format is always the same. This makes the 'Statement' readily recognisable and the location of information easy.

Figure 3.3 Departmental Statement of Income

	SCHEDULE	NET REVENUES	COST OF SALES	PAYROLL & RELATED EXPENSES	OTHER EXPENSES	INCOME (LOSS)
SUMMARY STATEMENT OF INCOME						
OPERATING DEPARTMENTS						
Rooms	1					
Food	2					
Beverage	3					
Telecommunications	4					
Garage & parking	5					
Golf course	6					
Golf pro shop	7					
Guest laundry	8					
Health centre	9					
Swimming pool	10					
Tennis	11					
Tennis pro shop	12					
Other operated departments	13					
Rentals & other income	14	_____	_____	_____	_____	_____
Total Operated Departments						
UNDISTRIBUTED OPERATING EXPENSES[1]						
Administrative & General	15					
Human resources	16					
Information systems	17					
Security	18					
Marketing	19					
Franchise fees	19a					
Transportation	20					
Property operation & maintenance	21					
Utility costs	22			_____	_____	_____
Total Undistributed Operating Expenses				_____	_____	_____
TOTALS		_____	_____	_____	_____	
INCOME AFTER UNDISTRIBUTED EXPENSES						
Management fees	23					
Rent, property taxes & insurance	24					_____
INCOME BEFORE INTEREST, DEPRECIATION & AMORTIZATION AND INCOME TAXES[2]						
Interest expense	25					_____
INCOME BEFORE DEPRECIATION, AMORTIZATION AND INCOME TAXES						
Depreciation and amortization	26					
Gain or loss on sale of property						_____
INCOME BEFORE INCOME TAXES						
Income taxes	27					_____
NET INCOME						_____

[1]A separate line for preopening expenses can be included if such costs are captured separately.
[2]Also referred to as EBITDA – Earnings Before Interest, Taxes, Depreciation and Amortization

- It is a tailor-made system for hotels and can be adopted by hotels of any size and anywhere. Time and money is saved because the design of an individual system for a hotel is unnecessary.
- The Uniform System facilitates the training of accounting and control personnel; only one generally accepted system has to be learnt.
- The system facilitates managerial mobility; there is no need to learn a new system when moving from one company to another.
- The Uniform System represents the 'best practice' in the hotel industry and, therefore, results in better quality of financial statements.

Many organizations adapt the principles suggested by the Uniform System of Accounts for their own purposes. The report in Figure 3.4 illustrates a monthly report layout for a contract catering business.

Profit versus cash

A business may be forecast to be profitable, but success will ultimately depend on there being sufficient cash available to generate sales. The difference between cash and profit is due to the timing differences incurred on the receipt of sales and on the payment of expenses, as well as depreciation. Current depreciation charges do not represent a cash outflow and therefore the cash-flow value will always be different to the profit figure. Cash flows also include capital items such as financing and fixed asset expenditures, neither of which would appear in the profit and loss account. The cash flow is considered to represent a more factual representation of state of the business and it is this rather than profit which is used for appraising long-term investments. Discounted cash-flow techniques are discussed in detail in Chapter 10.

The cash-flow statement

The principal aim of the cash-flow statement is to measure the liquidity of the business. The cash-flow statement is required to be produced in the company reports and this is shown as a historical picture summarizing how funds have been generated and how they have been used. Unlike the profit and loss account, the statement includes operating activities, sources of capital and capital expenditure items. The format of the published statement is regulated by FRS 1. This supersedes SSAP 10, Statement of Source and Application of Funds. A sample layout taken from the accounts for easyJet is illustrated in Figure 3.5.

The statement explains the increase or decrease in the cash balances over the year in terms of the cash inflows from operating activities, sale of fixed assets and the raising of additional finance compared with the cash outflows for interest and dividend payments, taxation and the purchase of fixed assets. The revised style of cash flow has the advantage that cash is the critical element rather than working capital changes, and this can easily be reconciled with the movements in the cash book.

Preparation of the published cash flow

All the information required for this statement can come from the profit and loss account and the balance sheets for the opening and the close of the year. Consider the following example.

Figure 3.4 Example of a monthly report layout

	Actual monthly	%	Budget monthly	%	Variance (£)	Variance B/W%	Budget YTD	%	Actual YTD	%	Variance (£)	Variance B/W%
Sales												
Cost of sales												
Gross profit												
Labour and staff costs												
Disposables												
Cleaning												
Laundry/uniform												
Equipment												
Rentals												
Management fee												
Net profit before overhead costs												

Figure 3.5 Cash-flow statement (easyJet)

Source: easyJet website (www.easyjet.com).

Cash flow information
for the year ended 30 September
Reconciliation of operating profit to net cash flows from operating activities

	2004 (£million)	2003 (£million)
Group operating profit	50.5	48.4
Goodwill amortisation	17.1	17.6
Depreciation of tangible fixed assets	25.3	30.1
Increase in debtors	(36.1)	(43.4)
Increase in creditors and provisions	103.7	24.5
Cash flow from operating activities	160.5	77.2

Consolidated cash flow statement

	Notes	2004 (£million)	2003 (£million)
Cash flow from operating activities		160.5	77.2
Committed contribution to associate		–	(1.9)
Returns on investments and servicing of finance	22	12.6	11.8
Taxation		(6.2)	(16.5)
Capital expenditure	22	(61.9)	(175.3)
Acquisitions and disposals	22	3.4	1.1
Cash outflow before management of liquid resources and financing		108.4	(103.6)
Management of liquid resources		4.8	68.6
Financing	22	66.5	11.1
Increase/(decrease) in cash in the year		179.7	(23.9)

Financing cash flow in includes £8.8 million (2003: £3.8 million) in respect of the exercise of employee share options.

Reconciliation of net cash flow to movements in net funds

	Notes	2004 (£million)	2003 (£million)
Increase/(decrease) in cash in the year		179.7	(23.9)
Cash inflow from the increase in debt	22	(57.5)	(7.3)
Cash inflow for decrease in liquid resources		(4.8)	(68.6)
Change in net funds resulting from cash flows		117.4	(99.8)
Exchange difference on loans		10.5	4.2
Increase/(decrease) in net funds for the year		127.9	(95.6)
Net funds at the start of the year		262.6	358.2
Net funds at the end of the year		390.5	262.6

Net funds at the end of the year comprises:

	2004 (£million)	2003 (£million)
Cash at bank and in hand	510.3	335.4
Bank loans	(119.8)	(72.8)
	390.5	262.6

£14.3 million (2003: £19.1 million) of the cash at bank and in hand is subject to restrictions governing its use.

Example

Treetops Hotel

Balance sheet		**Year ended**	
		2004	**2005**
		(£000)	(£000)
Fixed assets			
Freehold premises		65	100
Equipment and furnishings		84	126
Less depreciation		22	42
Net fixed assets		127	184
Current assets			
Stocks		66	72
Debtors		42	48
Cash balance		14	11
Current liabilities			
Creditors		45	56
Taxation		22	28
Dividend		15	20
Net current assets		40	27
Total assets		167	211
Less long-term liabilities		—	20
Capital employed		167	191
Financed by			
Ordinary shares		100	100
General reserve		41	51
Retained profits		26	40
Capital employed		167	191

Profit and loss account for the year ending 2005

		(£000)
Sales		250
Cost of sales		128
Gross profit		122
Operating costs		
Wages and Administration	28	
Depreciation	20	
		48
Operating profit		74
Interest payable		2
Net profit before tax		72
Corporation tax		28
Net profit after tax		44
Proposed dividend		20
Retained profit		24

The first step is to calculate the net cash inflow from operating activities. Companies are required to show this calculation as a note attached to the statement in the published accounts.

	(£000)
Operating profit	74
Add back depreciation	20
Adjust for changes in working capital by comparing the two balance sheets	
(Increase) or decrease in stocks	(6)
(Increase) or decrease in debtors	(6)
Increase or (decrease) in creditors	11
Net cash inflow from operating activities	93

An increase in current assets (stocks and debtors) represents an outflow of cash and this reduces the cash inflow value. An increase in creditors represents a cash-flow inflow as creditors are being used as a source of funds. From these workings the cash-flow statement can then be prepared.

Cash-flow statement for year ending 2005		(£000)
Net cash inflow from operating activities		93(+)
Returns on investment and servicing of finance		
Interest paid	2	
Dividend paid (taken from previous year)	15	
		17(−)
Taxation (figure actually paid)		22(−)
Investing activities		
Freehold premises	35	
Equipment and furnishings	42	
		77(−)
Financing		
Issue of long-term loan		20(+)
Decrease in cash		3

The change in the cash figure should reconcile with the cash balances shown in the two balance sheets.

Balance at 31/12/2004	14,000
Balance at 31/12/2005	11,000
Decrease in cash	3,000

The cash-flow statement has an important role to play as an internal control statement, where it will be produced in the form of a forecast as regularly as is required. This is commonly on a monthly basis, although weekly and even daily may be used. To illustrate the preparation of the cash flow the following information is to be used.

Example

A hotel is to start trading on 1 July. The following are the forecast trading data and expenditure for the first 4 months from 1 July to 30 October.

Sales	£300,000
Pattern of sales	July 35%
	August 20%
	September 15%
	October 30%
Credit sales	80% of each month's sales, payable in the following month
Cost of sales	50% of total sales, payable in the following month
Labour and staff costs	30% of total sales, payable in the month incurred
Fixed costs	
Salaries	£5,000 per month
Insurance	£10,000 for the year, of which £2,500 is payable in July and £7,500 payable in October
Property tax	£5,000 payable in September
Depreciation	£1,250 per month
Interest	£6,000 paid in October
Other costs	£1,250 payable on a monthly basis
Opening balance at bank	£(10,000) negative

The forecast cash flow is shown below:

	July	August	September	October
Cash inflows				
Sales – cash	21,000	12,000	9,000	18,000
Sales – previous month	nil	84,000	48,000	36,000
Total inflow	21,000	96,000	57,000	54,000
Cash outflows				
Cost of sales	Nil	52,500	30,000	22,500
Wages and staff	31,500	18,000	13,500	27,000
Salaries	5,000	5,000	5,000	5,000
Insurance	2,500			7,500
Property tax			5,000	
Interest				6,000
Other costs	1,250	1,250	1,250	1,250
Total outflow	40,250	76,750	54,750	69,250
Net flow	(19,250)	19,250	2,250	(15,250)
Opening balance	(10,000)	(29,250)	(10,000)	(7,750)
Closing balance	(29,250)	(10,000)	(7,750)	(23,000)

The profit for the period is £9,000. This can be reconciled to the cash balance by adding back the non-cash items including depreciation and cost of sales and deducting the credit sales. The difference is the opening balance value.

A review of the above figures indicates that although the business is just profitable there is a cash-flow difficulty leading to an increasing overdraft, and the cost of this overdraft has not been included in the figures.

The above example illustrates that it is possible to be profitable but still experience difficult trading conditions due to a lack of cash. As a result, for many businesses the forecast cash flow is an essential tool for predicting the future success of the business.

Legal requirements

Most businesses are required to publish a set of financial statements. These should be presented in the standard format to meet the requirements of the Companies Act and the guidelines embodied in the Statements of Standard Accounting Practice. Consequently, most businesses are required to produce a profit and loss account, a balance sheet, and a cash-flow statement, as well as a director's report, an auditor's report and detailed notes to explain and expand on the information presented.

The director's report should contain information such as the level of dividends to be paid, names and interests of the directors, and information regarding the nature of the business and details of employee policies and development. The Stock Exchange also requires a number of additions to the information disclosed to enable a full listing to be given.

Corporate governance

The late 1990s and the early twenty-first century business landscape has been dominated by the phrases 'corporate governance' and 'business accountability'. The publication of the Cadbury Report in 1992 formalized the growing interest in this area, and in the following 10 years the collapse of organizations such as Enron, Andersen and WorldCom ensured that interest in this topic has continued to grow.

Case study: What happened at Enron?

During the late 1990s Enron was a respected company in the USA, with a market value reaching $70 bn and a share price of $90 per share. In October 2001 Enron shocked the world when it announced results that included a loss of $638 m and the announcement that $1.2 bn of debt had been excluded from previous reported balance sheets. It is widely reported that the demise of Enron can be directly attributed to the use of creative and manipulative accounting practices to distort reported profits and asset security.

In the UK companies are governed by the Companies Acts, case law and the additional requirements set for companies listed on the London Stock Exchange. The recommendations arising from the Turnbull Report (*Guidance for Directors on the Combined Code*, Institute of Chartered Accountants of England and Wales, 1999) and the Combined Code on Corporate Governance (1999) require organizations to ensure that adequate internal control systems are in place. The guidance given in the Turnbull Report in relation to corporate governance indicates that a company's internal control system should:

- be embedded within its operations and not be treated as a separate exercise
- be able to respond to changing risks within and outside the company
- enable each company to apply it in an appropriate manner related to its key risks.

The importance of adequate internal control systems has become so prominent that there is now an expectation that companies will outline their commitment to corporate governance procedures in their annual report.

Case study: Four Seasons

The Four Seasons provides an orientation and education programme for new directors, thus imparting to them a deeper insight into the company's policies and functioning. An extract from their policy reads: 'All new directors will participate in this program, which should be completed within four months of a director first joining the Board of Directors. In addition, management will schedule periodic presentations for the Board of Directors to ensure they are aware of major business trends and industry practices as and when required.'

Source: Fourseasons website (**www.fourseasons.com**)

Summary This chapter serves to introduce the basic principles of accounting practice to provide the reader with an insight into the underlying principles of financial statement preparation. The balance sheet provides a historical snapshot of the business at a given moment in time and although this is useful for analysis purposes it should be remembered that the business is never static. There are essential differences between the profit and loss account and the cash flow which must be clearly understood in order to use these statements effectively. The profit and loss account shows the profitability of the business over a given period, whereas the cash flow emphasizes liquidity. The way in which these statements are used is summarized in Table 3.7.

Table 3.7 Time span of the key financial statements

	Past	*Present*	*Future*
Profit and loss account	Published statement	Management accounts	Budgeted
Balance sheet	Published statement		Budgeted
Cash flow	FRS1	Management accounts	Period basis

Questions

1 What is depreciation and how does it affect the accounts of a business?

2 Three main methods of depreciation are used in the UK. What are they and what are the advantages of each?

3 What is the concept behind the adjustments to the balances on various expenses and revenue accounts?

4 What is the logic behind showing the prepayments and accruals in the appropriate section of the balance sheet?

5 What are the roles of the balance sheet, the profit and loss account and the cash-flow statements?

6 Give six reasons why the accounting profit for a period will not necessarily result in an improvement in the business cash flow.

7 Give examples of balance-sheet items that may change the business cash position.

8 The hotel and catering industries have developed the Uniform System of Accounts. List the advantages of the Uniform System.

9 The primary financial objective of companies is usually said to be the maximization of shareholders' wealth. Discuss whether this objective is realistic in a world where corporate ownership and control are often separate, and environmental and social factors are increasingly affecting business decisions.

10 The Marchwood Leisure Group has been operating for a number of years, and its main activity is dining clubs. The actual results for 2003 and the comparative balance-sheet figures for 2002 are shown below:

31 May 02	**Marchwood Leisure, Balance Sheet**		31 May 03
(£000)	*Fixed assets*		(£000)
800	Freehold premises		1000
200	Equipment and furnishings		300
1000			1300
	Current assets		
60	Stock	50	
40	Debtors	60	
0	Bank	100	
100		210	
	Current liabilities		
70	Creditors	60	
50	Bank overdraft		
30	Taxation	50	
35	Dividend	60	
185		170	
(85)	*Net current assets/(liabilities)*		40
915	Capital employed		1340

	Financed by:	
700	Ordinary share capital	850
	Share premium account	110
200	General reserve	215
15	Profit and loss account	65
	Loan capital	
	8% debenture	100
915		1,340

Marchwood Leisure, Profit and Loss Account for the year ending 31 May 03

	(£000)
Sales	550
Cost of sales	200
Gross profit	350
Wages and administration costs	100
Depreciation	55
Other costs (including interest)	20
Net profit before tax	175
Corporation tax	50
Net profit after tax	125
Proposed dividend	60
Profit to reserves	65

Notes:

(a) No fixed assets were sold or revalued during the year

(b) The debentures were issued on 1 Dec 2002

You are required to:

(a) Calculate cash flow from operating activities from the above information

(b) Prepare the cash-flow statement in the published style. For your guidance a pro-forma follows.

	(£000)
Net cash flow from operating activities	
Returns on investments and servicing of finance	
Taxation	
Capital expenditure	
Equity dividends paid	
Financing	
Loans	
Capital	
Net increase/(decrease)	

(c) Reconcile the cash balance shown on the 2003 balance sheet with the net increase/(decrease) shown above.

(d) Summarize the aims of the cash-flow statement

British Association of Hospitality Accountants, Stage 1 Paper, July 2003

Practical activity

In light of recent accounting scandals in the USA, consider how these could have been prevented. What role, if any, do you think the accounting standards could play in ensuring that the preparation of the corporate accounts is true and accurate?

Further reading

Atkinson, H., Berry, A. and Jarvis, R. (1995) *Business Accounting for Hospitality and Tourism*, London: Thomson International Business Press.

Dick, G. (2004) *Introductory Accounting for the Hospitality Industry*, Melbourne: Hospitality Press.

Holt, A. and Eccles, T. (2003) Accounting practice in the post-Enron era: the implications for financial statements in the property industry, *Briefings in Real Estate Finance*, 2(4).

Kotas, R. and Conlan, M. (1997) *Hospitality Accounting*. London: Thomson International Business Press.

Owen, G. (1998) *Accounting for Hospitality, Tourism and Leisure*. Harlow: Longman Higher Education.

Useful websites

www.iasb.org/standards/summaries.asp   International Accounting Standards Board

http://www.icaew.co.uk/viewer/index.cfm?AUB=TB2I_26539&tb5=1&CFID= 1392568&CFTOKEN=84916671   Implementing Turnbull: a boardroom briefing published by ICAEW

http://www.icaew.co.uk/cbp/index.cfm?aub=tb2I_6242   Guidance from the ICAEW on the implications of the Turnbull Report

http://www.icaew.co.uk/cbp/index.cfm?AUB=TB2I_53432,MNXI_53432   Audit methodology, risk management and non-audit services: what can we learn from the recent past and what lies ahead?

http://www.accountancyage.com/News/1137823   Turnbull Report helps reduce risk

http://www.hospitalitynet.org/file/152001826.pdf   Raising the bar on corporate governance/What Sarbanes-Oxley means to the tourism, hospitality and leisure Industry/Deloitte

References

American Hotel & Motel Association (1996) *Uniform System of Accounts for the Lodging Industry* (9th edn), New York: Hotel Association of New York.

Field, H. (2002) *A Practical Guide to the Uniform System of Accounts for the Lodging Industry*, Wimbourne: British Association of Hospitality Accountants.

II External analysis

The Chartered Institute of Management Accountants (CIMA) in the UK defines strategic management accounting as: 'A form of management accounting in which emphasis is placed on information which relates to factors external to the firm, as well as non-financial information and internally generated information' (CIMA Official Terminology, 2000, p. 50). Several writers have put forward the notion that management accounting should be more outward looking, enabling a business to evaluate its competitive position relative to the rest of the industry sector by analysing sales volumes and cost structures for its competitors. The Best Practice Forum Research Report (2003) focusing on the hospitality and tourism industries states that a critical element in setting goals is to know what competitors are up to so that plans can be developed to meet the challenge and differentiate business from the competition. In the strategic management process an informed view of environmental influences and competitive forces is an essential part of the strategic planning process. Typically, a number of techniques can be used to assist in the process of environmental analysis, including:

- PESTLE analysis
- Portfolio models
- Competition analysis.

It is well understood that an understanding of the environment enables a business to develop a strategy to meet the demands of the future environment. The first stage of a formal analysis is to examine the global macroenvironment using a framework such as a PESTLE analysis. The aspects to be reviewed with this analysis are:

- **Political:** assessing the impact of political systems, laws and regulations, political stability and risk
- **Economic:** the rate of growth, pattern of consumption, rate of exchange, monetary and fiscal policy, interest rates, inflation, taxation levels and labour skills
- **Social:** factors such as demographics, culture, social factors, education and nationalism
- **Technological:** the impact of emerging technologies
- **Legislation:** the impact of national and world legislation
- **Environmental:** the impact of local, national and environmental issues.

The following chapters in this section consider how accounting information can be used to develop strategies to create sustainable competitive advantage. To do this, a range of portfolio models based on the work of Porter is described to provide a selection of tools for evaluating the competitive environment.

The accounting role is critical for producing information on competitors to help the business select its own strategy. The comparison of competitors' relative costs and investments will provide valuable information that can be used in the setting of pricing strategies. Ward *et al.* (1992) assert that the key to a cost comparison exercise lies in correctly predicting future levels of cost, and not in the measurement of historic relationships. This will enable the business to establish whether competitors are setting prices at levels that are sustainable in the long term. It may be that competitors are setting prices below their true cost levels to dominate the market and drive out local competition before increasing selling prices to improve profitability. However, the competitive situation is far more serious if competitors have already achieved long-term cost reductions and are able to offer lower prices for similar products or services without eroding the profit level per unit.

Consequently, there is most certainly potential for the management accounting information system to assist in the provision of information to enable the development of competitive strategies with the intent of pursuing competitive advantage, although evidence suggests that this is not widely understood in practice.

The following chapters consider the importance of cost control and revenue maximization in the context of maintaining competitive advantage.

References

Best Practice Forum (2003) Research Report 1. Key Elements of Best Practice prepared by the School of Management, University of Surrey.

CIMA Official Terminology (2000) London: CIMA.

4 | Managing costs

About this chapter

The effective management of costs is a major challenge for any organization. The benefits are obvious in that a reduction in costs will lead to an increase in the profit to sales ratio and an improved return on capital employed. Yet for many organizations the need for cost controls is only highlighted when costs have already started spiralling out of control or when revenue levels are falling during periods of intense competition or recession. This chapter considers first how routine performance can be monitored and controlled and then provides suggestions for a long-term approach to strategic cost reduction with the purpose of improving a business's opportunities for competitive advantage. The specific aspects to be covered are:

- the nature of costs
- costs for decision making
- monitoring routine performance
- investigating the cost base
- cost leadership
- competitive analysis
- Porter's approach to competitive advantage.

Learning objectives On completion of this chapter you should be able to:

- understand the meaning of different classifications of cost
- understand how to classify costs into different categories and apply techniques for determining the nature of costs
- construct breakeven, contribution and profit volume graphs
- apply cost–volume–profit analysis to varying sales-mix situations
- understand how a knowledge of cost structure facilitates competitive advantage.

Introduction

Costs can be classified in different ways depending on the source of the information and also on how the cost information is to be used (Table 4.1).

Table 4.1 Alternative approaches to the classification of costs

Basic cost elements	Direct and indirect costs	Fixed and variable costs
Materials Including food and beverage costs	**Direct** Materials Wages Expenses	**Variable costs** Costs that vary linearly with sales
Salaries and wages Costs associated with the employment of staff	**Indirect** Materials Wages Expenses	**Semi-variable** Costs that contain a variable element and a fixed element
Expenses Operating and overhead		**Fixed** Costs that remain constant regardless of the level of business activity over a 'relevant range' of activity

Essentially, all cost information can be used for control and planning purposes as follows:

- **control purposes**, where costs are matched to revenue to establish profitability for an area, product or market
- **planning purposes**, where information about costs is used to set pricing strategies, monitor profit margin and manage sales-mix profitability.

The basic cost element approach represents the simplest approach to classifying costs based on an analysis of the resources required to produce the product or service. There are three key cost elements:

- **materials**, which represent the cost of the components that make up the product, e.g. the cost of materials required to produce a restaurant meal or drinks cocktail
- **labour**, which includes all costs associated with rewarding personnel for their efforts, including uniforms, pensions and salary costs
- **expenses**, which include all other operating and overhead costs.

This approach forms the basis of the sequence of the basic profit and loss account.

A second approach is to divide costs into those that can be assigned to products, services, departments or particular activities, i.e. *direct costs*, and those that cannot be assigned, i.e. *indirect or overhead* costs. Examples of direct costs also include the basic cost elements, but this time these costs are directly attributable to a specific area of the business:

- materials: cost of sales, e.g. ingredients
- labour: restaurant manager's salary
- expenses: laundry of table linen.

In this example all these costs are clearly directly attributable to the restaurant within a larger operation such as a hotel.

Examples of indirect costs include all indirect material costs, labour costs and expenses included in the operation, such as:

- property rentals
- general manager's salary
- energy costs.

Some businesses try to allocate indirect costs to products and services; however, this is often problematic, as it is usually difficult to arrive at a basis of apportionment that is truly representative of how the cost has been accumulated.

The third category of cost classification considers cost behaviours in relation to revenue or volume. This is done by defining two basic cost types:

- fixed costs
- variable costs.

Fixed costs are those that remain unchanged in total over a given period of volume of activity, whereas variable costs change proportionately with a change in the level of activity. Fixed costs remain constant over a period of activity or sales volume known as the 'relevant range'. Beyond the relevant range the fixed costs will start to increase. In cost per unit terms this means that the cost per unit falls for fixed costs as volume increases, whereas the variable cost per unit remains the same regardless of volume of units sold. This can be demonstrated graphically and this is illustrated in Figures 4.1 and 4.2.

Many costs have both a fixed and a variable element. Energy consumption, for example, can clearly be partly fixed and partly variable. This cost is illustrated in Figure 4.3.

Classifying costs in this way provides a powerful tool in analysis terms, in that the contribution, which is the interim profit before fixed costs are deducted, can be used for a series of decision-making activities as well as being the essential determinant of breakeven point. The key relationships are:

$$\text{Sales revenue} - \text{Variable costs} = \text{Contribution}$$

Figure 4.1 Fixed costs

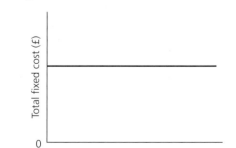

Figure 4.2 Variable costs

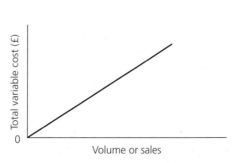

Figure 4.3 Semi-variable costs

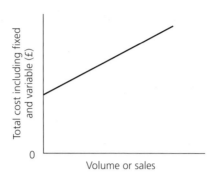

and

$$\textbf{Contribution} - \textbf{Fixed costs} = \textbf{Profit}$$

This can then be used with the relationship fixed costs divided by the contribution per unit to establish a breakeven point in units, that is, the level of trading where neither a profit nor a loss is made.

For example, given the following information:

	Per unit (£)
Sales	10
Variable costs	4
Contribution	6
Fixed costs	£60,000 in total

it can immediately be seen that the breakeven point must be 10,000 units because each unit provides a contribution of £6 towards the total fixed costs. The proof being:

Sales	10,000 × £10	100,000
Variable costs	10,000 × £4	40,000
Contribution	10,000 × £6	60,000
Fixed costs		60,000
Profit/(loss)		Nil

The breakeven point can be illustrated graphically, as demonstrated in Figure 4.4. When drawing the graph it is important to ensure that:

- the horizontal axis is used to plot sales (£) or volume of business
- the vertical axis is used to plot sales and costs in monetary terms
- the graph scales start from zero at the origin
- the graduation of the scales is equally spaced.

The following sequence of instructions will help you to draw an accurate graph:

- Draw the fixed cost line which represents the fixed costs over the relevant range of activity.
- Draw the variable cost line from the origin to the maximum level of sales volume.
- Draw the sales line from the origin to the maximum level of sales volume.
- Draw the total cost line from the point on the vertical axis where fixed costs occur and add the variable costs.

Figure 4.4 illustrates how the breakeven or cost–volume chart should appear.

Figure 4.4 Breakeven chart

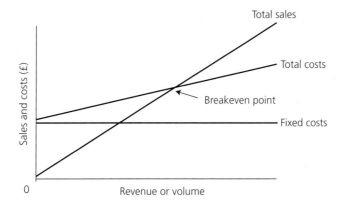

Forecasting required profit

A certain level of required profit can be also be built into the equation. If an operation requires a level of profit of £20,000, possibly to meet a return on equity consideration, then this figure can be used with the cost information to establish the required level of sales, as the following workings demonstrate.

$$\frac{\text{Required profit + Fixed costs}}{\text{Contribution per unit}} = \text{Required volume of sales}$$

Using the previous data

$$\frac{20,000 + 60,000}{£6} = 13,333 \text{ units}$$

Margin of safety

The margin of safety illustrates how much sales activity can fall by before a loss will occur. Using the previous example, if the breakeven volume of sales is 10,000 units and the forecast level of sales is 15,000 units the percentage margin of safety is calculated as:

$$\frac{\text{Expected sales} - \text{Breakeven sales}}{\text{Expected sales}} = \frac{15,000 - 10,000}{15,000}$$

$$= 33\%$$

The following examples illustrate breakeven calculations in practice.

Example

Yellow Hammer Tours sells adventure holidays direct to the public via the internet and has the capacity to organize and sell 3,000 tours per year. The average unit cost and selling price per tour is as follows:

	(£)
Selling price	1,500
Variable costs:	
Accommodation and meals	500
Flight and transfers	250
Other costs	200

Fixed overhead costs are £350,000 per annum for up to 3,000 tours and the forecast sales for the year are 2,000 tours.

One can start by calculating breakeven point arithmetically. The contribution, that is the selling price minus variable costs per tour, is £550. The total fixed costs are £950,000 and so the breakeven point in number of tours is:

$$\frac{950,000}{550} = 1,727 \text{ tours}$$

The margin of safety is:

$$\frac{\text{Expected sales} - \text{Breakeven sales}}{\text{Expected sales}} = \frac{2,000 - 1,727}{2,000}$$

$$= 13.65\%$$

In this example the breakeven point was calculated using the contribution per unit. However, when selling a range of products or services the use of contribution per unit is not always possible.

Breakeven and sales mix

The reality for many hospitality organizations is that a combination of products is sold, each with their own cost structure and resulting contribution per unit. The overall contribution and resulting breakeven point then become dependent on the actual sales mix achieved, as the following example demonstrates.

Example

The Regent Hotel has prepared the following budget for the forthcoming month:

Total sales		£400,000
Sales mix	Rooms	50%
	Food	30%
	Beverage	20%
Cost of sales	Food	40%
	Beverage	35%
Other variable costs		
	Rooms	£40,000
	Food	£45,000
	Beverage	£35,000
Fixed costs		£170,000

In this situation it is not possible to calculate the contribution per unit because each department will be selling numerous products, each with their own selling price and resulting contribution. Instead, the relationship between total sales and total contribution, known as the C/S ratio, is used. To calculate the overall C/S ratio and the resulting breakeven point from the above data the following workings are required.

	Rooms	Food	Beverage	Total
Sales	200,000	120,000	80,000	400,000
Cost of sales	–	48,000	28,000	76,000
Gross profit	200,000	72,000	52,000	324,000
Variable costs	40,000	45,000	35,000	120,000
Contribution	160,000	27,000	17,000	204,000
Fixed costs				170,000
Net profit				34,000
C/S ratio	80%	22.5%	21.25%	51%

The resulting breakeven point is calculated using the fixed costs as follows:

$$\frac{170,000}{51\%} = £333,333 \text{ in sales}$$

If the sales mix were to change to, say

Rooms	40%
Food	40%
Beverage	20%

then the resulting C/S ratio would change and a new breakeven point would need to be calculated. A simple approach to calculating the new weighted C/S ratio is by using the percentage points as follows:

	C/S ratio	Sales mix	Percentage points
Rooms	80%	40%	32 (80 × 40%)
Food	22.5%	40%	9 (22.5 × 40%)
Beverage	21.25%	20%	4.25 (21.25 × 20%)

The new weighted C/S ratio is the sum of the percentage points, 45.25%.
   The resulting breakeven point is:

$$\frac{170,000}{45.25\%} = £375,690.60 \text{ in sales}$$

Breakeven analysis is an essential tool for assessing the viability of a new business and most feasibility studies for a new investment will include a review of the breakeven point, as the following example illustrates.

Example

A small company operating a number of restaurants is searching for a location to open another. A possible opportunity has been identified and the following forecasts have been made:

1 This operation requires an investment of £5,500,000 to purchase the site, furniture and equipment and the balance for working capital.

2 The shareholders of the company have £3,000,000 of their own to invest and will borrow the remainder at 10%.

3 Estimates for the first year of trading are that food and beverage cost will be 30%, variable labour costs will be 15% and other variables will be 5% of total sales.

4 Other cost estimates are:

Management salaries	£950,000
Depreciation	£350,000
Insurance	£100,000
Other costs (excluding interest on loan)	£50,000

5 The company requires a return of 20% on its own initial investment.

Based on the figures given, the forecast profit and loss statement for the first year of trading will appear like this:

	£	%
Revenue	4,600,000	100.0
Cost of sales	1,380,000	30.0
Gross profit	3,220,000	70.0

(continued)

Labour costs	690,000	15.0
Variable expenses	230,000	5.0
Contribution	2,300,000	50.0
Fixed costs excluding interest	1,450,000	31.5
Profit before interest	850,000	18.5
Interest	250,000	5.4
Net profit	600,000	13.0

In order to calculate the revenue figures a bottom–up approach is required. The profit required by the shareholders is 20% of the shareholder investment. The interest payable will be based on the loan of £2,500,000 borrowed at a rate of 10%.

The breakeven point is calculated from the total fixed costs divided by the C/S (contribution to sales) ratio.

$$\frac{1,700,000}{50\%} = £3,400,000 \text{ revenues}$$

This can be proven as follows:

	£	%
Revenue	3,400,000	100.0
Cost of sales	1,020,000	30.0
Gross profit	2,380,000	70.0
Labour costs	510,000	15.0
Variable expenses	170,000	5.0
Contribution	1,700,000	50.0
Fixed costs excluding interest	1,450,000	42.6
Profit before interest	250,000	7.3
Interest	250,000	7.3
Net profit	Nil	0.0

CVP assumptions

This approach is known as cost–volume–profit (CVP) analysis and provides a powerful tool for assessing the viability of a business. There are, however, several assumptions associated with the CVP analysis with which it is important to be familiar. Drury (2005) identifies these as:

- All other variables remain constant.
- There is a single product or constant sales mix.
- Total costs and total revenue are linear functions of output.
- The analysis applies to a relevant range of fixed costs only.
- The analysis applies only to a short-term horizon.
- Costs can be accurately divided into their fixed and variable elements.

We are now going to consider this final point, which highlights that the difficulty in using CVP analysis often falls not in the analysis, but in the initial classification of costs into those that are fixed and those that are variable in nature. However, there is a number of simple, as well as more sophisticated, statistical techniques available to assist in this exercise and the reader is recommended to review the further reading.

The following example demonstrates what is known as the high–low approach to cost analysis.

Example

The following sample of costs and activity levels was recorded for a food servery:

	Covers	
	1800 £	2400 £
Labour	9,000	11,400
Food costs	12,600	16,800
Administration costs	6,000	6,000

Labour costs are analysed by taking the difference between the costs and dividing by the additional covers, the assumption being that the additional cost must be a variable cost as fixed costs remain constant:

$$\frac{11,400 - 9,000}{2,400 - 1,800} = £4$$

This procedure isolates the variable cost per unit. From this the variable costs may be deduced as being:

$$2,400 \times £4 = £9,600$$

and so the fixed costs must be:

$$11{,}400 - 9{,}600 = £1{,}800$$

Food costs are proven to be totally variable because, after dividing the cost by the covers, the food costs remain constant at £7 per cover:

$$\frac{16{,}800 - 12{,}600}{2{,}400 - 1{,}800} = £7 \text{ per unit}$$

Administration costs are purely fixed costs as the same level of cost is recorded for differing levels of volume.

Another approach using a range of data is demonstrated as follows.

Example

A department has the following breakdown of its revenue and employment costs for the past year:

	Revenue (£)	Salaries (£)
January	49,100	22,800
February	49,000	22,600
March	52,300	23,900
April	48,800	22,500
May	69,200	29,800
June	93,500	38,400
July	107,600	43,800
August	89,100	37,200
September	69,100	30,500
October	60,900	26,800
November	57,500	25,600
December	55,200	24,600

With these data the fixed and variable costs can be estimated by applying the high–low method to the July and February figures as follows. By using the highest set of data, that is revenues of £107,600 and corresponding costs of £43,800, along with revenues of £48,800 and costs of £22,500, the additional variable costs arising from the additional sales can be calculated:

$$\frac{43{,}800 - 22{,}500}{107{,}600 - 48{,}800} = \frac{21{,}300}{58{,}800}$$

The variable costs are 36.2% of sales. This means that the fixed costs can be calculated approximately:

Revenue	Total cost	Variable cost	Fixed cost
49,100	22,800	17,774	5,026
49,000	22,600	17,738	4,862
52,300	23,900	18,933	4,967
48,800	22,500	17,666	4,834
69,200	29,800	25,050	4,750
93,500	38,400	33,847	4,553
107,600	43,800	38,951	4,849
89,100	37,200	32,254	4,946
69,100	30,500	25,014	5,486
60,900	26,800	22,046	4,754
57,500	25,600	20,815	4,785
55,200	24,600	19,982	4,618

An alternative approach would be to plot the values on a graph with revenue on the horizontal axis and costs on the vertical axis. To ensure accuracy it is essential to ensure that:

- the graph scales start from zero at the origin
- the graduation of the scales is equally spaced
- the pairs of figures are accurately plotted.

In practice it is highly unlikely that the points will form a perfectly straight line, but if there is a relationship between revenue and costs the points plotted will approximate to a straight line. From this it is possible to determine the fixed costs and the variable cost, as illustrated by Figure 4.5.

The CVP approach can also be used to help explain why some businesses are more risky in nature than others. Consider the CVP graphs in Figure 4.6.

Restaurant A illustrates an operation with lower fixed costs and hence a lower breakeven point. This means that lower sales are required to achieve a profit and if sales revenue falls the loss will be relatively small. Restaurant B illustrates a high fixed cost operation where the breakeven point is much higher, but once this has been achieved the resulting profitability will be much higher. The traditional approach to investment in the hospitality industry, that is direct equity invest-ment, means that many operations have substantial fixed costs in terms of salary

Figure 4.5 Relationship between costs and volume

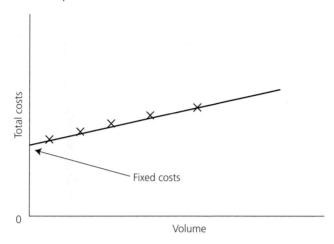

Figure 4.6 Two businesses with varying cost structures

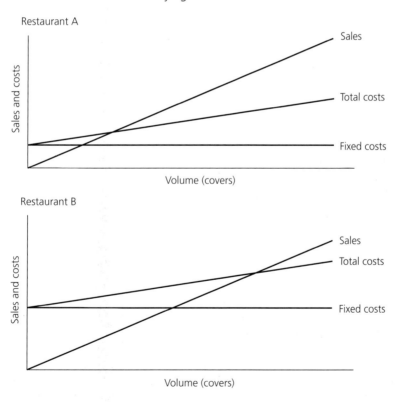

costs, property operation and maintenance costs and the servicing of finance. The high-risk nature of this type of investment has led to the growth of other forms of expansion using techniques that serve to reduce risk; these are discussed in further detail in Chapter 10.

Costs for decision making

For the purposes of decision making it is often useful to consider the relevant costs associated with the project. These are costs that will be incurred as the result of taking the decision. In many cases the relevant costs are the variable costs and these may be used in the decision-making process. In reality the variable costs may only be used in the short term and in situations where spare capacity exists. In the long term it is likely that both fixed and variable costs will need to be considered as relevant costs.

In most decisions it is also necessary to consider the nature of the opportunity cost. This can be defined as the benefit forgone as a consequence of taking an alternative course of action. No cash exchanges hands; the cost results from for-going an alternative that requires no transaction. These costs are often not clearly understood and are then left out of the decision-making process.

Finally, a sunk cost is defined as one that has already been incurred and cannot be recovered. It is considered to be not relevant in the decision-making process and should be left out. In the following example the different types of costs are identified.

Example

XYZ is a food manufacturer specializing in cook–chill meals. An unexpected order has been received for which labour and production-line capacity are available. The two main ingredients required are:

- Ingredient A, which is used regularly in the existing process and 1,000 kg is required for this order. The existing stock holding is 1,500 kg purchased at 85 p per kg. The current replacement cost is 90 p per kg.

- Ingredient B, which is currently in stock with a stock holding of 500 kg purchased at 60 p per kg. This order requires 300 kg to be used. Without the order the entire stock would be either wasted or sold off as waste products at 30 p per kg.

	Ingredient A	Ingredient B
Relevant cost	90 p/kg	30 p/kg
Sunk cost	85 p/kg	60 p/kg
Opportunity cost		30 p/kg

Monitoring routine performance

This is usually carried out as part of the budgetary control process where variances are used to compare actual performance with budgeted values. This area is covered in some detail in Chapter 6. The essential requirement for effective budgetary control procedures is a system for analysing revenues and costs incurred in the organization. This normally means breaking the organization down into areas of responsibility known as budget centres or cost centres. Responsibility is then assigned to individuals for the management of the sales and costs in those areas. The three types of responsibility centre are:

- cost centre
- profit centre
- investment centre.

Typically an organization will comprise cost centres where only servicing activities take place such as marketing, personnel and training and administration, and profit centres where trading activities take place. The performance of a profit centre is based on a comparison of revenues and costs. An investment centre is often the complete operation where overall profitability can be compared to the investment. Variances are normally considered in terms of cost types such as materials, labour and expenses, and the comparison to budget is normally made on the basis of the cost of the resource (price per unit) and the volume used in the process. A typical layout for a regular report comparing budget to actual performance is illustrated in Figure 4.7.

The budgeted figures are based on standard costing procedures to forecast the spend at a given volume and the actual results are then compared to this. It may then be useful to prepare a flexible budget statement that reflects actual volumes at standard or target cost to provide a means of effective comparability with the actual results. This is illustrated in Chapter 6.

The system of flexing is certainly useful for monitoring performance, but often the data required to produce the flexed statements are not available and variances in practice are often calculated simply by comparing original forecasts with the actual performance.

Figure 4.7 Report comparing budget to actual performance

	Yearly budget (£)	% to sales	Budget to date (£)	% to sales	Actual to date (£)	% to sales	Variance (£)	Variance (% B/W)	Projected end of year (£)	Projected variance to budget (£)	Projected variance to budget (% B/W)
Sales											
Cost of sales											
Gross profit											
Wages											
Operating costs											
Net profit before fixed costs											

Investigating the cost base

Costs that provide the greatest scope for improvement are often the indirect or overhead costs, which are usually fixed in nature. These are often the greater proportion of costs in any case and deserve further attention. It is frequently assumed that because they are fixed in nature they cannot be effectively controlled or reduced. In practice, other costs that are directly attributable to revenue levels are much harder to reduce without reducing the quality of the product or service, although considerable management time is spent in tracking them. To reduce variable costs effectively a long-term view of the production process is required and this will be discussed later.

The nature of overhead costs can be investigated using techniques such as zero-based budgeting (ZBB), a technique that has its origins in the public sector. This technique requires the relevance of all costs to be questioned during the budgeting process, rather than relying on an incremental approach where last year's performance is the starting point for setting this year's budget. This technique is described in more detail in Chapter 6 with relevance to the hospitality and tourism industries. ZBB can produce substantial benefits, but it is a time-consuming activity and requires considerable expertise on the part of the operational manager to be used effectively.

An approach that has attracted considerable attention in recent years, particularly in the manufacturing sector, is activity-based costing (ABC).

Activity-based costing

This approach focuses on indirect costs and attempts to establish links between expenditure and the activities carried out by the organization. This contrasts with the traditional approach of allocating overheads arbitrarily to departments on the basis of revenue, floor space, head count or any other base deemed to be appropriate. ABC has its origins in the manufacturing sector, but is now being more widely applied in many different types of organization. The process requires the identification of the key activities which take place in the organization and establishing a cost centre for each of those activities. The next step is to determine the cost driver for that activity; that is, the events that can be described as the significant determinant of the cost of the activity. Finally, a unit cost should be derived for each activity and these costs are assigned to each product on the basis of the demand for the activity.

This is probably better understood if it can be applied to a practical situation. In the case of a hotel, major activities performed include receiving reservations, checking in, room servicing, billing and checking out. Examples of cost drivers that may be appropriate to these activities include:

- the number of reservations received
- the number of guests arriving at the front desk
- the number of guests in house and the number of point-of-sale transactions.

The next stage is to divide the cost by the total number of driver units to calculate the cost per unit of activity. Finally, the cost of activities is traced to products according to the product demand for activities by multiplying unit activity costs by the quantity of each activity that a product consumes. Hence, the process attempts to measure as accurately as possible the *total* actual cost of each activity in the organization, rather than focusing specifically on direct or variable costs.

Cost leadership

For companies competing on price, cost leadership is vitally important to achieve as it enables the operation to achieve increased market share by providing the best value for money to the customer. It also enables the operation to strengthen its position of competitive advantage by using the higher financial returns to improve quality, customer service and product innovation. Cost leadership means that a business seeks to achieve the status of being the lowest cost supplier to the market. This does not mean that the business is the lowest priced supplier, but there is the potential to reduce price during periods of intense competition. Being cost efficient provides businesses with the opportunity to develop a strong competitive advantage. The management guru Michael Porter has written extensively on this theme and says that:

> its cost position gives the firm a defence against rivalry from competitors, because it can still earn returns after its competitors have competed away their profits through rivalry (Porter, 1980).

Porter has argued that there are only two alternative routes to competitive advantage, these being cost leadership and differentiation, with there being little advantage in being the industry average competitor pursuing a 'stuck in the middle position'. The alternative competitive positions are illustrated in Figure 4.8.

Other writers argue that such a polarized approach is a dangerous strategy to pursue and that practice suggests that it is possible to be both cheaper and better. Certainly, customers in the hospitality and tourism sectors are demanding evidence of constantly improving levels of cost, quality, reliability and innovation.

Achieving long-term cost leadership requires a strategic approach in that the long-term nature of costs needs to be considered. Short-term measures for cost reduction such as operational cuts in staffing levels, material costs and operating costs normally cannot be sustained and inevitably lead to a drop in product and service quality. Instead, a long-term approach is required, with a 'spend to save' policy. Lynch (2000) describes the main routes to strategic cost reduction as:

- Designing in cost reduction: this is based on designing the product or service carefully during inception so that it is cheaper to deliver.
- Supplier relationships: using relationships with suppliers to achieve long-term cost reductions has been popular with some of the UK's large-scale catering operators, who have been able to drive down unit costs through changing specifications and centralized purchasing to take advantage of bulk buying.

Figure 4.8 Alternative competitive positions

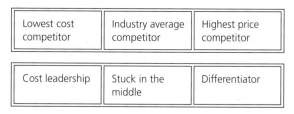

- Economies of scale and scope: unit costs can fall as the business increases in size and processes are streamlined to take advantage of bulk buying.
- The experience curve: the learning organization will be able to achieve cost reduction as it becomes more experienced in the preparation and delivery of products and services.
- Capacity utilization: the hotel industry in particular has significant high fixed costs and achieving the best use of space, for example, can achieve cost reductions per unit.

Conventional approaches to cost analysis tend to be based on a historical analysis of costs focusing on a single accounting period at a time. The approach tends to be introspective, operations based and reactive to short-term crisis. A strategic approach has a wider focus, looking forward, analysing costs as they change throughout the product life cycle. The aim should be to consider the external environment, which is the competition, in addition to internal factors, and to be proactive in analysing information.

A limited approach to cost management often occurs because the responsibility for cost cutting usually lies solely with operating managers rather than being part of the strategic planning process. Frequently, costs are only managed during crisis situations and many important costs are ignored. All too often employees hold negative perceptions of the cost-cutting activity and personal relationships and emotions stand in the way of objective action. As a consequence exercises in cost reduction are neither followed up nor maintained, while the wrong costs are often cut first because they are the easiest to eliminate.

Increasingly, the concept of value chain analysis is viewed as an approach for both achieving increased customer satisfaction and managing costs more effectively. The value chain illustrated in Figure 4.9 connects all the individual parts of the business process together. Drury (2005) suggests that the key to success when using the value chain concept is to view the value chain from the customer's perspective and assess their satisfaction with each component.

To summarize, the obstacles most likely to prevent costs being managed in a strategic way are:

- top management attitudes
- the dominance of return on investment as a measure of performance preventing further investment spend
- the failure to recognize the importance of spending to save.

Figure 4.9 The value chain

Source: Reproduced with permission from Drury (2005) *Management Accounting for Business.*

Profit planning

The profile of business costs is a critical element in profit planning. The cost structure, also called operating leverage, is measured in terms of the proportions of fixed costs and variable costs present in the business structure. An understanding of the influence of cost structure on profits is a crucial element in management decision making.

The hospitality and tourism sector is characterized by a wide range of cost structures found in different types of business. In Chapter 1 the profile of the sector was considered and the following list of operations put forward:

- hotels
- restaurants
- pubs, bars and nightclubs
- contract food service providers
- membership clubs
- events
- gambling
- travel services
- tourist services
- visitor attractions
- youth hostels
- holiday parks
- self-catering accommodation
- hospitality services.

Each of these elements of the sector will experience a differing cost structure. Typically, owned hotels, for example, have high fixed costs, whereas the contract catering sector is typified by a low fixed cost structure. The term sensitivity analysis is used to describe a technique used to measure the effect of cost structure on profitability. The technique enables the manager to establish which factors are critical to a decision, with the critical factors including unit volume, selling price, variable costs and fixed costs. Profit multipliers are used in sensitivity analysis to determine the effect of a percentage change in critical factor on the level of profit.

$$\text{A profit multiplier} = \frac{\%\ \text{Change in net profit}}{\%\ \text{Change in critical factor}}$$

In general terms, the profits generated by a business with a high fixed cost structure are relatively sensitive to changes in critical factors. This suggests that the profits are potentially more at risk than for businesses with low fixed cost structures. Cost structure has implications for management decision making.

Case study: British Airways

Fuel warning takes shine off BA profits surge

British Airways has posted its best annual profits since 1997 but warned that the surge in oil prices, which dragged the airline near the red by the end of the period, was set to raise fuel bills by more than one-third.

The company, Europe's second-biggest airline, reported an 80 per cent rise to £415 million in pre-tax profits for the year to the end of March. A 3.3 per cent rise in turnover, helped by higher cargo volumes, more than outpaced a 1.6 per cent rise in costs.

The company, which has cut thousands of jobs and revamped its routes after the aviation down-turn prompted by the September 11 attacks, met a target of cutting its cost base by £450 million within two years, helping operating margins rise by 1.5 points to 6.9 per cent.

"These are good results, driven by continued cost control and strong demand for our products," Rod Eddington, who steps down in September as the BA chief executive, said.

The margin increase has, for the first time in seven years, triggered a bonus scheme which it will hand to BA's non-managerial staff, giving payouts of at least £612 each.

However, the full-year figure disguised a slowdown in the January-to-March period reflecting a decline in fares amid tough industry conditions. Passenger revenues fell by 1.5 per cent despite an increase in the number of travellers carried.

Aviation fuel costs were, at $143 a gallon, 36 per cent higher than a year before and 5.4 per cent up on the quarter before.

British Airways estimated that fuel costs would rise by £400 million, or 35 per cent, this financial year, more than outstripping a rise of up to 5 per cent, or about £370 million, expected in revenue rises.

'Quite clearly the headwinds are still pretty strong', Mr Eddington said, also noting that some rival US carriers were shielded by Chapter 11 bankruptcy protection and 'received substantial government support'.

BA also reported a £205 million increase in its pension deficit to £1.4 billion despite a doubling in company contributions.

The company, which cut its dividend in 2001, once again failed to announce a payout.

The report, nonetheless, was welcomed by analysts.

'They are performing very well in what is a very challenging environment,' Edward Legget, the investment analyst at Standard Life, said.

At Panmure Gordon, Gert Zonneveld said: 'We must give the company credit for what has been achieved. There is further potential to improve the competitiveness of the company, particularly the move into Heathrow Terminal 5, which gives the company a great opportunity to address outdated and inefficient working practices.'

Source: *The Times Online*

Competitive analysis

The process of competitive analysis covers a number of key characteristics of a business. These include:

- the external attractiveness of the different products and/or market opportunities measured

- using the growth in the market in total
- the competitive position of the individual business in terms of current market share and relative cost levels.

These characteristics are often hard to measure in practice, although a profiling approach, which is based on matrix analysis, is often used.

Market development

The nature of competitive strategy is very much influenced by the stage of development of the product in the marketplace. The stages are defined as being:

Stage 1: product launch
Stage 2: sales growth
Stage 3: competitive shakeout
Stage 4: maturity
Stage 5: decline.

Techniques for analysing how each stage might be identified were discussed in Chapter 2.

During the launch stage competitive advantage is established by virtue of the fact that a new product has been launched in the marketplace ahead of the potential competition. The focus for competitor analysis at this stage will be on the relative levels of development and launch costs. However, this type of information is often difficult to obtain.

As the industry moves into the rapid growth stage the key factor is the growth in market share and the focus switches to monitoring marketing expenditure. This information is more readily available in that the level of marketing activity is easily visible and it is therefore simpler to evaluate.

Once the product can be determined as being in the mature stage the basis of competition is frequently selling price and the key success factor to obtaining competitive advantage is in the effective management of costs to ensure that in a highly price-sensitive market profit levels are maintained. This exercise is obviously vitally important to many business operations to sustain competitive advantage throughout the maturity stage which, in practice, is proportionately considerably longer than the other stages of the product life cycle.

The competitor analysis should not be simply limited to relative cost comparisons, however. Relative selling prices and customer perceptions should also be monitored. Products that are perceived to have a higher value in the eyes of the customer do not need a lower cost base because the premium selling price compensates the resulting profit levels. Therefore, relative cost comparison exercises should start from an appreciation of the strategic product positioning that the competitor is seeking to achieve.

Sources of competitive information

The problem with achieving effective competitor analysis lies in obtaining good, reliable and meaningful information. It is not always necessary to obtain absolute values as quite often relative financial data, that is data relative to one's own business, are sufficient. The management accountants within the business should be sufficiently experienced to be able to apply their own knowledge of cost structures to develop data drawn from the competition. The overall aim is to build up a comprehensive database about the competition that is continually being updated. The information contained within this can be drawn from a number of sources without in any way resorting to unethical forms of industrial espionage. A varied range of sources is listed in Table 4.2.

Table 4.2 Sources of competitor information

Library research	Annual reports
	Press/journal material
	Investment analysts' reports
	Government reports
	Published market intelligence
	Company literature
	Company history
	Academic case studies
	Computer-based information services
	Competitors' advertising
Interviews	Journalists
	Academics
	Others with specialist knowledge
Direct contact	Visits to other establishments
	Physical observation
	Physical analysis of product
Conferences	Industry associations
Primary market research	Consumer surveys
	Industrial market research
Soft information	Own staff and management
	Mutual suppliers
	Mutual customers

Porter's approach to achieving competitive advantage

Michael Porter (1995) offers a three-step approach to achieving competitive advantage. The steps are:

- analysis of industry structure
- choosing a competitive strategy
- implementation of strategy.

Analysis of the industry structure enables firms to gain a good understanding of the cost structure of competitors and assess where advantages can be gained. This is discussed in more detail in the following paragraph using Porter's five forces model. Selecting a strategy for competitive advantage requires careful planning, and Olsen, West and Tse (1998) suggest that for firms to achieve long-term sustainability, they should combine several of their unique products and services into a number of competitive methods in such a way that it will be difficult for others to imitate. The final step is then the careful implementation of the strategy.

Analysis of industry structure

The structure of the industry is determined by the pressure from five competing forces acting on the business. These are:

- the threat from new entrants
- the bargaining power of suppliers
- the bargaining power of buyers
- the threat of substitutes
- rivalry between existing competitors.

This is often illustrated diagrammatically, as shown in Figure 4.10. Each force will now be analysed in detail.

Barriers to entry

The threat of entry by new competitors is often influenced by the economies of scale, brand loyalty and cost advantages already being achieved by the existing players in the market, along with the capital required for entry. This force can have a significant effect in the hospitality industry, where all of these conditions can apply.

An entry barrier is anything that represents a significant economic disincentive to a business to invest in a particular industry. In the hospitality industry the size

Figure 4.10 Current and potential competitor analysis (using the Porter model as a basis)
Source: Ward (1992) *Strategic Management Accounting.*

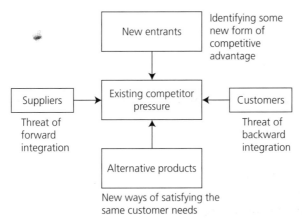

of the investment required to set up the business often acts as a significant barrier to possible new entrants. The cost structure may also serve as a barrier, particularly when fixed costs are high and higher volumes are required to achieve profitability. Finally, another common barrier comes from the use of heavily marketed brands to try to create customer loyalty.

Power of suppliers

The power of the suppliers is derived from the availability of resources and may have a more significant effect for, say, operations setting up in developing economies. The conditions that make suppliers more powerful include those situations where there are no substitute products available for the buyer to switch to, or where the cost of switching supplier is too high to be viable.

Power of buyers

The power of buyers is derived from the level of supply and demand and the homogeneity between product suppliers. The power that buyers can exert is increased when several buyers unite or when there are suppliers and few costs are incurred in switching supplier. The threat from buyers is also increased when there is a real risk that the buyer will consider backward integration, that is, expanding by buying out a supplier in an attempt to achieve satisfactory prices and quality.

Substitute products

To identify the level of threat from substitute products it is necessary to identify those products and services that perform the same function. Often these products are situated in industries that seem quite remote from the industry in question. For example, within the leisure industry there is a whole range of leisure activities each vying for customers' limited leisure time and spending power.

Existing firms

Rivalry among existing firms can occur in a number of ways, including price competition, new products and increased levels of customer service. The degree of rivalry depends on a number of features related to industry structure. Numerous or equally competitive competitors may cause instability by attempting to make strategic moves while hoping to remain unnoticed. Where there is low market growth the level of competition can intensify as firms attempt to expand by capturing market share from other firms. This intensifies still further where there is little opportunity for product differentiation. High levels of competition often mean that profitability is eroded, but high exit barriers can prevent firms from moving into other more profitable areas.

Exit barriers arise when the business is supported by high-cost dedicated assets that have limited alternative uses, such as hotels. Exit costs may also include redundancy settlements and wasted material costs.

The level of rivalry is also dependent on the market position. It is most intense during the mature stage of the product life cycle and results in a condition called shakeout, when the less profitable operations are forced to retire. Consequently, the higher the pressure from the five forces the less attractive the industry as profit levels are constantly being reduced and it is increasingly difficult to maintain market position.

Competitive strategy

The next stage in Porter's approach is to decide upon a competitive strategy. Porter suggests that there are only two generic competitive positions, these being cost leadership and product differentiation.

- **Cost leadership** involves achieving competitive advantage through overall lowest cost compared to competing firms.
- **Differentiation** involves identifying those product or service characteristics that customers perceive as valuable and meeting those needs better than any of the competition, and as a result a premium charge can be made.

Strategy implementation

The final stage is implementation of the strategy, and Porter has produced the 'value chain' model to illustrate how this final stage can be achieved. The value chain comprises a grouping of the primary and secondary activities of the organization which 'up' the product or service, or both, provided to the customer. This is illustrated in Figure 4.9.

A business can be described as having a collection of activities that are performed to design, produce, market, deliver and support its product. The way in which an organization does this is a reflection of the organization's history, structure and past strategies, and the nature of the activities. It may be useful at this stage to illustrate how this chain might apply to a hotel operation.

- **Inbound logistics:** these are the activities concerned with receiving, storing and distributing the input resources in the system. Practical examples include bookings received from customers using a variety of reservation capture methods.
- **Operations:** this stage converts the inputs into the final products and/or services of the organization, i.e. the management of the whole experience which converts needy customers into satisfied customers.
- **Outbound logistics:** this stage is concerned with the collection, storage and distribution of products and services to the customers, i.e. the service distribution points such as room service and restaurants.
- **Marketing and sales:** these are activities designed to attract further purchases during the period of the customer stay.
- **Service:** these activities ensure that customers enjoy their purchased goods and services and are associated with customer care and after-sales service.

Porter's approach has been designed with the intention of providing a framework for classifying the various areas of the organization in order to understand how the various activities interrelate and contribute to the firm's competitive position.

The aim is to understand what resources exist in the organization and how they may be used more effectively.

Summary The management of costs is an essential part of any business and should be carried out throughout the life of the business and not just in times of crisis. The routine control of costs can effectively be achieved through the use of budgetary control systems based on assigning areas of responsibility to individuals and monitoring the variances that occur between expected and actual performance. In the long term a strategic view of cost management is required, which may mean moving away from the traditional approaches to cost monitoring. A strategic view means that all levels of managers in the organization should be reviewing the cost base and seeking ways of achieving long-term cost savings that are sustainable. This may mean incurring expenditure to save in the long term, but thereby ensuring that the organization can achieve competitive advantage through control of the cost base. Monitoring the competition can provide a wealth of information to assist an organization in establishing its position in the marketplace.

Questions

1 Define fixed and variable costs.

2 Give examples of the following for a hotel and resort operation:
   (a) direct materials
   (b) direct labour
   (c) indirect materials
   (d) indirect labour
   (e) direct expenses.

3 Explain the meaning of each of the following and give three examples of each for a travel operator:
   (a) variable cost
   (b) fixed cost
   (c) semi-variable cost

4 Contribution for decision making

   The Westgate Hotel operates at an average of 85% capacity and offers three types of bedroom. The information on the rooms is shown below.

	Family	Twin/Double	Single
Number of rooms available per night	100	150	100
Average tariff per room per day	£120	£95	£85
Cleaning time per room	120 min	90 min	70 min
Daily cost of consumables per room	£10	£8	£6

Owing to a staff shortage on one particular day the number of available cleaning hours is only 300. The fixed costs of the hotel including the salaries of the cleaning staff are £15,000 per day.

You are required to:

(a) Calculate the contribution per room.

(b) Calculate the most profitable combination of rooms to be made available given the staff shortage.

(c) Calculate the profit if all the rooms are available and the revised profit given the staff shortage.

(d) The hotel can use agency staff to fill the shortfall but the cost per labour hour is 20% higher than the usual staff. Comment on the viability of using the agency staff and illustrate your answer with workings. Give your conclusions as to whether the agency staff should be used.

British Association of Hospitality Accountants, Stage 2 Paper, July 2004

5 Breakeven analysis and sales mix

The following figures relate to the Zena Restaurant for the monthly accounts for June:

	Starters	Main course	Sweets and coffee	Total
Sales mix	30%	60%	10%	100%
Variable costs	30%	40%	20%	
Fixed costs				£120,000

You are required to:

(a) Calculate the breakeven sales revenue per period, based on the sales mix assumed above.

(b) Prepare a contribution breakeven chart illustrating the above figures.

(c) Calculate the impact on the breakeven point of a change in sales mix to:

Starters	20%
Main course	65%
Sweets and coffee	15%

(d) Explain the assumptions underlying the cost–volume–profit analysis technique.

(e) Explain how a business with multiple products can use cost–volume–profit analysis.

British Association of Hospitality Accountants, Stage 2 Paper, July 2004

6 Breakeven and sales mix

The Foxglove Restaurant has prepared the following budget for the forthcoming quarter:

Total sales		£750,000
Sales mix		
	Food	70%
	Beverage	20%
	Other	10%
Cost of sales		
	Food	30%
	Beverage	25%
	Other	80%
Labour		
	Fixed	£95,000
	Variable	20% of sales
Other fixed costs		£175,000

(a) Calculate the contribution and the contribution to sales ratio for each area and the total net profit for the year.

(b) Compute the effect of the following changes in sales mix and cost of sales percentage on the contribution and the total net profit:

Sales mix		Cost of sales	
Food	65%	Food	30%
Beverage	25%	Beverage	28%
Other	10%	Other	85%

(c) Discuss the effect of these changes on the breakeven point and the margin of safety.

7 Breakeven and selling price

A proposed restaurant operation is scheduled to open in a few months. The owner seeks your advice on pricing and gives you the following information:

Total capital investment	£500,000
Target return on investment	15%
Annual fixed costs other than depreciation	£100,000
Depreciation	£60,000
Operating costs	£750,000
Cost of food and beverage	30% of sales

The restaurant will have 150 seats and an average seat turnover per day of 2.5. The restaurant will be open for 320 days per year.

(a) Calculate the average spend per meal.

(b) Calculate the breakeven point for the operation.

(c) Calculate the margin of safety.

8   Feasibility study
A small company operating a number of restaurants is searching for a
location to open another restaurant. Two possible opportunities have been
identified and the following forecasts made regarding each one:

Option 1: This operation is to be leased under the terms of a management
contract with present revenues of £600,000 a year, operating variable costs
of £450,000 and fixed costs of £75,000. In addition to these costs the lease
contract calls for the company to pay an annual rental of 5% of sales plus a
fixed amount of £10,000 per year.

Option 2: This operation requires an investment of £550,000 to purchase the
site, furniture and equipment and the balance for working capital. The
company has £300,000 to invest and will borrow the remainder at 10%.
Estimates for the first year of trading are that food cost will be 30%, variable
wage costs will be 15% and other variables will be 5% of total sales. Other
cost estimates are:

Management and salaries	£55,000
Depreciation	£35,000
Insurance	£10,000
Other costs (excluding interest on loan)	£50,000

The company requires a return of 20% on its initial investment.
Ignore taxation.

You are required to:

(a) Prepare a trading statement for each option to meet the criteria
specified.

(b) Calculate the breakeven point for each option in terms of sales.

(c) Evaluate each option in terms of risk and profitability and make
appropriate recommendations for the selection of one of the options.

9   Compare the following operations in terms of the nature of their costs:

(a) A luxury restaurant

(b) A staff canteen

(c) Catering at a tennis tournament

(d) A five-star hotel operation

(e) A budget-style motel.

Practical activity

Techniques for monitoring the competitive environment

It is not necessary to monitor every competitor in the market place and indeed it is highly unlikely that this would be achievable. Instead, monitoring just a handful of competitor operations can provide useful information about the competitive position of a business. Data based on sales can be analysed in the following manner.

	Sales (£ 000)	Market share (%)	Relative market share
Firm A			
Year 1	700	19.4	
Year 2	1,000	20.4	
Year 3	1,200	20.8	
Firm B			
Year 1	1,400	38.9	2.0
Year 2	2,200	44.9	2.2
Year 3	1,200	50.0	2.4
Firm C			
Year 1	1,000	27.8	1.4
Year 2	1,200	24.5	1.2
Year 3	2,000	23.6	1.1
Firm D			
Year 1	500	13.9	0.7
Year 2	500	10.2	0.5
Year 3	400	5.6	0.3
Total			
Year 1	3,600	100.0	
Year 2	4,900	100.0	
Year 3	7,200	100.0	

Relative market share is calculated by dividing each competitor's market share percentage by that for firm A.

The main points that arise from this analysis are:

- Firm A's sales are increasing from year to year by 42.9% in year 2 and by 50% in year 3.
- Firm B is maintaining its proportion of the market.
- Firm B is achieving higher market growth by capturing market share from firms C and D.

Therefore, firm A needs to ensure that its own market share is not likely to be eroded by the strategy pursued by firm B. It may well then be possible to characterize firm B's strategy in terms of Porter's cost reduction focus or differentiation focus strategies. Firm A needs to ensure that it is not stuck in the middle. Consequently, such an analysis yields very useful information for firm A without requiring the entire market to be defined and analysed.

Further reading

Harris, P. and Hazzard, P. (1992) *Managerial Accounting in the Hospitality Industry*, Cheltenham: Stanley Thornes.
Pearson, G. (1990) *Strategic Thinking*, London: Prentice Hall.
Porter, M. (1980) *Competitive Strategy: Techniques for Analysing Industries and Competitors*, New York: Free Press.

Useful websites

www.drury-online.com
www.netmba.com/strategy/value-chain/
www.absoluteastronomy.com/encyclopedia/P/Po/Porter_generic_strategies.htm
www.quickmba.com/strategy/generics.html

References

Drury, C. (2005) *Management Accounting for Business*, London: Thomson.
Olsen, M. D., Tse, E. C. and West, J. J. (1998) *Strategic Management in the Hospitality Industry* (2nd ed), New York: John Wiley.
Porter, M. E. (1980) *Competitive Strategy: Techniques for Analysing Industries and Competitors*, New York: Free Press.
Porter, M. (1985) *Competitive Advantage: Creating and Sustaining Superior Performance*, New York: Free Press.
Ward, K. (1992) *Strategic Management Accounting*. Oxford: Heinemann.

5 | Managing pricing strategies

About this chapter

This chapter reviews the various pricing methodologies available to the hospitality and tourism industries for the pricing of accommodation, food, beverages and other activities. The review of accommodation pricing techniques considers formulistic approaches to pricing such as the rule of thumb method and the Hubbart formula, which are based on cost plus calculations, as well as market demand approaches such as yield management. Food and beverage pricing is considered with specific reference to sales mix and approaches to menu analysis for maximizing gross profit in percentage and cash terms. In theory, price setting appears to be a simple task, but in reality the pricing process is complicated by market, economic and psychological influences and, as a result, the pricing decision requires input from financial, marketing and operational managers to ensure that the resulting pricing policy is based on the correct information.

Learning objectives On completion of this chapter you should be able to:

- describe how the optimum sales volume and selling price are determined using economic theory
- understand the principles of cost-based approaches to pricing
- apply cost-based pricing techniques to commodities such as accommodation, food and beverages, and other tourism services
- make pricing decisions based on market conditions.

Introduction

The principal aim of any pricing policy should be to increase revenue without sacrificing volume, while increasing profitability and ensuring long-term business value. It should also aim to change customer buying behaviour by responding to influences from the competitive environment. A knowledge of economic theory provides a suitable basis for introducing the cost information required for pricing decisions.

Economic theory

Economic theory describes the sensitivity of customer demand to price as the price elasticity of demand. Demand is described as elastic when a change in price results in a change in the buying behaviour of customers. This relationship is illustrated in Figure 5.1.

The points marked A and B in Figure 5.1 represent two of the many possible price/quantity combinations. As the price falls the quantity demanded increases. Inelastic demand arises where the customer buying decision is unaffected by price changes. Figure 5.2 illustrates the price elasticity of demand where there is elastic demand and inelastic demand. When demand is inelastic an increase in demand has only a minimal effect on quantity purchased, whereas with elastic demand a change in price results in a significant change in quantity demanded.

Figure 5.1 The demand curve

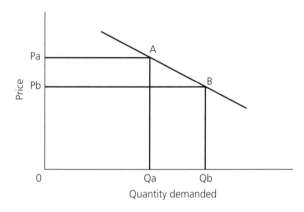

Figure 5.2 Price elasticity of demand: (a) inelastic demand; (b) elastic demand

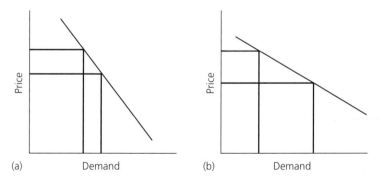

Price and the product life cycle

The product life cycle was introduced in Chapter 2. Pricing strategy should be considered in the light of the positioning of the product or service in relation to

Figure 5.3 Relationship between the product life cycle and pricing strategy

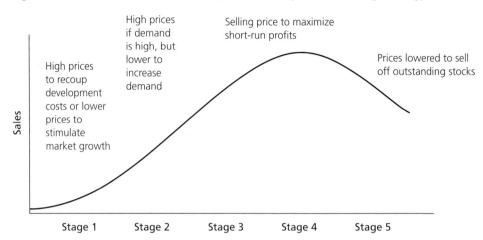

the product life cycle. Figure 5.3 illustrates the relationship between product life cycle and price.

Cost-based approach to pricing

The overall aim of an effective pricing policy is to ensure that the profit per product is maximized while maintaining a perception of value for money in the eyes of the customer. Despite this aim, the traditional approach to pricing tends to be based on cost-plus techniques, where a mark-up is added to the cost of producing the product. The cost of the product can range from simply analysing the food cost, in the case of menu pricing, to attempting to achieve a total cost per product. However, this level of detail is reliant on adequate information being available to enable fixed or indirect costs to be allocated to individual products in a satisfactory manner, particularly where there are several products being provided.

When the pricing policy is based solely on direct costs or on material costs the difference between the selling price and those costs must be sufficient to cover all other costs and provide an adequate level of profit. The following example illustrates a mark-up policy of 200% on cost in a restaurant.

Example

A restaurant produces one dish which is made from food costs to the value of £3. The restaurant has forecast to sell 10,000 of these dishes over a set period with forecast variables at 25% of sales and fixed costs of £12,000.

$$\text{Selling price} \quad = \quad \text{£3 plus 200\%}$$
$$= \quad \text{£9}$$

Therefore

Sales	=	£90,000
Food cost	=	£30,000
Variable costs	=	£22,500
Fixed costs	=	£12,000
Net profit	=	£25,500

The profit required to meet investors' target returns is often used as the basis for establishing the total revenue for an operation where costs can clearly be predicted. The required profit is added to the estimated cost figures to produce a value for total sales. This figure is used with volume forecasts and sales-mix predictions to arrive at selling prices for individual products and services.

Price setting

The economic theory of supply and demand argues that as an item becomes scarcer its price should increase and that there is a direct relationship between price and demand. In the hospitality industry this simple relationship is complicated by the seasonality of the business giving rise to differing demand patterns, and the multiple numbers of products available in a restaurant, for example, where sales are interrelated.

The hospitality industry also differs from the manufacturing industry in terms of the product. Although products may be very similar, no two establishments offer the exact same product and service. There will always be some difference in terms of the product itself and the nature and quality of service. This factor means that it is difficult for operators to use the competition prices as a guideline, but it also gives the operator far greater scope for achieving product and therefore price differentiation.

One approach might be deliberately to charge more than the competitors and use product differentiation to justify the higher price. However, the cost of raising quality should be considered in relation to the increase in selling price, and continual monitoring is required to ensure that the customer still perceives the product to be good value.

Alternatively, an operation may choose to price the product at a level below the competition. This tactic can be dangerous in that unless real cost savings can be made without undermining quality the profit per product will drop without a sufficient corresponding increase in sales volume. This in turn may lead to a price-war situation with a downward spiral of price cutting, which leads to profit reduction for all operators and the possibility of bankruptcy. Although the economic principles of supply and demand and price elasticity apply to the hospitality industry, generally a restaurant does not increase its prices on a Saturday night when it is fully booked, preferring instead to turn customers away.

The accepted pricing practice is to set the published prices at the maximum and then, particularly in the case of rooms, to discount to maximize utilization during the poor trading periods.

Accommodation pricing

Managing the room resource in hotel operations requires achieving a careful balance between maintaining room rate and achieving maximum occupancy, where a relatively small increase in room rate may be worth a drop in occupancy in terms of profitability. However, room occupancy percentage remains the critical determinant of success for many operators, particularly where substantial sales can be generated in other trading areas in the hotel.

Hotel occupancy levels are commonly viewed to be directly related to the size of the hotel, average room rates, conference facilities, hotel ownership and location. Severe discounting may serve to maintain volumes in a period of recession, but the effect of this can have a dramatic downward effect on profitability and the cash-flow levels of the operation.

Hoteliers throughout Europe have faced difficult trading conditions throughout the early years of the twenty-first century, with falling average room rates and occupancy volumes. To compensate for this it is natural that management attention should turn to cost cutting and improving cost controls to maintain profitability, with staff costs often being the first to be cut.

There are various approaches to setting the room rate, ranging from those that are simply formulistic to an extensive analysis of target profit levels and costs, and these will be discussed in detail. However, a successful approach to room pricing requires an accurate knowledge of the markets to which the product is attractive and a clear knowledge of price elasticity patterns. The yield management (YM) approach to pricing does just this, and with the advent of widespread use of computerized reservation systems, is now used extensively. As a result a detailed discussion of this approach will follow later in the chapter. The following discussion considers the alternative approaches practised for setting room rates.

Rule of thumb method

In an operation where the majority of income is derived from room letting, one approach is to base the average room-rate calculation on the capital cost for building one room. It should be reasonable to assume that there would be a fairly direct relationship between the cost of the building and the room rate to be charged. The rule of thumb states that £1 of room rate should be charged for each £1,000 invested in building the room. If a room costs in capital costs £100,000 to build, the average net room rate is calculated to be £100. This relationship is based on the assumptions that the hotel is fairly large (several hundred bedrooms), with other departments such as food and beverage, and that the operation will achieve 65–70% average room occupancy.

This approach is used as a very general guide only and can lead to incorrect pricing strategies where the emphasis is purely on historical costs.

Profit-based pricing techniques

This approach is sometimes referred to as the 'bottom–up' approach to pricing or the 'Hubbart formula' and was originally developed for the American Hotel and

Motel Association. This method is based on accurate forecasts for operating costs and for room occupancy. The sales figure is calculated by summing the target profit with the fixed and variable costs. This total figure is then subdivided to arrive at different rates for different room types. The following example demonstrates the method in practice.

Example

Forecast projections for a 100-bedroom hotel operation are given below.

Investment details	(£)
Fixed assets	2,500,000
Working capital	150,000
Total net assets	2,650,000
Financed by:	
Owner's equity	2,000,000
10% mortgage debenture payable 2010	650,000
	2,650,000

Trading forecasts

– average of 70% occupancy

– forecast profits for other departments £400,000

– owners require a 20% return on equity invested

	(£)
Net profit required	400,000
(based on after-tax target percentage return on equity)	
Corporation tax	133,333
(at 25% of profit before tax)	
Profit before tax	533,333
Interest	65,000
(relating to mortgage debenture)	
Depreciation	250,000
(10% straight-line method on fixed assets)	
Insurance and licence	20,000
(forecast)	
Property operation	520,000
(forecast)	
Administration	55,000
(forecast)	
Management salaries	400,000
Less profit from other departments	(400,000)
(forecast)	
Operating expenses for accommodation	274,920
(forecast at 26% of revenue)	
Accommodation revenue required	1,718,254

Forecast rooms sold annually

The forecast room occupancy percentage should be an accurate forecast for the likely number of rooms sold based on current achievable levels in similar operations. An accurate forecast will improve the reliability of the rate-setting calculation.

$$100 \text{ rooms} \times 365 \text{ nights} \times 70\% \text{ occupancy} = 25,550$$

$$\text{Average room rate required} = \frac{1,718,254}{25,550}$$

$$= £67.25$$

The rate calculated from this approach is simply the average room rate before VAT. From this, rates for room types and market segments will need to be calculated.

Setting the room rate

Single and double rates can be calculated by considering historical double and single occupancy rates. Using the data generated in the example given above, if twin occupancy is 60% of room sold and single occupancy is then 40%, and a 20% difference is required between twin and single rates, the calculation would be:

$$(60\% \times 60\% \times 100 \text{ rooms} \times 365 \times 1.2R)$$
$$+ (40\% \times 60\% \times 100 \times 365 \times R) = £558,558$$

where R represents the single rate. This solves to:

$$15,768R + 8,760R = £558,558$$

$$R = \frac{558,558}{24,528}$$

$$= £22.77$$

The double rate will be £27.32.

This type of algebraic formula could be expanded to include other room type and market segments as long as the occupancies for each type could be forecast.

Room pricing options

The simplest approach would be to offer all rooms at one rate. The advantage of this approach is that it is easy to administer and to communicate to customers. However, the approach fails to respond to peaks and troughs in demand by recognizing customer price sensitivity and as a result fails to maximize revenue.

Alternatively, room rates can be set by room type depending on the room characteristics. This approach is also fairly simple to administer, but is useless where all rooms are uniform. Even if the hotel has different room types it is still limited by the stock of each of those room types and consequently the approach becomes product led rather than market led.

Another approach is to use price segmentation; that is, to introduce logical restrictions on the booking in return for a discounted rate. This allows customers to have access to lower rates in return for reduced flexibility and differentiates those who are willing and able to pay higher prices from those who are willing to change their behaviour in exchange for a lower price. Such an approach enables the hotel to penetrate new markets without encouraging existing business to trade down. It is more difficult to manage than the other approaches and requires the support of a room management package such as a YM system.

Accommodation markets

The transient hotel market, excluding groups, may be crudely classified into two markets, business and leisure, and each market has its own booking pattern characteristics.

Leisure travellers	Business travellers
Advance bookings	Short booking lead times
Quality required varies	Tend to require high quality
Destination flexible	Destination predetermined
Highly price sensitive	Less price sensitive
Stay longer	Short-term stay, avoiding weekends

Hotel pricing strategies should take advantage of these differing market characteristics by attempting to expand the price-elastic markets while ensuring that inelastic business revenues are maintained. Practically, this means managing capacity to ensure that an appropriate number of rooms is left available at high rates to accommodate the late-booking business market. The industry has long been at ease with charging different rates to different markets and although business customers may feel that they are subsidizing the holiday market any rate that exceeds the variable cost of providing the product ensures a contribution towards fixed costs.

The strategy of matching rates to customer behaviour has been less well received, particularly where customers who pay one rate later realize that they could have negotiated a cheaper rate. The key to success with this strategy is to ensure that the rules are clearly structured and logical. This approach to pricing is likely to become more popular particularly where the increased use of technology means that customer markets can be defined by the guests' arrival and departure patterns rather than by status.

Room rate discounting

Discounting is a widespread practice in the hotel tourism industry and is particularly suited to a product based on minimal variable costs and substantial fixed costs. Providing that a room is sold at a price in excess of variable costs, some contribution to fixed costs will be made. This knowledge has led to an almost unchecked approach to room rate discounting by some operators. Often there is no methodology at all to determine how discounts are to be offered and the customer is forced to enter into a haggling procedure to achieve the best rate. Rate cutting can generate more revenues, but this is not always transferred to the bottom line when operating profit per occupied room is falling owing to expenses increasing at the rate of inflation.

The YM technique, as described earlier, provides a formal approach to room discounting which focuses on price and market segment using technology to develop a room pricing policy. More recently this technique has become known by the term 'revenue maximization'.

Yield management

The process of YM involves controlling the rooms' inventory to maximize sales by adjusting room rates in response to the level of rooms booked for a future arrival date. Most hoteliers are well practised at lowering prices to stimulate sales when demand is low, but generally the process of discounting is not supported by any clear methodology, resulting in disgruntled customers and often less revenue achieved than is possible. The practice of YM broadens the scope of the price-setting process by focusing on the rooms available and pricing of the rooms.

The concept of a method for maximizing occupancy and revenue is not new. The airline industry has used the technique for many years with a great deal of success. When airlines cannot fill all of the seats on an aircraft with full-fare customers they try to fill them with customers paying discounted rates. An empty seat represents an opportunity lost owing to the perishable nature of the product. The airline must decide how many fares to discount while making sure they have enough seats left to sell to late booking full-fare-paying customers to maximize the possible revenue. Consequently, YM techniques have been essential for managing a fixed capacity efficiently.

Comparisons can easily be drawn between the management of airline seats and hotel rooms, where fixed capacity exists and the products are sold in easily segmented markets with variable levels of demand often well in advance of the consumption date. The cost structures of the two industries are also similar, both being capital intensive with high fixed costs, while the marginal cost of selling one more airline seat is minimal and the same is true for the selling of a hotel room. Despite the similarities in the two industries the hotel industry has been slow to accept the advantages that YM can offer; however, evidence now suggests that more and more operators are examining the potential of the technique. This may be reflective of the industry, where the vast majority of businesses are individually owned.

Calculating room yield

The two main factors used by management to measure performance in room revenues are occupancy and average room rate. Both of these should be maximized to ensure that the full potential revenue of the room is achieved. The yield is an integrated statistic based on actual potential revenue and is calculated using the following example.

Example

Hotel A has 100 rooms and a rack rate of £100. The following sales mix represents the pattern of business for one night:

Rack rate	25% at £100
Corporate rate	15% at £80
Walk-in trade	3% at £50
Travel agency	3% at £45
Groups	10% at £30

This results in total revenue of £4,285, occupancy of 56 rooms or 56%, and rate per available room of £42.85.

The 'yield statistic' is expressed as follows:

$$\text{Yield} = \frac{\text{Realized revenue}}{\text{Potential revenue}}$$

Potential revenue is the maximum sales that could be obtained if all the available rooms were sold at full rack rate and realized revenue is the actual sales generated. The yield statistic for the previous example would be:

$$\frac{£4,285}{100 \text{ rooms} \times £100} = 42.85\%$$

In terms of room sales, many combinations of occupancy and achieved room rates could generate equal revenue and yield percentages, as the following figures for hotel A illustrate.

Average room rate	Occupancy (%)	Realized revenue (£)	Yield (%)
100	42.85	4285	42.85
90	47.61	4285	42.85
80	53.56	4285	42.85
70	61.21	4285	42.85
60	71.42	4285	42.85
50	85.70	4285	42.85

The yield statistic can also be expressed as a combination of occupancy percentage and average room rate. It can be calculated by multiplying the average rate ratio by the actual room occupancy percentage, where the average rate ratio is calculated by expressing the average rate as a percentage of the average maximum potential rate. Given the data in the example above,

$$56\% \text{ occupancy} \times \frac{76.52}{100} = 42.85\% \text{ yield}$$

This simple statistic provides a single value for measuring a hotel's performance and forms the basis of YM. The purpose of the approach is to maximize room yield by managing both the room rate and the occupancy percentage so that when demand exceeds supply the customer pays more and when demand is low the price is discounted, while ensuring that each customer pays the maximum possible price.

Critics of YM have identified the fact that not all these combinations of occupancy and rate as illustrated in the above example produce the same level of profitability. By introducing a marginal cost of servicing a room, of say £10 per room, the hotel's contribution to fixed costs can be calculated.

Occupancy (%)	Realized revenue (£)	Servicing cost (£)	Contribution (£)
42.85	4,285	429	3,856
47.61	4,285	476	3,809
53.56	4,285	536	3,749
61.21	4,285	612	3,673
71.42	4,285	714	3,571
85.70	4,285	857	3,428

The room's contribution can be seen to fall as occupancy increases and rates fall. However, the effect of the fall in the room's contribution arising from discounted room prices may be outweighed by the resulting increase in food and beverage revenue derived from increased volumes.

Yield management system requirements

To use the system effectively, it is essential to have a clear understanding of the markets in which the business operates. This will be achieved by analysing historical data in terms of the patterns of demand, the market segments and price elasticity. Demand analysis is essentially based on clearly defining the product and differentiating the main market segments to identify the levels of demand from each market segment at different times of the year, thereby predicting the number of rooms needed to meet each segment's needs.

Specifically, the system must contain information relating to customer booking patterns and behaviour and the timing of demand in each market segment. This will need to be supported with data relating to the policy and volumes of overbooking and a clear knowledge of the impact of price changes on demand patterns and occupancy. Producing this level of information is a task of enormous complexity, but the process can be assisted with the use of expert system packages. These are software packages containing a knowledge base that allows the system to approach and solve problems by interpreting the 'facts' based on decision rules written into the software.

Problems specific to hotels

In certain circumstances YM practices translated directly from the airline industry may fail to adjust to the complexities offered by the hospitality industry. The key problem arises when a guest, having stayed one night, decides to extend the stay for one or more nights. If the first night's stay is determined to be a low-demand, low-rate reservation, problems will arise if the ensuing nights of stay are during high-demand periods. Similar problems arise where a customer wishes to stay through a period of both low and high demand. The solution in this case might be to offer an average of the high and low rates generated.

Resistance to change

In the early years of use, research by Jones and Hamilton (1992) identified two major problems in the technique. The first was that there is a tendency for the complexity of the system to overwhelm the user so that the concept of the system was never clearly understood and, as a result, the human interface with the system was often ignored. It became apparent that the key to success was in ensuring that everyone in the organization, including managers and operators, understood what the process was about, and this could be done by simplifying the jargon that is often associated with running the system.

Secondly, the effective use of the system depends on the accuracy of the forecast data, and although technology can effectively plot the historical trends the final forecasts should also be reviewed by the management team to ensure that the forward projections for demand are as accurate as possible. Existing reward systems based on sales volume, occupancy and average room rate may be inappropriate. Instead, it may be possible to introduce rewards to those personnel who implement the new techniques and suggest improvements for the operational use of the system. This may serve to overcome the potential for employee demotivation arising from the perception that the reservation or sales job has been deskilled.

Customer perceptions

The airline industry has successfully used differential rates for many years and customers appear to be used to the fact that they are charged different rates for the same flight. However, the issue of fairness can affect the maximization of profits. In general, customers feel that price rises are fair when costs increase and the price rise has been incurred simply to maintain profits and not to increase them. To convince customers of the fairness of the system while maximizing price, one approach is to increase the reference price, that is, the rack rate, in the knowledge that virtually all customers will pay less than this.

Research drawn from surveys on hotel guests has established that customers express satisfaction with yield management practices when information on the different pricing options is available, when a substantial discount is given in return for cancellation restrictions and when different prices are charged for products that are perceived to be different. This would indicate that improved communication with the customer is necessary to ensure complete acceptance of the approach. Finally, research has indicated that customers perceive unacceptable practices to include:

- offering insufficient benefit in return for booking restrictions
- imposing severe booking restrictions such as non-refundable, non-changeable restrictions on discounted rooms
- not informing customers of the availability of discounted rates.

The future for yield management

Developments in external computerized reservation systems (CRSs) have had a significant effect on the use and extension of YM applications. It is already possible to interface YM systems to external CRSs, widening the potential for the use of YM systems. However, many organizations are still some way off this position and need to upgrade their internal systems to match the standards inherent in external CRSs. In the longer term the application will need to be interfaced market-segment profit analysis (MSPA), which enables decisions to be made on the basis of profit rather than revenue maximization. The MSPA approach identifies the costs within each 'activity centre' in the hotel, enabling profit values and margins to be calculated for each market segment. The development of this approach requires further research and more advanced technology, but it is already clear that an emphasis on profit rather than revenue will, in the long term, realize the full potential of a YM system.

Food and beverage pricing

Restaurant management has traditionally been based on unsophisticated techniques for establishing menu item prices, and the most commonly used approach has been simply to multiply the food cost by a factor of three or even four to produce a target gross profit percentage. Alternatively, the average spend per customer can be determined in the same way as average room rates by using a bottom–up, profit-based approach. Again, the problem with a cost-based approach lies in the accurate forecasting of costs and volumes.

Pricing menu items

A common approach to menu pricing is to calculate the standard cost to produce one of each menu item. This cost is then multiplied by a factor to achieve the target gross profit, as the following example demonstrates.

Standard cost	£1.00
Multiplication factor	3
Selling price	£3.00
Gross profit %	67%
Gross profit	£2.00

Naturally, this is a mechanistic approach and in reality the price should be set to reflect what the market will pay. As a result, some items will have a higher gross profit percentage than others and the combination of products sold, otherwise known as the sales mix, then becomes important.

It is also important not to rely solely on gross profit percentages; often it is the cash gross profit figure that is important, as the figures in Table 5.1 demonstrate. It would be preferable to sell more of menu item 1 than menu item 2, despite the lower gross profit percentage.

Sales mix

This is defined as the combination of menu items sold from the menu. The sales mix will influence the average spend per cover and the resulting achieved gross profit percentage, as the figures in Table 5.2 demonstrate. This combination of menu items produces an average spend of £2.33, a gross profit percentage of 51% and gross profit in cash terms of £71.50. If the sales mix were to change the effect would be that shown in Table 5.3.

These variables make the setting of food menu selling prices particular complex and the problems are equally valid for establishing beverage prices. This, in turn, makes the process of controlling gross profit percentage a time-consuming exercise in practice and for many operations the exercise can never be accurately completed owing to the range of information required.

Fixed price menus

British restaurants have been slow to introduce fixed price menus where the customer pays one price for a three-course meal without choice or a reduced price for

Table 5.1

Menu item	Cost price (£)	Selling price (£)	GP (%)	GP (£)
1	5.00	10.00	50	5.00
2	2.00	6.00	67	4.00

GP: gross profit.

Table 5.2

Menu item	Quantity sold	Selling price (£)	Total sales (£)	Cost price (£)	Total cost (£)	GP (%)
1	10	4.00	40.00	2.00	20.00	50
2	15	3.00	45.00	1.00	15.00	67
3	20	2.00	40.00	1.50	30.00	25
4	10	1.00	10.00	0.20	2.00	80
5	5	1.00	5.00	0.30	1.50	70
Total	60		140.00		68.50	51

Table 5.3

Menu item	Quantity sold	Selling price (£)	Total sales (£)	Cost price (£)	Total cost (£)	GP (%)
1	15	4.00	60.00	2.00	30.00	50
2	15	3.00	45.00	1.00	15.00	67
3	15	2.00	30.00	1.50	22.50	25
4	5	1.00	5.00	0.20	1.00	80
5	10	1.00	10.00	0.30	3.00	70
Total	60		150.00		71.50	52

two courses. The practice has been common in Europe for many years, with fixed price menus available in all types of operation. However, many top London hotel restaurants are now benefiting from offering a set-priced lunch menu based on buffet items or limited choice. The reasoning is that customers prefer to know what the maximum price will be without being caught out with cover charges, service charges and separate charges for bread, vegetables and coffee. For many operations the appeal of fixed menus is a full restaurant at lunchtime, which improves staff morale and is good for the image of the hotel.

Demand-based menu pricing

Increasing profits can either be achieved by reducing expenses, the usual targets being food and labour costs, or by raising the selling price. In recessionary times this latter option may appear to be out of the question. However, the reality is that for a high fixed cost operation a 1% increase in price will have a considerably more substantial effect on profitability, as the following example illustrates.

Example

Assume:

Selling price	£10
Variable cost	£2
Volume of	2000 units
Fixed costs	£10,000

	Original data	Increase selling price (10%)	Reduce costs by 10%
Sales	20,000	22,000	20,000
Variable costs	4,000	4,000	3,600
Fixed costs	10,000	10,000	9,000
Net profit	6,000	8,000	7,400

These figures clearly illustrate that where possible selling price should be maximized by considering the most that a customer is likely to spend on that item before the value/price relationship is lost. This approach can be developed further using techniques described as menu analysis.

Approaches to menu analysis

An approach to menu analysis called menu engineering was proposed in 1982 by Michael Kasavana and Donald Smith. This is a portfolio approach whereby menu items are classified in terms of those with highest contribution margin and highest sales volume. Contribution margin is defined in this case as the difference between selling price and direct costs. Menu items could then be plotted in terms of a grid as shown in Figure 5.4, and managers seek to choose those menu items with the lowest direct costs.

The bias in this approach may result in favouring high-price items that maximize contribution, resulting in a strategy that eventually decreases demand and profitability. Similar approaches using different variables have been proposed by Miller (1980) using food cost percentages, Pavesic (1983) using the combination of food cost percentage, contribution margin and sales volume, and Hayes and Huffman (1985) using individual profit and loss statements for each menu item based on direct and allocated costs. Pavesic's approach using a combination of three variables attempts to overcome the bias inherent in the earlier approaches. The target is to achieve a sales mix that optimizes the cash contribution margin, defined by Pavesic as sales less food costs, and total sales revenue while achieving the lowest food cost percentage. The menu items are then classified into the following groups:

- standards: high contribution margins, high food cost percentage
- primes: high contribution margins, low food cost percentage

Figure 5.4   Kasavana and Smith's approach to menu analysis

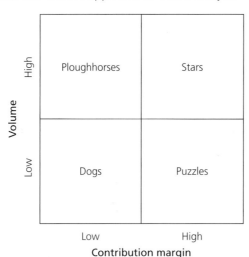

- sleepers: low contribution margins, low food cost percentage
- problems: low contribution margin, high food cost.

Pavesic offers the following explanation. Primes are often the speciality dishes that can be priced at whatever the market will bear, while standards are often popular items that are offered on most menus and need to be priced keenly. The sleeper category includes new items being test marketed to see how the clientele responds to them. The final group is made up of the 'problem' items and these should be eliminated from the menu. Pavisec suggests that maximum contribution will be achieved when the predominant sales mix is made up of primes and standards, while sleepers are used to diversify the menu and attract new clientele to the establishment.

The approach offered by Bayou and Bennett (1992) is different to those previously offered, in that instead of using average cost, each menu item is individually costed in full. However, the cost allocation task is not simple when numerous sales-mix possibilities exist. An approach to segment profitability as described by Bayou and Bennett can be a useful approach to ensuring that all menu items are priced to achieve minimum levels of profitability. Profitability analyses can be performed at several levels ranging from (a) the entire restaurant, through (b) individual business operations such as breakfast, lunch, dinner and banqueting and (c) product groups, to (d) individual menu items.

Decisions based on contribution margin are useful for pricing short-term decisions such as bidding for a banquet, where knowledge of contribution levels can suggest the lowest bidding strategy. Any selling price in excess of variable costs will provide a contribution towards fixed costs. Completion of the above analysis may indicate that one segment is not profitable. However, it may be decided that pricing to achieve a loss in one segment is acceptable when that segment draws custom to the restaurant.

Summary This chapter introduces the reader to the various pricing methodologies that are available to the hospitality industry. All pricing strategies need to consider both internal factors such as cost and target returns, and external factors such as the competition and market demand.

Questions

1 What does the price elasticity of demand measure?

2 What are the limitations of cost plus pricing?

3 Describe the different types of pricing policy that can be applied in the hospitality and tourism sectors.

4 Pricing accommodation
  The Lexus International Hotel has 100 rooms and is expected to achieve an average occupancy of 80%. The owners of the hotel expect a net profit after tax of 20% of the investment.

The following data are available for the hotel:

Owner's investment	£2.5 million
Loans (10%)	£1.0 million
Selling and distribution costs	£225,000
Administration expenses	£355,000
Bar and restaurant staff costs	£165,000
Target food and beverage cost of sales %	30%
Target annual profit for the restaurant	£40,000
Accommodation staff costs and expenses	£355,000

The taxation on profits is 25%.

You are required to:

(a) Calculate the total accommodation revenue required per annum to meet the targeted returns and forecast costs.

(b) Calculate the average room rate.

(c) Discuss the advantages and disadvantages to the above approach to pricing.

British Association of Hospitality Accountants, Stage 2 Paper, July 2004

5 Pricing food items

Clarendon Caterers Ltd has been researching its pricing policy for the operation of a new restaurant in London TV which will operate for 50 weeks of the year. The capital cost of the venture will be £900,000 and the company requires an annual net profit of 15% of this figure. The restaurant is expected to have a maximum turnover of 1,000 covers per week. Labour costs, rental, maintenance and other fixed costs will total £2,875 per week when open.

The company proposes the following menu structure, together with anticipated food cost and sales-mix percentages.

	Cost % of selling price	Sales mix %
Appetisers	30	23
Main course	40	56
Sweets	35	12
Beverages	40	9
		100

You are required to:

(a) Calculate the annual net profit required.

(b) Calculate the overall gross profit percentage required.

(c) Set the selling price for a complete meal, and the individual courses based on the anticipated number of covers and required net profit. Ignore VAT.

(d) Calculate the breakeven point per week in sales revenue, number of covers and occupancy percentage.

(e) Write a short report to the Managing Director indicating the actions that could be taken to achieve the net profit required if the actual number of covers sold fell below expectations.

6 Pricing accommodation

The Raven Hotel is a 40-bedroom hotel being built for and owned by Raven Group (Europe) plc.

For this venture the following forecasts are available:

(a) Investment

	(£000)
Land and buildings	2,110
Furniture and equipment and working capital	382
Total investment	2,492

(b) Financing of the investment

Debt: long-term loan at 18% p.a. gross	1,492
Owners have invested some of their own money and expect an after-tax return of 15% on	1,000
Total finance	2,492

(c) Projected occupancy is 80% of available room accommodation for a 52-week accounting period open 7 days per week

(d) Corporation tax is calculated at 25%

(e) The debt and equity rates of return are to be calculated on a calendar year basis

(f) Rooms department operating expenses (wages, supplies, laundry, etc.) are 27% of the required room sales.

(g) **(i)** Fixed charges

	(£)
Depreciation, insurance, etc.	183,000

(ii) Undistributed operating expenses

Administrative and general	38,300
Marketing	28,900
Energy costs	35,100
Repairs and maintenance	28,800
Total	131,100

(h) Departmental information

Food and beverage	
Sales	£575,000
Direct wages	15% of sales
Direct expenses	10% of sales
Cost of sales	35% of sales

You are required to:

(a) Prepare a financial statement from the above information to include:

    (i) required room sales for the year

    (ii) average room rate.

(b) What would the hotel's average rate per guest be if 60% of rooms sold were for double occupancy, with the remaining rooms for single occupancy?

(c) If the hotel did operate with 60% of rooms sold being for double occupancy and management wanted a £15 spread between single and double room rates, what would these rates be?

Practical activity

Research the terms 'yield management' and 'revenue maximization' on the internet.

Further reading

Brotherton, B. and Mooney, S. (1992) Yield management – progress and prospects, *International Journal of Hospitality Management* 11(1): 23–32.

Cross, R., Hanks, R. and Noland, R. (1992) Discounting in the hotel industry: a new approach, *Cornell Hotel and Restaurant Administration Quarterly*, February.

Jones, P. (2001) Menu development and analysis in UK restaurant chains, *Tourism and Hospitality Research* 3(1).

Kelly, T., Kiefer, N. and Burdett, K. (1995) A demand-based approach to menu pricing, *Cornell Hotel and Restaurant Administration Quarterly*, February.

LeBruto, S., Ashley, R. and Quain, W. (1997) Using the contribution margin aspect of menu engineering to enhance financial results, *International Journal of Contemporary Hospitality Management* 9(4).

Morrison, P. (1996) Menu engineering in upscale restaurants, *International Journal of Contemporary Hospitality Management* 8(4).

Relihan, W. (1989) The yield management approach to hotel-room pricing, *Cornell Hotel and Restaurant Administration Quarterly*, May.

Useful websites

www.netmba.com/marketing/product/lifecycle/
www.pcma.org/templates/Conferon/charts/Ch3_2.htm
http://ite.pubs.informs.org/Vol3No1/NetessineShumsky/NetessineShumsky.pdf

References

Bayou, M. and Bennett, L. (1992) Profitability analysis for table-service restaurants, *Cornell Hotel and Restaurant Administration Quarterly*, April.

Hayes, D. and Huffman, L. (1995) Menu analysis: A better way, *Cornell Hotel and Restaurant Administration Quarterly* 25(4), February.

Jones, P. and Hamilton, D. (1992) Yield management: putting people in the big picture, *Cornell Hotel and Restaurant Administration Quarterly*, February.

Kasavana, M. and Smith, D. (1992) *Menu Engineering*, Michigan: Hospitality Publishers.

Miller, J. (1980) *Menu Pricing and Strategy*, New York: Van Nostrand Rheinhold.

Pavesic, D. (1983) Cost/margin analysis: a third approach to menu pricing and design, *International Journal of Hospitality Management* 2(3): 127–134.

III Internal appraisal

An essential part of the strategy process is to compile a position audit or capability profile, which includes considering the conditions that exist inside the firm. The prime objective of internal appraisal is to establish a clear picture of the organization in terms of its resources and capabilities, which requires identifying and tabulating resources and also evaluating the management utilization of those resources. Internal appraisal involves reviewing the main functional areas of the business, accounting and finance, marketing, operations, personnel, and research and development. The financial area is an important aspect of internal appraisal in that a review of the key financial data provides an immediate insight into the health of the company. In general, the first area for inspection is the historical financial results of the company, which are analysed through ratio analysis. Although the results are retrospective they are important in that they are reflective of the effectiveness of past management decisions. The internal analysis should also encompass a review of current resources and existing accounting procedures for budget setting and control and performance measurement. The following three chapters focus on these important aspects of internal appraisal, providing tools and techniques for implementing effective budgeting procedures, cash management and performance measuring mechanisms.

6 | Making budgets work

About this chapter

This chapter considers the role of the budgeting process as a key factor in implementing the strategy of an organization. Budgeting has an essential role to play in converting all elements of the strategic plan into actual financial statements to provide a standard for performance for the short-term future, set in the context of the long-term aims and object-ives of the organization. If used correctly, the process ensures that the organizational resources such as capital and labour are allocated efficiently and effectively, and at the same time provides a vehicle for departmental co-ordination and communication. This chapter considers the role of budgeting with reference to the following issues:

- budgetary planning process
- behavioural issues
- budgetary control
- improving the effectiveness of the budgeting process.

Learning objectives   On completion of this chapter you should be able to:

- prepare a SWOT analysis in the planning process
- prepare a budgeted trading account, cash flow and balance sheet
- understand how to analyse variances in terms of price and volume
- understand the behavioural aspects of budgeting.

Introduction

Technology has enabled budgeting and forecasting to become embedded at an operational level in the hospitality and tourism industries. Departmental managers can expect to work to weekly budgets for revenues and costs and be required to reforecast revenues and costs on a regular basis. Achievement against budget is usually a critical element in departmental performance. However, successful budgetary planning and control systems require certain conditions to be in place. Best practice in budgetary planning and control depends on:

- **frequency and timeliness** of management reports, and in the hospitality and tourism industries this means daily business reports, weekly trading reports and monthly reporting packs
- **flexibility** in preparing budgets by introducing rolling budgets rather than relying on an annual fixed budget
- **accountability and ownership** to ensure that departmental managers feel motivated to raise actual performance to meet budget expectations
- **transparency and access** to financial data and measures, to ensure that managers can lead teams to achieve maximum performance
- **accuracy** in reporting to ensure that managers are working with comparable figures and have confidence in the information for decision making.

Budgeting and the strategic planning process

The budget provides a short-term plan for the organization and is normally prepared for up to a year ahead. This plan should be drawn from the long-term plans of the organization, providing a scheme for the implementation of the organizational goals and objectives. The budget should be more than just an extension of last year's actual results with incremental increases for revenues and costs. However, for many organizations the budgeting process is reduced to this basic exercise, which ensures that each year more and more slack and inefficiency is built into the budgeted values. Instead, the budget-setting exercise should reflect the current activities of the business, allowing for a distinction between two types of activities:

- **maintenance activities**, which are a continuation of existing activities
- **development activities**, which can be considered to be new opportunities in terms of products or markets or both.

A maintenance budget reflects an organization pursuing well-established activities, whereas a development budget should reflect changes in strategic direction such as divestment or changes in product or market base. A budget for a business planning to launch a new product or concept will require allowing for capital expenditure and high levels of marketing costs, whereas a business in the mature stage or entering the decline stage of the product life cycle will need to budget for substantially reduced marketing and investment costs and will focus on the cutting of critical costs.

The purpose of budgets

The successful implementation of the budgeting process should achieve a number of aims. These include enabling the organization to:

- **quantify future plans**: the budgeting process compels operational managers to look ahead and set short-term targets. This enables shortfalls in sales and resources to be identified and provides the opportunity for measures to be implemented to overcome these difficulties

- **set performance objectives and targets**: the budgeting process provides the opportunity to set targets to raise operational performance by increasing management motivation levels
- **co-ordinate departmental activities**: the preparation of the sales budget for each trading department forces the different departments to co-ordinate with each other. This is particularly true in a hotel, where the restaurant sales budget is dependent on the forecast room occupancy levels
- **communicate plans and objectives**: the budgeting process provides a formal opportunity for higher level managers at divisional regional levels to set targets based on the long-term objectives of the organization
- **control business performance**: the process provides a standard based on expected revenues and costs to which actual performance can be compared. Variances between actual and planned performance can then be identified and inefficiencies targeted and eliminated.

However, the budgeting process in its entirety can be time consuming and, therefore, costly in terms of management time and resources. Critics of the process argue that the cost and time involved are not justifiable because the end result is based on many unknown factors and the actual performance will almost certainly be different. This criticism needs to be considered in the light of the overriding benefit of the budgeting process, which is that it forces managers to consider all relevant factors likely to affect their business and plan for the effective use of resources, and this requires both an internal and an external analysis.

Finally, it can be argued that the budgeting process encourages managers to spend up to budget. Certainly, it is true that this can occur towards the budget year end when responsibility centre managers note that they have not utilized the full value of their expense budget for, say, stationery and are tempted, as a result, to spend more than is required. This effect can be minimized, however, through effective communication and participation in the budgeting process.

Determination of goals and objectives

The budget is the translation of the organizational business and financial goals into actual values. The nature of organizational objectives has already been discussed in detail in Chapter 1, where it was concluded that goals may range from profit or revenue maximization through to just pure survival tactics. The short-term planning in the organization should aim to achieve long-term objectives, but invariably conflict can arise. For example, maximizing return on capital employed in the short term may mean that the long-term future of the business is compromised. Emphasizing the maximization of this ratio means that there is a temptation to increase profits artificially by cutting expenditure in areas such as maintenance, training and marketing, while plans for further investment in assets are curbed. Therefore, it is far better to use more than one yardstick for setting targets and assessing performance. The planning process is based on three types of objective, all of which are closely related. These are known as business, operational and financial objectives and may be described as follows:

- **Business objectives** relate to markets, economic and business conditions, organizational style and personnel policies.
- **Operational objectives** are based on realistic levels of activity given the supply of resources available. A limiting factor is a scarce resource that impedes the operation or growth of business activities.
- **Financial objectives** are incorporated into the budget and are used to evaluate actual performance. They relate directly to the budget-setting process and may be expressed in a variety of forms, which may include targets set as follows:
  - **absolute terms**, e.g. sales to reach £2 million
  - **relative terms**, e.g. sales to increase by 10% on the previous year
  - **a range**, e.g. stock to sales to be between 10 and 15%
  - **a ratio**, e.g. return on total assets to be 16%
  - **a maximum**, e.g. debt to equity ratios not to exceed 50%
  - **a minimum**, e.g. dividend cover to be at least twice.

Allen and Myddelton (1992) provide a summary of what a financial budget must aim to provide and identify the main areas that a business must consider when trying to improve its performance. These are illustrated in Figure 6.1.

Figure 6.1 Financial split of operating objectives in budgeting
Source: Allen and Myddelton (1992) *Essential Management Accounting.*

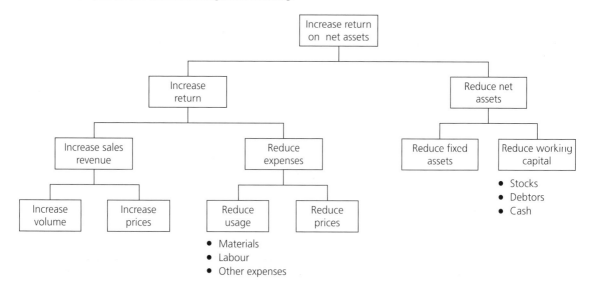

Planning to achieve organizational goals

Most organizations aim to produce a series of budgets for all levels in the operation. Using a typical hotel unit as an example, it is made up of a number of departments, some of which are classified as trading areas, such as the restaurants or the rooms division, and other departments provide support services such as marketing, personnel and maintenance. Each of these areas is required to produce a budget from which a master budget may be prepared. A master budget is the set of consolidated budgeted statements for all the areas within a unit, and these may then be consolidated with other units to produce an overall master budget for a division or for the business in total depending on its structure.

Consequently, for the majority of organizations where there is a number of scattered units, it is usual to operate a decentralized system where control is devolved to the budget centres. These can be defined as areas in the organization where responsibility has been devolved to a manager and the accounting reports and information have been tailored to match the responsibilities of that manager. Budget centre types can be categorized into three types: investment, profit and cost centres. These are defined as follows:

- **An investment centre** is an area where the manager is responsible for revenues, costs and assets employed, e.g. a hotel division within a large group. The traditional measures of performance for this group include return on capital employed, asset turnover and profitability to sales.

- **A profit centre** is an area where the manager is responsible for both revenues and costs, e.g. the restaurant within a hotel operation.

- **A cost centre** is an area where managers are responsible for costs only, such as the marketing, personnel and maintenance departments.

Normally the responsibility for a department is assigned to an individual manager who must accept responsibility for that area and as a result receives regular reports, known as management accounts, containing details of all the controllable costs. An example of a layout for such a report is illustrated in Figure 6.2.

Successful implementation of this process for responsibility accounting can lead to much higher actual performance, particularly where participation and communication are encouraged. Many of the larger hotel companies assign profit centre responsibilities to individual unit managers, with investment responsibilities being held at area or divisional management level. However, with the increased emphasis on decentralization and empowerment this is likely to change, with unit managers taking increased responsibility for investment decisions.

Responsibility accounting will not be successful where managers are held responsible for costs over which they exert no, or only partial, control. This situation can occur in organizations where costs are allocated or apportioned to departments from the centre or where a system for transfer pricing exists. Solutions for overcoming these problems are discussed in more detail in Chapter 4.

Figure 6.2 Management accounts sample layout

	Actual monthly	%	Budget monthly	%	Variance £	Variance %	Budget ytd	%	Actual ytd	%	Variance £	Variance %
Sales												
Accommodation												
Food												
Beverage												
Other												
Total												
Cost of sales												
Food												
Beverage												
Other												
Gross profit												
Labour and staff costs												
Energy costs												
Insurance												
Disposables												
Cleaning												
Laundry/ uniform												
Equipment												
Rentals												
Net profit before overhead costs												

Administration of the budgeting process

Having established areas of responsibility within the organization, the administrative control of the budgetary process should be considered. This requires a key person in the organization, usually the accountant, taking responsibility for the budgeting process throughout the period of preparation. This involves setting guidelines to ensure that the budget is prepared to a standard format in the appropriate timescales. A typical sequence of activities is shown in Figure 6.3.

It is usually desirable for individual managers to participate in the budgeting process. In some organizations the budget is imposed from the top without participation from or consultation with those managers who will execute the budget. This is generally considered to be a less effective approach for raising performance levels compared with an environment where managers can engage in participation and negotiation. However, where managers are given the freedom to participate time should be allowed for the negotiation process.

Figure 6.3 Sequence of activities in the budgeting process

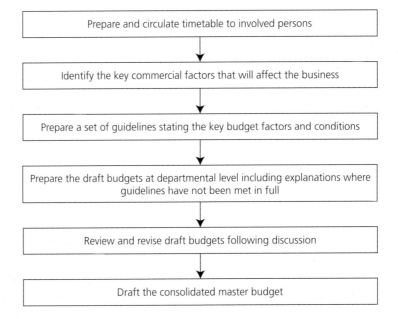

The budget period

This may vary from one organization to the next, but for the preparation of a fixed budget it is usually 1 year in length and is often dependent on the natural business year. In the hospitality and tourism industries the seasonal nature of trading means that the control periods within the budget will need to be accurately determined. Traditionally, the budget period is split into 12 periods coinciding with the calendar months. The disadvantage with this procedure is that the periods are of different length and will straddle the weeks, with one budget period often ending mid-week. An alternative approach is to use 13 budget periods each of 4 weeks in length. A business that is reliant on virtually all seasonal trade would then need to split the budget month down further into a week-by-week budget to take account of factors such as bank holidays. Traditionally, one year is planned in detail and this year is then worked through almost to completion before the next budget is considered. This results in, first, an intensive period each year when the budget is being prepared and, secondly, a period at the latter end of the year when the manager is working without a short-term plan. The use of a rolling budget provides the solution, where a month or quarter is continually being prepared to add to the budget year while the current month or quarter drops out of the time-frame.

The process of communication

Each responsibility centre is required to prepare its own forecast of what it hopes to achieve and the resources it intends to use. To harmonize the forecasts of the various centres and to avoid interdepartmental conflict a budget committee should be constituted. The various heads of department form the membership and the accountant assumes the role of budget officer or budget co-ordinator. This process ensures, first, that individual budgets complement each other and, secondly, that the lines of communication between departmental heads are open. During the budgeting process in the preparation of a fixed budget it is important to communicate the following points to those involved in the budgeting process:

- a statement of the objectives of budgetary planning and control and the procedures to be used to ensure uniformity of approach
- a definition of responsibilities for each person involved
- a timetable for the preparation of the budget
- the budget and control periods
- the responsibility centre for the preparation of each budget
- the cost codes to be used for cost collection and classification
- the standardized report layouts to be used by each unit to assist in consolidation.

Information technology has a vital role to play in providing a medium for the distribution of standardized forms for data entry. Many organizations are now using technology that enables managers to enter budgeted figures onto computerized management accounting packages, which allow for the manipulation of data and the consolidation of information at head office level.

Preparation of the budget statements

There are potentially three forms of budgeted statements to be prepared. These are:

- the trading account or operating budget
- the cash flow
- the balance sheet.

However, it is not always necessary for all responsibility centres to prepare all three statements. Centres termed as profit centres may only need the operating budget, while the investment centre of which the profit centre forms a part will find all three statements of value. In the larger multiunit organization it is often the case that individual units prepare the operating budget and the other statements are only prepared at a higher level in the organizational structure. This may be appropriate in an organization where much of the accounting activity takes place centrally, such as the payment of suppliers and the receiving of outstanding monies from customers. However, self-accounting units should also prepare forecast cash flow and balance sheets. The operating budget may be divided into further areas of responsibility with key personnel being responsible for achieving specific targets such as average room rate, revenue per available room (RevPAR) and cost of sales percentages.

Budget layouts

Many hospitality operators use a version of the layout recommended by the Uniform System of Accounts when preparing their budgeted statements. This system is described in detail in Chapter 3 and is essentially a uniform accounting system which was introduced in 1969 by the Economic Development Council particularly for hotels and caterers. The standard system provides a basic layout for profit and loss accounts, balance sheet and cash flow, and distinguishes three operating departments:

- rooms
- food and beverage
- liquor and tobacco.

To control the financial operation of the hotel several levels of control are suggested by the system. The system is described in more detail in Chapter 3.

Forecasting revenue

The starting point for the preparation of a budget is normally to estimate the sales revenue for the period. There are numerous factors to be taken into account, both internal and external to the organization. These include:

- **past actual figures** based on customer volumes, selling prices and sales mix
- **current anticipated trends**; consequently, it is important not to start the budgeting process too early to allow for the most up-to-date information to be used
- **economic factors** such as trading conditions, inflation rates and unemployment levels, in addition to details regarding planned local activities and events
- **the competition**, including general information and projections as well as current advance bookings

- **capacity restraints**, which will limit the sales budget by the level of capacity and resources available (known as limiting factors). It is important that these factors are clearly identified and their effects reduced or eliminated entirely.

There are several key resource constraints relevant to the hospitality and tourism industry. The most obvious is in the form of physical constraints that may hinder sales growth, such as total room availability, total bed night availability, total restaurant covers and bar space. These may be coupled with constraints relating to labour such as shortages of skilled staff and limited management skills, as well as equipment capacity restraints and limited capital available for expansion. To capture the impact of these factors it can be useful to prepare a SWOT analysis for the business based on a review of the above factors. The SWOT analysis technique was discussed in detail in Chapter 2. This analysis can then be used to inform the preparation of the budget.

Sales trend analysis

This approach to forecasting future sales is based on the use of product demand curves or the product life cycle. A description of the principles of the product life cycle is included in Chapter 2. To predict the trend in future sales, past sales figures are collected and are plotted on a graph against time. This shows the sales trend and indicates the stage in the product life cycle that has been reached. This methodology is much improved upon with the use of time-series analysis, which attempts to eliminate the seasonal nature of past data and seeks to establish the underlying trend through averaging. This technique is demonstrated with the following example.

Example

The Ferdinand Hotel has had the following occupancy percentage levels during the past 3 weeks.

Day	Week 1	Week 2	Week 3
Mon	68	67	67
Tue	75	80	77
Wed	85	95	90
Thu	82	84	87
Fri	62	49	48
Sat	65	60	58
Sun	53	48	46

This technique is based on averaging historical data to calculate the underlying trend. To calculate the trend data (column 4, below) it is necessary to calculate a 7-day average. The adjusted trend values (column 5) represent the deviation between the average trend values and the actual (column 1 – column 4).

1 Day	2 Occupancy %	3 7-day total	4 Trend value	5 Trend adjusted
Mon	68			
Tue	75			
Wed	85			
Thu	82	490	70	12
Fri	62	489	70	−8
Sat	65	494	71	−6
Sun	53	504	72	−19
Mon	67	506	72	−5
Tue	80	493	70	10
Wed	95	488	70	25
Thu	84	483	69	15
Fri	49	483	69	−20
Sat	60	480	69	−9
Sun	48	475	68	−20
Mon	67	478	68	−1
Tue	77	477	68	9
Wed	90	475	68	22
Thu	87	473	68	19
Fri	48			
Sat	58			
Sun	46			

The following table illustrates the average of the trend deviations for each day of the week.

	Mon	Tue	Wed	Thu	Fri	Sat	Sun
				12	−8	−6	−19
	−5	10	25	15	−20	−9	−20
	−1	9	22	19			
Total	−6	19	47	46	−28	−15	−39
Average	−3	9.5	23.5	23	−14	−7.5	−19.5
Adjusted average	−1.29	7.79	22.33	21.29	−12.29	−5.79	−17.79

The variations around the basic trend line are almost complete, but there is one more step to take. The average weekly variations need to be corrected so that they add up to zero; therefore, the total of the variations is spread across the 7 days so that the final total of the variations goes to zero.

To achieve this, all the averages are summed and divided by 7, as follows:

$$\text{Sum of the averages} = -3 + 9.5 + 23.5 + 23 - 14 - 7.5 - 19.5$$
$$= 12$$

This is then divided by the number of days in the week = 1.71.

This adjustment is added to each of the averages to calculate the adjusted average, as the following table illustrates.

	Mon	Tue	Wed	Thu	Fri	Sat	Sun
Forecast trend line	68	68	68	68	68	68	68
Adjusted average	−1.29	7.79	22.33	21.29	−12.29	−5.79	−17.79
Forecast	66.71	75.79	90.33	89.29	55.71	62.21	50.21

The forecast trend line is estimated by plotting the trend line and extending this line into the future to read off the future trend values.

Sales mix and average spend

Trend analysis and moving averages provide an approach for forecasting future sales levels based on historical data. To calculate sales from a zero base it is necessary to determine the predicted sales volumes, average spends and sales mix. This can require some research to determine what the sales volumes and business mix will be. It is possible to access statistics for a specific sector on sales patterns, occupancy levels and average room rates, for example, and these are available from some of the large accounting firms specializing in hospitality and tourism.

Preparation of the operating budget

Having determined the likely level of sales for the budget period, the next step is to determine the level of resources required to service those sales. An important requirement in forecasting costs is an understanding of cost behaviour. Once this has been established the problem of predicting the future level of the cost item is almost solved. An inspection of past records will clearly highlight those costs that are variable and those that are fixed, but the difficulty arises when attempting to classify semi-variable costs, that is, those with both a fixed and a variable element. A range of methods is available for assisting in this process, ranging from the simple high–low method to more complex techniques such as multiple regression analysis. The first of these methods is illustrated in Chapter 4. The reader is advised to consult the further reading at the end of this chapter for references to a statistical-based approach.

The cash budget

Knowledge of the company's cash cycle is essential to the success of any business. Many unit managers in large hospitality and tourism organizations feel that the cash budget is unimportant and requires little attention as the company as a whole will always have plenty of cash to support cash-flow problems at individual sites. However, to produce a company cash-flow forecast the requirements of individual sites need to be consolidated to produce an overall picture. A small change in debtor days at each operation in a large multinational organization will have a significant effect on the company's overall cash flow, as will a change in strategic direction in terms of the customer base, say from individuals to company account business. To summarize, the cash-flow statement assists in the management of the company's finance by disclosing the peaks and troughs within the budget period, indicating where extra funds will be needed. Short-term needs may be met from short-term sources such as overdrafts, but normally long-term funding is preferable even for supporting the working capital needs of a seasonal business.

The majority of cash flows will contain all or many of the following transactions:

- net cash generated from trading operations
- sales and purchases of fixed assets
- issue and redemption of equity, i.e. shares
- long-term borrowings and redemption of debt
- changes in working capital requirements.

Balance sheet

The asset budgets serve several purposes by ensuring that all assets, both fixed and current, are planned for in the budget. Charges are made to the operating budget in respect of depreciation for new assets acquired or coming on stream during the budget year, and when new facilities start to trade the related income and costs are to be incorporated into the operating and cash budgets. The relationship between the components of the budgeted balance sheet can then be monitored using ratio analysis. Working capital ratios and asset management ratios can be used futuristically when applied to the budgeted values to ensure that the financial targets being forecast are both realistic and efficient.

Example

Blue Tulip Restaurants Ltd
Balance Sheet as at 31 December 2004

	Cost £	Depreciation £	Net £
Fixed assets			
Tangible assets			
Freehold premises	3,355,000	80,000	3,275,000
Furniture and fittings	575,000	125,000	450,000
Kitchen equipment	720,000	150,000	570,000
		355,000	4,295,000
Current assets			
Stock		6,500	
Debtors		43,500	
		50,000	

Less: Creditors – amounts due for payment within 1 year			
Trade creditors	68,000		
Bank overdraft	10,000		
		78,000	
Net current (liabilities)			(28,000)
			£4,267,000

Financed by:
Capital and reserves

	Authorized £	Issued £
Share capital		
Ordinary shares of £1 each fully paid	5,000,000	3,000,000
Reserve		
Retained profit		1,267,000
		£4,267,000

The restaurant group is a private company and the directors work in the business. In discussions with the bank manager it has been suggested that in future budgetary planning techniques should be used. As a result, an operating budget and a cash budget need to be prepared for each of the months of January and February 2005, and a budgeted balance sheet as at 28 February 2005.

The following information has been forecast:

(a) Sales: January £150,000, February £160,000.

Three-quarters of the sales are for cash, the other quarter is on 1 month's credit.

(b) The gross profit on sales has been calculated at 70%.

(c) Direct wages are payable in the month incurred: January £30,000, February £32,000

(d) The level of stock remains at £6,500 throughout the period. All purchases are on 1 month's credit.

(e) Direct expenses are payable the month incurred: January £15,000, February £16,000.

(f) Creditors are paid in the following month less a 5% cash discount.

(g) Depreciation is calculated on the straight-line method at the following rates:

Land and buildings	5% per annum
Furniture and fittings	10% per annum
Kitchen equipment	20% per annum

Where new assets are purchased, depreciation is calculated on a monthly basis.

(h) Selling and promotion expenses are allocated: January £10,000, February £12,000. However, these are not payable until March.

(i) Establishment expenses are allocated: January £20,000, February £20,000. All are payable in the month incurred.

(j) Additional kitchen equipment to cost £120,000 is planned to be purchased in February 2005. Allow depreciation for the whole of the month.

(k) Administrative expenses (which include directors' salaries) are forecast to be January £15,000, February £16,000. All are payable in the month incurred.

Profit and loss account

	January	February
Sales	150,000	160,000
Cost of sales	45,000	48,000
Gross profit	105,000	112,000
Labour costs	30,000	32,000
Direct expenses	15,000	16,000
Depreciation:		
Land and buildings	13,979	13,979
Fixture's and fitting	4,792	4,792
Kitchen equipment	6,000	7,000
Selling and promotion	10,000	12,000
Establish expenses	20,000	20,000
Administrative expenses	15,000	16,000
Add back: discount on creditors	3,400	2,250
Profit/(loss)	(6,371)	(7,521)

Cash flow

	January	February
Cash inflows		
Cash sales	112,500	120,000
Sales debtors	43,500	37,500
	156,000	157,500
Creditors	64,600	42,750
Labour	30,000	32,000
Direct expenses	15,000	16,000
Selling and promotion	—	—
Establish expenses	20,000	20,000
Administrative expenses	15,000	16,000
Kitchen equipment		120,000
Net flow	11,400	−89,250
Opening balance	(10,000)	1,400
Closing	1,400	−87,850

	Cost	Depreciation	Net
Fixed assets			
Freehold premises	3,355,000	107,958	3,247,042
Furniture and fittings	575,000	134,584	440,416
Kitchen equipment	840,000	163,000	677,000
Current assets	4,770,000	405,542	4,364,458
Stock	6,500		
Debtors	40,000		
Less creditors	46,500		
Trade creditors	48,000		
Bank overdraft	87,850		
Selling and promotion expenses	22,000		
			(111,350)
Financed by			4,253,108
Share capital			3,000,000
Reserves			1,253,108
Retained profit			4,253,108

The budgetary control process

Having prepared and agreed the budget for the forthcoming period a key factor in the success of the budgeting process is the level of monitoring that then takes place to compare actual results with those that were planned. This level of control is supported by a system for variance accounting, where the planned activities of the organization are compared with the actual results and the differences analysed. Broadly speaking, there can be many potential causes for variance. These range from those that have occurred owing to external factors such as economic, social, legal and political changes, changes in competition and changes in supply conditions, to those that have arisen owing to changes and inefficiencies in the operating systems. Effective variance accounting is based on establishing individual unit selling prices and costs in a process known as standard costing. This enables performance to be monitored in terms of both price and volume changes.

Standard costing in food cost management

This approach provides a method for identifying the causes of the variation between actual and budgeted results and can exist only where firm standards of performance are capable of being set. A fast food outlet is a good example of an operation where standardized products are sold and where it is then possible to establish standard ingredient costs designed to hold constant over a determined period. The process of standard costing requires the setting of five standards for

- **purchase prices**, where each unit has a set selling price
- **purchase specifications**, where each ingredient is clearly specified
- **portion sizes**, where each dish is specified in terms of size
- **yields**, where weight changes in the cooking process are identified
- **recipes for production**, to ensure that a uniform procedure is followed.

The standard cost of the final recipe represents what the cost should have been if there was minimal waste and maximum efficiency and the supporting standards were followed. The use of such an approach has distinct advantages in that by presetting the standard the best methods and materials for the product are determined and variances may be produced that indicate where the actual costs have varied against the standard. It may also mean that targets are set against which employee performance may be measured, as well as assisting in the training of staff. Such activity focuses management attention on the shortfalls; this is known as 'management by exception'. Finally, the process can also improve the quality of pricing decisions because the business has accurate information about costs.

However, standard costing can be a difficult system to administer in practice to ensure that all records are maintained, and time consuming to set up in the first instance as all dishes need to be costed. Computer technology can certainly assist where purchasing and inventory control packages can be linked to menu costing options to provide up-to-date costed dishes.

The operational restraints imposed by standard costing can be disliked by employees as procedures and products are likely to be significantly preset, leaving little scope for individual creativity. However, standard costing processes ensure that a consistent quality is maintained. As a consequence, standard costing is used most effectively in fast food-style operations with semi-skilled or unskilled labour.

Flexible budgeting

A budget prepared in advance of the trading period set at an assumed level of activity is called a fixed budget. This original budget can then be used in comparison with the actual data. However, this comparison is less meaningful when actual activity is significantly different to the budgeted activity. Where standard unit costs are available or where the proportions of fixed and variable costs have been calculated, it is possible to calculate a revised budget based on the actual level of sales using the budgeted levels of costs. This revised budget is called a flexible budget. This approach can be used to monitor variances caused by changes in volume, changes in sales mix and operating cost inefficiencies.

The following example illustrates the use of a flexible budget.

Example

The following figures have been extracted from the fixed budget for the Bay Restaurant for budget period 5.

Budgeted covers	3,200
Average spend	£12.00
Gross profit %	60%
Labour and expenses	30%
Fixed costs	£2,500

The actual results were:

Covers	4,500
Average spend	£10.00
Gross profit	£27,900
Labour and expenses	£13,000
Fixed costs	£2,900

The following table illustrates how the results might be analysed.

	Fixed budget	Flexible budget	Actual	Variance
Covers	3,200	4,500	4,500	
Average spend	12.00	12.00	10.00	
Sales	38,400	54,000	45,000	9,000A
Gross profit	23,040	32,400	27,900	4,500F
Labour and expenses	11,520	16,200	13,000	3,200F
Fixed costs	2,500	2,500	2,900	400A
Net profit	1,340	2,900	1,200	1,700A

The variances can be summarized as follows:

Variance due to volume	2,900 − 1,340 = 1,560F
Variance due to operations	2,900 − 1,200 = 1,700A
Variance overall	1,340 − 1,200 = 140A

Using budgets to motivate

The budgeting process is often used not only to plan ahead, but also for target setting and for raising individual performance. Traditional theories of motivation focus on the identification of specific factors such as pay systems, working conditions and self-fulfilment as being associated with producing increased levels of motivation. There have been various industrial studies conducted on the theme of employee motivation and performance with relation to budgets, across a range of industries. In general, these have concluded that difficult goals produce either very good or very bad results compared with goals of normal difficulty and that difficult goals lead to reduced effort on the part of those managers who are less mature and experienced and who have less self-confidence. Results from various sources of research indicate that:

- Budgets have no motivational effect unless they are accepted by the managers involved as their own personal target.
- Up to the point where the budget target is no longer accepted, the more demanding the budget target the better the results achieved.
- Demanding budgets are also seen as more relevant than less difficult targets, but negative attitudes result if they are seen as too difficult.
- Acceptance of budgets is facilitated when good upward communication exists. The use of departmental meetings was found to be helpful in encouraging managers to accept budget targets.
- Manager reactions to budget targets were affected both by their own personality and by more general cultural and organizational norms.

Based on the work of Otley (1987).

The relationship between budget difficulty and the ensuing level of performance can be shown graphically and is illustrated in Figure 6.4. This shows that a budget level that is perceived as being more likely to be achieved will motivate a lower level of performance. Consequently, to improve performance the budget level should be set in excess of the average performance likely to be attained.

Figure 6.4 Relationship between budget difficulty and the ensuing level of performance

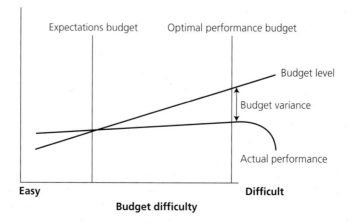

Improving the effectiveness of budgeting

The effectiveness of budgeting relies on reducing slack or bias by ensuring that forecasts are accurate during the budget preparation stage and by ensuring the timeliness of reporting of the actual results. Bias in budgeting is a major problem and detecting bias in the budget-setting process can sometimes be impossible. Bias occurs when a manager incorporates a certain amount of slack into the budgeted figures. There are various reasons for doing this, but it occurs mainly when the manager's performance is being assessed against the budgeted targets. Slack may be built into sales by understating what is possible, or into costs, thereby masking potential overspends. Alternatively, in tough environments managers may set unachievable budgets to divert attention away from current poor performance. Delays in reporting the actual results against the budget delays the taking of corrective action, which may in the long term reduce management motivation. Consequently, a system of 'flash' reports may be useful, which report rough numbers relating to sales and key costs such as materials and wages within a few days of the end of the budget period, with the complete results coming no more than a week later. The incremental approach to budget setting is widely used and is based on the assumption that a budget will grow each year as a result of inflation or with the provision for 'natural growth'. As a result, gradual changes in the business may be overlooked. These may be basic changes such as differences in the cost structure or the customer base. Even without such changes occurring the traditional approach ensures that previous overspends and inaccuracies are compounded each budget period.

An alternative is zero-based budgeting (ZBB), which is an approach that challenges the existence of all items in the budget.

Zero-based budgeting

The concept of ZBB relies on the assumption that levels of expenditure in previous periods do not justify continuation of that spending in future periods; instead, all spending must be justified each year. This approach is most useful in the control of indirect, overhead costs such as marketing, maintenance and training. Each activity in the organization is scrutinized and the expected outcome determined. These activities are then ranked based on the following criteria:

- the activity's objectives in relation to the organization's overall objectives
- the required budget for the activity
- justification for the outcomes of the activity against cost.

The main differences between traditional techniques of budgeting and ZBB are summarized in Table 6.1, which has been taken from the work of Allen and Myddelton.

One of the key elements in successful implementation of ZBB is the decision unit. A decision unit represents an activity carried out in a particular area of an operation. The number of units required varies depending on the size of the organization, and a large organization would expect to have several units for each type of overhead expense. Each unit should contain just one or two employees and the associated costs. Once the decision units have been established the department head must prepare an analysis for each separate unit in his or her responsibility.

Table 6.1 Traditional budgeting versus zero-based budgeting

	Traditional budgeting	Zero-based budgeting
Frequency	Annual	Every 3–5 years
Time and effort	Often significant	Very substantial
Starting point	Last year's budget/actual	Zero
Basis for budget	Last year +/− %	Separate decision packages
Amount	Single sum	Range of cost–benefit options
Involves	Manager and boss	Cross-functional team
Needs awareness of	Function	Whole business
Priorities	Not stated	Ranks 'mosts' and 'wants'
Alternatives	Not stated	Detailed review

For each decision unit the following will need to be documented:

- the unit's objective
- the unit's present activities
- justification for continuation of the unit's activities
- a list of alternative ways of carrying out the activities
- selection of recommended alternatives
- budget required.

Ranking process

To determine how money will be spent in the organization it is necessary to rank all activities in order of importance to the organization. This may be achieved by using committees who may approve automatically the first 50–60% of all activities, and the remainder is ranked by middle and top management. The completed ranking process and approved expenditures constitute the new budgets for those areas or departments.

Advantages of ZBB

The detail required to complete ZBB successfully is extensive and therefore time consuming, requiring a management team that knows the whole business very well. This may present difficulties in an industry where staff and management turnover is traditionally very high. However, the advantages of ZBB are that the process:

- concentrates on the cash value of each department's activities and budget and not on percentage increases

- can reallocate funds to the department or activity providing the greatest benefit to the organization
- provides a quality of information about the organization that would otherwise not be available
- involves all levels of management and supervision in the budgeting process
- obliges managers to identify inefficient or obsolete functions within their areas of responsibility.

Summary The preparation of a detailed budget will be of value to most operations by helping to quantify the short-to medium-term objectives and plans. This will then provide a benchmark against which actual performance can be compared and action taken to improve future results. A checklist for effective budgeting will include:

- establishing attainable goals or objectives
- planning to achieve these goals or objectives
- comparing actual results with those planned and analysing the differences
- taking corrective action if required
- improving the effectiveness of budgeting.

Questions 1 Preparing a budgeted trading account

Produce a budgeted trading account for three different annual revenue levels: £800,000, £900,000 and £1,000,000, using the following information:

Food costs: 40% of sales
Variable labour expenses: 25% of sales
Fixed labour costs: £60,000
Other variable costs: 12% of sales
Other fixed costs: £120,000
Taxation rate: 30%

2 Preparing a cash-flow budget

The budget year for a catering business starts in July. The following are the forecast trading data and expenditure for that year from 1 July 200x to 30 June 200x.

Sales	£1,500,000
Sales mix	Food: 60%
	Beverage: 40%
Pattern of sales	July–September: 35%
	October–December: 20%
	January–March: 15%
	April–June: 30%
Credit sales	20% of each quarter's sales, payable in the following quarter
	Outstanding debtors from the previous year are £300,000

Cost of sales	Food: 40%
	Beverage: 35%
	(stocks remain constant throughout)
	Cost of sales follows the pattern of sales
	and is payable in the month incurred

Fixed costs

Salaries	£300,000 a year, payable monthly
Insurance	£100,000 a year, of which £25,000 is payable in January and £17,000 in October
Property charges	£25,000 payable in September
Depreciation	£15,000 for the year
Interest	£26,000 a year, half of which is payable in September and half in March
Other costs	£25,000 a year, payable on an equal monthly basis

Capital expenditure

Finance	Purchase of equipment for £215,000 in January
Opening balance at bank	£(10,000) negative

You are required to:

(a) Prepare a cash budget on a quarterly basis.

(b) Prepare an operating budget for the year in total and reconcile the budgeted profit figure to the closing cash balance.

3 Preparing a budget
A new hotel is to open for business on 1 August. It is expected that the preceding month will be devoted to staff training and other start-up requirements.

The following are the forecast trading data and expenditure for the first month from 1 July 2005 to 30 June 2006.

Sales	£6,600,000
Pattern of sales	July–September:20%
	October–December:20%
	January–March:15%
	April–June:45%
Credit sales	20% of each quarter's sales, payable in the following quarter
Variable costs:	35% of total sales, payable within the quarter in which they were incurred

Fixed costs

Salaries	£1,650,000 a year, payable monthly
Insurance	£28,000 a year, of which £16,000 is payable in January and £12,000 in October
Property tax	£250,000 payable in September
Maintenance, etc.	£27,000 payable in December and £23,000 payable in January
Depreciation	£300,000 for the year
Vehicle running costs	Road tax £1,200; insurance £3,200; petrol, oil and mainte-nance £10,200; depreciation £6,000. The tax and insurance

are payable in July, and the petrol, etc., are payable equally each month

Interest £160,000 a year, half of which is payable in December and half in June

Other costs £124,000 a year payable on an equal monthly basis

You are required to:

(a) Prepare a cash budget on a quarterly basis.

(b) The budgeted net profit for the year is different to the cash-flow balance. Explain why this differs from the closing cash balance.

(c) Does the cash budget reveal any problems? How would you overcome this?

4 Flexible budgeting

Elite Holidays is a holiday resort open 365 days per year. The manager of the restaurant in the holiday resort is required to work with a budget and reviews performance weekly and monthly. The period accounts for June monitor revenue and costs against the period budget, highlighting any variances.

	Actual (£000)	Budget (£000)	Variance (£000)
Covers	38,666	41,700	3,034
Revenue			
Food	254	333	−79
Beverage	155	230	−75
Other	55	63	−8
Total revenue	**464**	**626**	**−162**
Cost of sales			
Food	64	73	9
Beverage	36	46	10
Other	28	30	2
Total cost of sales	**128**	**149**	**21**
Direct wages	138	184	46
Direct expenses	44	50	6
Administrative expenses	25	32	7
Sales and marketing expenses	10	12	2
Energy costs	3	4	1
Maintenance	10	8	−2
EBITDA	**106**	**187**	**−81**

EBITDA: earnings before interest, tax, depreciation and amortization.

You are required to:

(a) Explain what is meant by the terms 'fixed budget' and 'flexible budget', and state the main objective of preparing flexible budgets.

(b) Prepare a revised performance statement using flexible budgeting. Your statement should show both the revised budget and the revised variances. You should assume that:

  (i)   Direct wages are £100,000 fixed costs

  (ii) Direct expenses are £35,000 fixed costs

  (iii) Administration, sales and marketing, energy and maintenance are fixed costs.

(c) Comment on the performance of the restaurant using the table above and your workings from (b).

(d) 'Budgets are set to help managers achieve objectives'. Comment on this statement and discuss how effective you believe budgets are for motivating the performance of a department.

British Association of Hospitality Accountants, Stage 2 Paper, July 2004

5 Moving averages

The Allen Hotel has had the following occupancy levels during the past 3 weeks.

Day	Week 1	Week 2	Week 3
Mon	68	67	67
Tue	75	80	77
Wed	85	95	90
Thu	82	84	87
Fri	62	49	48
Sat	65	60	58
Sun	53	48	46

You are required to:

(a) Forecast the daily occupancy level for week 4 by using the 7-day moving average method to establish the 'trend line' and then adjusting for seasonal variations.

(b) Briefly describe the main reasons for preparing sales forecasts and the limitations of the method used above.

British Association of Hospitality Accountants, Stage 2 Paper, July 2004

6 Standard costing

The following information relates to a contract catering company providing employee feeding at a pharmaceutical company.

Budget

Number of covers sold	50,000
Average spend per head	£1.60
Food cost as percentage of sales	50%
Variable labour cost (% of sales)	20%
Fixed labour cost	£10,000
Fixed overhead	£10,000

At the end of the year the total results were:

Actual

Number of covers sold	55,000
Sales revenue	£97,000
Food cost	£48,000
Variable labour	£20,000
Fixed labour	£9,000
Fixed overhead	£10,000

You are required to:

(a) Prepare a statement for the year showing the fixed budget, the flexible budget, actual results and variances.

(b) Evaluate the results you have prepared and suggest possible causes for the variances.

(c) Briefly explain the following terms:

    (i) standard cost

    (ii) standard price

    (iii) food price variance

    (iv) food usage variance.

(d) Describe the limitations of fixed budgets and comment on the practical value of flexible budgeting for a particular sector of the hotel and catering industry.

7 The Place To Eat is a new fish restaurant in a central location in a busy city centre.

The owner has prepared the following forecasts for the first quarter of trading:

Sales	£32,000
Cost of sales is budgeted at 30% of sales	
Other expenses are fixed and per quarter are:	
Wages	£6,800
Salaries	£10,000
Rent and rates	£6,500
Depreciation	£3,500

You are required to:

(a) Produce a simple budget from these values.

(b) Prepare a flexible budget showing the effect of an increase/decrease in sales of 10%.

8 The balance sheet of the Peter's Restaurants Ltd at 1 April 2005 was as follows:

	Cost	Depreciation	Net
Fixed assets			
Freehold premises	900,000		900,000
Kitchen equipment	195,000	39,000	156,000
Furniture and fittings	130,000	13,000	117,000
	1,225,000	52,000	1,173,000
Current assets			
Stock		1,500	
Debtors		16,000	
Less creditors – amounts falling due within 1 year			
Creditors	36,000		
Bank overdraft	31,500	67,500	
Net current liabilities			(50,000)
			1,123,000
Financed by:			
Share capital		Authorised (£)	Issued (£)
Ordinary shares of 10p each fully paid		1,200,000	1,000,000
Reserve			
Profit and loss account			
Retained profit			123,000
			1,123,000

The company has not previously used budget planning procedures, and *you are required to* prepare an operating budget and a cash budget for:

(a) Accounting period 1: 2 April to 29 April 2005

(b) Accounting period 2: 30 April to 26 May 2005

(c) Accounting period 3: 28 May to 24 June 2005

(d) Budgeted balance sheet at 24 June 2005.

(e) You are also required to prepare a short commentary for management based on your figures that should include an analysis of the key ratios.

The following information has been forecast:

(i) Sales: accounting period 1 £80,000; accounting period 2 £90,000; accounting period 3 £100,000. Four-fifths of all sales are for cash, one-fifth is on one accounting period's credit. All debtors pay promptly: no cash discount is allowed.

(ii) The gross profit on sales has been calculated at 55% for accounting period 1; 60% for accounting periods 2 and 3.

(iii) The level of stock remains at £1,500 throughout the period. All purchases are on one accounting period's credit. A cash discount of 2.5% is deducted when payment is made.

(iv) Direct wages, payable in the accounting period incurred: accounting period 1 £20,000; accounting period 2 £24,500; accounting period 3 £26,000.

(v) Direct expenses, payable in the accounting period incurred: accounting period 1 £4,000; accounting period 2 £4,500; accounting period 3 £5,000.

(vi) Depreciation is calculated on the straight-line method, at the following rates: furniture and fittings 10% on cost; kitchen equipment 20% on cost. The depreciation charge is allocated to accounting periods on the basis of 1/13th for each period. When new assets are purchased depreciation is calculated on an accounting period basis.

(vii) The unissued ordinary shares are to be issued to shareholders for cash, at their par value, in accounting period 3.

(viii) The bank overdraft will be cleared.

(ix) A new issue of 500,000 10% preference shares of £1 each, at par, is to be made in accounting period 3. Authorised preference capital will be 1,000,000 shares of £1 each.

(x) Additional kitchen equipment to cost £5,200 is to be purchased for cash in accounting period 3. Allow depreciation for this accounting period.

(xi) Selling and promotion expenses are allocated as follows: accounting period 1 £3,000; accounting period 2 £4,000; accounting period 3 £4,500. Accounting periods 1 and 2 are payable in accounting period 3. Accounting period 3 expenses are not payable until accounting period 4.

(xii) Establishment expenses are: accounting period 1 £2,500; accounting period 2 £3,000; accounting period 3 £3,200, all payable in the accounting period incurred.

(xiii) Administration expenses are: accounting period 1 £6,000; accounting period 2 £6,500; accounting period 3 £7,000, all payable in the accounting period incurred.

Further reading

Emmanuel, C., Otley, D. and Merchant, K. (1990) *Accounting for Management Control*, London: Chapman & Hall.

Ezzamel, M. and Hart, H. (1987) *Advanced Management Accounting*, London: Cassell.

Harris, P. (1994) *Managerial Accounting for the Hospitality Industry*, Cheltenham: Stanley Thornes.

Useful websites

www.bestpracticeforum.org/WhatIsBP/PTPBookletBoostProfits.pdf
www.accaglobal.com/publications/studentaccountant/2377529
www.acca.co.uk/publications/accountingandbusiness/45679?

References

Allen, M. and Myddelton, D. (1992) *Essential Management Accounting*, New York: Prentice Hall.

Otley, D. (1987) *Accounting Control and Organisational Behaviour*, Oxford: Heinemann/CIMA.

7 | Management of working capital

About this chapter

In Chapter 3 cash flow was discussed in detail and guidelines were given for the preparation of the cash flow in accordance with FRS 1 guidelines. The monitoring of cash flow is a vital task for managers. In this chapter the concept of working capital will be introduced and each aspect of working capital will be discussed with regard to the control and monitoring of each component.

Learning objectives On completion of this chapter you should be able to:

- understand the importance of liquidity
- understand the significance of cash-flow management versus profit management
- apply techniques for controlling inventory levels
- understand the importance of managing debtor levels
- apply techniques for monitoring creditors.

Introduction

A key feature consistent with many business failures in the UK is that businesses have been too late in realizing the importance of short-term and long-term cash availability. Obviously achieving profit is important, but maintaining sufficient cash funds for financing the payment of suppliers (trade creditors) and for financing long-term management decisions is the successful route to achieving strategic objectives. When there are insufficient funds in the form of cash the business may at worst face liquidation if creditors are not being paid, but such a shortage also limits the ability of a business to pursue a strategy of expansion through revenue growth. This chapter considers the management of working capital in total, as well as a review of the key aspects of each of the component including:

- working capital cycles
- working capital ratios
- debtors
- creditors
- stock
- cash.

Working capital

Working capital is normally defined as the cash value of current assets less the current liabilities. According to the Association of Chartered Certified Accountants (ACCA) the primary objective of working capital management is to ensure that sufficient cash is available to:

- meet day-to-day cash-flow needs
- pay wages and salaries when they fall due
- pay creditors to ensure continued supplies of goods and services
- pay government taxation and providers of capital dividends
- ensure the long-term survival of the business entity.

Poor working capital management can lead to:

- overcapitalization (and therefore waste through underutilization of resources and hence poor returns)
- overtrading (trying to maintain a level of sales that is higher than working capital can sustain; for businesses that extend credit terms, more sales mean more debtors and higher working capital demands).

When the assets exceed the liabilities this is known as positive working capital, where current assets are funded partly from the current liabilities such as trade creditors and bank overdrafts and also from long-term sources of funds such as bank loans or equity. Negative working capital arises when current liabilities exceed current assets. In this case current liabilities are funding both current assets and a proportion of long-term assets.

In general, a business should seek to minimize the level of each type of current asset held such as stock, debtors and cash, and maximize the benefits from short-term financing arising from the delayed payment of creditors. However, other factors influence the working capital policy, such as the possibility of lost sales through not offering credit to potential customers, lost sales through holding insufficient stocks and increases in operating costs due to poor supplier relationships. The management of working capital should be based on achieving a balance between these factors. The problem lies in the fact that the level of funds required is constantly changing, particularly where there are seasonal sales that will affect stock, debtor and creditor levels. As a result, forecasting working capital requirements becomes difficult in cases where the level of future sales and the timing of cash flows are not known with accuracy. However, it is essential that every attempt is made to predict accurately the business cash requirements, and the increasing importance of monitoring the levels of cash generated in an operation is now widely recognized.

A business can increase profits through cost cutting or creative accounting, but there is no corresponding increase in cash flows following these activities. Therefore, the monitoring of cash flows and not profits is, in many cases, the true measure of the health of the business. There are various approaches to monitoring cash levels and working capital requirements and these will now be considered.

Working capital cycle

Unfortunately, to maintain liquidity the level of available current assets must be kept sufficiently high to cover payments to outstanding suppliers when they fall due. These cash balances mean that the business incurs an opportunity cost for interest lost or the earnings that could have been made if the cash had been invested elsewhere. The exact amount of idle cash held can be managed effectively by understanding and controlling the cash operating cycle. This specifies the period taken in days between the cash payment to suppliers for goods and the cash being received from customers for sales. In a manufacturing industry a large portion of the cash cycle will focus on days required to manufacture the finished product from the raw materials, and the incomplete finished goods are known as work in progress. The usual cash operating cycle is illustrated below.

Days raw materials held in stock	x days
Days needed to produce goods	x days
Days finished goods held in stock	x days
Days debtors take to settle accounts on receipt of goods	x days
Less	
Days taken to pay trade suppliers	x days
Equals	
Cash operating cycle	x days

The typical hotel operation requires stock for almost instant use and the emphasis is not on the management of the stock cycle but on ensuring that sufficient stocks are held for service without incurring the costs associated with overstocking. In simplified form, the chain of events in a hotel operation that will affect the working capital cycle is shown below.

Days raw materials held in stock	x days
Days debtors take to settle accounts on receipt of goods	x days

Less
Days taken to pay suppliers   *x* days

Equals
Cash operating cycle   *x* days

Whenever a business is able to gain credit from suppliers this in effect finances part of the cash operating cycle. Consequently, large businesses such as hotel chains and contract caterers can operate with shorter operating cycles if they are able to secure better credit terms from suppliers. Any delay in the time taken to receive cash from outstanding customers or additional time given in the credit terms offered will increase the length of the cycle. This can eventually lead to the running down of cash resources and may lead to liquidation. The problem for manufacturing businesses lies in the length of time taken for stock to be sold as finished goods following purchase as raw materials. This is less of an influencing factor for hotel and catering organizations, where stocks are of a lower value in cash terms and because of their perishable nature are much faster moving.

The key factor for successful control of the working capital cycle for a service type of operation is in the management of debtors and creditors. However, in the case of large-scale production kitchens there are similarities with the traditional manufacturing approach, as the following example illustrates.

Example

The Canford Kitchen produces a range of speciality meals using cook–chill processes, which it distributes to a number of different brands of fast food restaurants. The table below gives information extracted from the accounts for the past 3 years.

	Year 1 (£)	Year 2 (£)	Year 3 (£)
Sales	864,000	1,080,000	1,188,000
Cost of goods sold	756,000	972,000	1,098,000
Purchases	518,400	702,000	720,000
Debtors (average)	172,800	259,200	297,000
Creditors (average)	86,400	105,300	126,000
Raw material stock (average)	108,000	145,800	180,000
Work in progress	75,600	97,200	93,360
Finished goods (average)	86,400	129,600	142,875

Assume all sales and purchases are on credit terms.
  Days taken are worked out as follows:

	Year 1	Year 2	Year 3
$\dfrac{\text{Raw materials}}{\text{Purchases}} \times 365$	76.0	75.8	91.3
$\dfrac{\text{Trade creditors}}{\text{Purchases}} \times 365$	(60.8)	(54.8)	(63.9)
$\dfrac{\text{Work in progress}}{\text{Cost of sales}} \times 365$	36.5	36.5	31.0
$\dfrac{\text{Finished goods}}{\text{Cost of sales}} \times 365$	41.7	48.7	47.5
$\dfrac{\text{Debtors}}{\text{Sales}} \times 365$	73.0	87.6	91.3
Total length of cycle	166.4	193.8	197.2

Overtrading

This is a term used when a business is financing too high a level of sales activity with insufficient working capital. The situation can occur where sales are increasing more rapidly than the cost base through rapid growth, or when costs are rising quickly due to inflation. In each case the business faces a cash shortfall situation. Overtrading is more likely to affect a business selling on credit terms than a cash-orientated business.

Measures for managing working capital

There are several performance evaluation techniques for monitoring the level of working capital. These include the calculation of a range of ratios based on the relationships that exist between the different types of current assets and current liabilities, and also specific ratios for managing each type of asset. When calculated using internally reported values drawn from management accounts the results provide a useful tool for monitoring and evaluating performance. However, when values are taken from the published balance sheet it is important to remember that the financial statements are drawn up following a number of conventions and rules, and that the asset values are simply those at that point in time and the relationships may have considerably changed since that date.

The current ratio

This provides a measure of the balance between the assets and liabilities. Usually a business would seek to achieve a ratio in excess of 1:1, which communicates confidence to short-term creditors by confirming the ability of the business to meet all of its short-term debts. Many textbooks on accounting advocate a ratio of 2:1, that is, current assets at twice the value of current liabilities, as being a safe measure. In practice, the trading patterns of the business will dictate the level of a 'safe' ratio. In restaurants, for example, current assets will consist of cash and fast-moving stocks, with possibly few or no debtors. Therefore, all assets are in a fairly liquid state and it would not be unusual to see a consistent ratio of 1:1 or less with no working capital difficulties being experienced. Alternatively, a hotel operation may have a considerable level of debtors and slow-moving stocks, and the most efficient ratio will be higher than 1:1.

The acid-test ratio

Liquid assets are normally taken to be debtors and cash, whereas stock may take longer to realize. However, it may also be relevant to exclude some of the debtors as well if the outstanding balances are difficult to realize. The target for the ratio is normally about 1:1, but again differences in industry operating practice mean that these benchmarks should not be adhered to rigidly.

Managing debtors

Ideally, if all sales could be for immediate cash payment, liquidity problems would be less likely to occur. Unfortunately, in many sectors of the hospitality industry it is expected that credit will be available and in many cases this serves as a marketing toll to attract further business. The optimum level of debtors outstanding is established by achieving a balance between the cost of giving credit and the additional profits to be generated from credit sales. The cost of granting credit to a customer includes:

- **Loss of interest:** the supplier is in effect giving the customer an interest-free loan during the period in which the amount is outstanding.
- **Reduced purchased power:** during the period that the debt is outstanding the supplier may suffer from insufficient funds to buy stock or pay staff.
- **Administrative costs:** maintenance of a sales ledger will incur costs for record-keeping and staffing.
- **Cost of bad debts:** these occur when an outstanding debt is not paid. The greater the length of debtor days the greater the risk of bad debts occurring.

However, costs are also incurred when credit is denied, the most significant being the loss of customer goodwill and sales.

In the hotel and tourism industry credit is extended at various levels, ranging from the house accounts where credit is extended during the guest's stay until the point of checkout when payment is made, to authorized credit extended to customers where the balance outstanding is shown on the sales (city) ledger. Credit is also extended when a guest pays by credit card, where billing is made to the credit card company, usually incurring commission charges.

Credit policy

To avoid excessive bad debts an effective policy for giving credit should be established. This should be communicated to staff through training sessions and company manuals with standard forms for collecting credit information. The company policy regarding credit should include guidelines on who should be granted credit and references required, how much credit is to be granted and the length of credit period to be extended. The credit application form should be the most accurate document on customer details available and is, therefore, worth reviewing carefully. When preparing a credit application form the following checklist should be considered:

- Are these reasonable questions?
- Would I give out such information?
- Is it necessary and relevant?
- Will the customer find it easy to answer?

In addition to the credit application form there are many sources available for gathering information about customer credit worthiness. These include:

- credit ratings supplied by credit agencies such as Dunn and Bradstreet
- banks
- trade associations
- own company experience.

To ensure that debtor management is efficient it is important to monitor that invoices and statements are sent out promptly and accurately. The sooner the invoice is sent out the sooner the customer will deal with it. An accurate, clear invoice will also improve the speed with which the invoice is paid. Payment terms should be clearly worded; for instance, '30 days net' means payment on the 30th day without taking discount, but this is not very clear to the customer. A more accurate message to the customer would be 'Please pay within 30 days of the invoice date' or 'Please ensure payment reaches this office by the 25th of the month following the month of the invoice'.

A courteous but firm system of reminders and collection procedures should be operated, and the sending of statements, reminders and telephone contact calls should all be logged. The monitoring of debtor levels can be greatly assisted by computer technology and for many hotels this was one of the first areas to undergo computerization. Most computer packages should be able to produce an ageing analysis of debtors, a list of accounts that have exceeded their credit limit and an average debtor payment period calculation. With this information available it is important to ensure that debtor information is conveyed to other departments such as reservations to prevent credit terms being continued when large debts are already outstanding.

Late payment of bills is clearly damaging to any type of business, but it particularly affects the smaller business. These types of business are often at the mercy of much larger businesses who deliberately delay payment for financial advantage. To avoid the problems associated with collecting debts it may be relevant to consider debt factoring and offering discounts for prompt payment.

Debt factoring

In recent years there has been a growth in the use of external debt collection agencies and there are various services available depending on the needs of the individual business. A more common arrangement is one in which the factoring organization will pay invoices immediately up to an agreed percentage of the sales ledger, say 80%, and receive in return a fee, which may be 1.5% of the invoice total. Consequently, the business receives an immediate injection of cash, but there are some disadvantages that should be considered. The most significant of these is that the outstanding customers will be contacted by the factoring company; this may give the wrong impression to the customer and with some contracts the debt reverts to the company after, say, 60 days. However, the advantages of factoring should not be dismissed because the process relieves the supplier firm of the administrative and financial burdens of granting credit, but at a cost. To evaluate the cost effectiveness of factoring it is necessary to evaluate the benefits, which may include reduced overdraft costs, reduced bad debts and reduced administration costs, and compare these with the cost of the factoring service.

Cash discounts

Discounts off the total amount outstanding may be offered to the customer for early payment, but care should be taken to ensure that the customer really is eligible. The offering of a cash discount is becoming less frequent and has never really been adopted by the hotel industry. In many cases the cost of discounting may mean that this is not a viable approach to reducing debtors. If a customer is offered terms of say '2/30, net 60', this means that payment is due within 30 days and will result in a 2% discount; otherwise the full amount is due within 60 days. The customer has two options: he can either pay 2% less on day 30 or he can pay the full amount on day 60. The extra 30 days' credit costs the customer 2%. This works out at approximately $360/30 = 12$ times per year or an annual interest rate of 24%.

The calculation can be worked out more precisely using the following formula:

$$l(\text{interest rate}) = (1 + \text{Discount rate}) - 1$$

that is

$$l = (1 + 0.02) - 1$$
$$= 26.8\%$$

Unless the supplier's cost of borrowing is more than this figure it is uneconomic to offer this level of discount. The following example illustrates a cost–benefit analysis calculated from the viewpoint of the creditor.

Example

The following details relate to a debt of £1,000 owed by Sunshine Food Products to a food wholesaler. The terms are payment within 10 days to receive a discount of 5% or full payment within 30 days. The food company has an overdraft facility on which interest is payable at 15%. Should the food company take up the offer of the discount for early payment?

Benefit if the cash discount is accepted is a saving of £50 arising from £1,000 × 5%.

Benefit if the discount is rejected is a saving in overdraft costs because the business would have 20 more days' use of the money, which represents:

$$£950 \times \frac{20}{365} \times 15\% = £7.81$$

Therefore, the benefit of discount outweighs the cost of the overdraft incurred.

Interest charges

The reverse of offering a discount for early payment is to charge interest for late payment. The difficulty in practice is in enforcing the payment of the interest. As mentioned earlier, it is often smaller businesses who suffer most from the late payment of invoices.

Bad debts

The cost of offering additional credit should be compared with the benefits of incurring additional sales. The following example illustrates the cost–benefit analysis.

Example

The current level of sales is £20,000 per month with an average credit period of 1 month. If the credit period is lengthened it is anticipated that sales will increase and some bad debts will be incurred. There are considered to be three options, the first of which is to continue with the existing policy.

Increase in credit period	Increase in sales above £20,000 per month	Percentage bad debt
Nil	Nil	Nil
1½ months	£4,000	1
2 months	£10,000	10

The bad debt is only incurred on the new sales. The variable costs are known to be 60% of sales. Fixed costs are £50,000. There will be no increase in stocks required. Total investment in net assets, excluding debtors, will be fixed.

	Current situation (£)	Increase by 1½ months (£)	Increase by 2 months (£)
Sales	20,000	24,000	30,000
Sales p.a.	240,000	288,000	360,000
Variable costs	144,000	172,800	216,000
Contribution	96,000	115,200	144,000
Bad debts	—	480	11,000
	96,000	114,720	133,000
Fixed costs	50,000	50,000	50,000
Profit	46,000	64,720	83,000

Despite the bad debt increasing by extending credit to 2 months, this does provide an increase in profit.

The additional investment in debtors at cost is as follows, assuming that the cost of capital is 15%:

Debtor level	20,000	36,000	60,000
Value at cost	12,000	21,600	36,000
Opportunity cost	1,800	3,240	5,400

It is still worth offering additional credit to increase sales.

Debtor ratios

Ratios can also be used for debtor management and probably the most widely used is the debtor collection period. This is calculated as follows:

$$\text{Debtor days} = \frac{\text{Average debtors} \times 365}{\text{Annual credit sales}}$$

This value indicates the average time between the sale being recorded and payment being received. The ratio may be calculated annually or on a weekly or monthly basis, substituting the relevant number of days. Most businesses calculate an average for the debtors in total and also values for individual accounts. The following timescales are averages of the periods normally used.

0–40 days	Acceptable credit period
40–60 days	Chase letter normally sent
60–90 days	Second chase letter sent and personal calls made to the company

The average number of days for debtors in the UK is considered to be approximately 45 days, with the very large businesses taking much longer. Beyond 90 days it may be possible to retrieve bad debts through the courts, but this is normally not worth the time and cost involved. It is better, therefore, to operate an effective credit policy to minimize the possibility of debtors being written off as bad debts in the first place.

Managing creditors

The process for paying suppliers is influenced by three important factors:

- interest costs
- administrative costs
- supplier relationships.

Creditors are an important source of short-term finance and it is beneficial to delay payment. Discounts may be offered by some suppliers as an attempt to improve payment settlement times. However, these should only be considered where the discount is greater than the opportunity cost of early payment, as demonstrated by the previous example.

Large companies often take more than 30 days to settle an invoice and this is due partly to administrative factors, particularly where invoices for individual units are settled centrally. Invoices for each supplier may be processed on a certain day each month and where the payment day is missed the supplier will need to wait until the following month. However, delay in payment may well be intentional, with companies taking advantage of suppliers who fail to follow up on outstanding invoices. Failure to pay on time may well damage supplier relationships and this could result in less co-operation from suppliers, increased prices, and delayed or erratic deliveries. A different approach to creditor management, based on Japanese management principles, focuses on the relationship with suppliers, where communications are fostered to improve service and to reduce the need for extensive stock-holding. Companies who have taken this approach have reduced the number of suppliers used and have involved the supplier in strategic decision-making processes.

The management of creditors is achieved through the production of regular reports containing the credit payment period ratio, which is calculated as follows:

$$\text{Creditor days} = \frac{\text{Average or period end creditors} \times 365}{\text{Total purchases}}$$

The value calculated gives the number of days for which credit is taken.

Inventory control

Stock or inventory may be defined as any current asset held for conversion into cash. In manufacturing industries stock-holdings may account for almost half of the total assets employed and consequently stock management will require careful planning and control. In these types of business the stock is classified into three types:

- **raw materials:** stock held in the state in which it was purchased without any work having taken place
- **work-in-progress:** stock that has been partially converted into the final state; the value is made up of raw material costs plus labour and expenses
- **finished goods:** completed goods awaiting delivery to the customer.

In typical hospitality organizations the stock-holding levels are likely to be much lower, and stock is often held solely in the raw material state, with the transition to finished goods taking place at the point of consumption.

Stock will comprise food and beverage, which will be fairly fast moving, and also items such as disposables and stationery. The overall objective of inventory control is to minimize the costs associated with stock-holding without losing potential sales through not having sufficient stock available. The cost of stock comprises three elements: the purchase price, the holding costs and the cost to the business of being out of stock.

The cost of holding stock includes costs associated with the following:

- lost interest on money tied up in stock
- storage space
- staffing and insurance
- risk of obsolescence and pilferage
- purchasing costs.

The cost of being out of stock is difficult to calculate accurately. It is not easy to quantify the cost of the loss of customer goodwill and potential lost sales when insufficient stocks are available. Other costs may be incurred where production is halted in other areas causing a delay in services, through the loss of flexibility that exists when there is buffer stock and the administrative costs incurred from placing lots of small orders.

Stock management should include the use of models where appropriate and also stock turnover ratios. The use of these methods will depend on the nature of the stock. An effective stock-control system will not necessarily classify stock items in the same way.

Both the Pareto principle and the ABC method are based on the condition that a small percentage of items comprises the greatest value of stock. The Pareto principle works on the assumption that 80% of the value of the stock may be held in only 20% of the items. This may be close to reality in hotel operations, where liquor stocks often have the largest value per item. The ABC or 123 method of stock control is based on the principle that stock is classified into three groups depending on an item's value and degree of usage. The distribution of the value of these items may typically be illustrated as follows:

	% Stock volume	*% Stock value*
Category A	10	50
Category B	30	35
Category C	60	15
	100	100

Category A stocks will be essential items where the probability of a stock out is much higher and therefore levels must be monitored closely. Category B stocks will require less control and category C stocks almost no control. In practice, all stock items can be effectively monitored using computerized inventory systems and in many hospitality organizations these have replaced traditional stock-recording systems such as the bin cards used for liquor stocks.

Stock management models

The quantity of stock ordered each time depends on the balance between the costs of holding stock and the costs of a stock shortage. A common model is the economic

Figure 7.1 Graph of the stock level against time for some item of stock

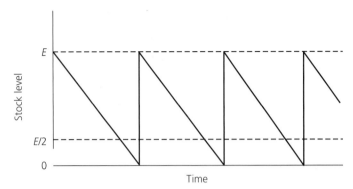

order quantity (EOQ) model, which calculates the most efficient order quantity for each item given the costs involved. Many models operate on the assumption that the stock levels fall evenly over time until the stock runs out, when it is replaced by a stock delivery, as illustrated in Figure 7.1.

In the figure, an amount (E) of stock is delivered at time 0. This is steadily used until the stock level drops to 0, at which point a new consignment (amount E) arrives. The average level of stock is $E/2$.

The calculation is as follows:

$$EOQ = \frac{\sqrt{2CoD}}{Ch}$$

where EOQ = economic order quantity, Co = cost of ordering, D = annual demand, and Ch = cost of holding stock.

The assumptions underlying the model place limits on the use of the model in the hospitality industry. They are that there is a known constant stock-holding cost and a known constant ordering cost, the rates of demand are known and there is a known constant price per unit. The seasonality of the hospitality industry may, in many cases, render the model almost totally useless. However, the model may have useful application in the food production industries where production is constant.

The following example illustrates how the model is used.

Example

Ingredient X is required on a regular basis throughout the year. It is estimated that the annual demand is 4095 kg and the cost of holding 1 kg in terms of refrigeration costs and other costs amounts to £4.00. It is estimated that it costs £4.85 to place and process a purchase order.

The EOQ is calculated using the formula:

$$EOQ = \frac{\sqrt{2CoD}}{Ch}$$

Using the given values,

$$EOQ = \sqrt{\frac{2 \times 4.85 \times 4,095}{4.00}}$$

$$= 99.65\,kg$$

Assuming that demand is constant over the year, purchase orders need to be made

$$\frac{4,095}{99.65} = 41.36 \text{ times per year}$$

which is approximately equivalent to every 8 days.

Stock ratios

Stock control can be improved with the use of ratios. These are most effective when compared with budget, target or forecast figures. The most useful ratio is the stock turnover ratio, which is calculated as follows:

$$\text{Stock turnover} = \frac{\text{Cost of sales}}{\text{Average value of stock}}$$

The greater the number of times the stock turns over the more efficient the stock control. The value can also be expressed in terms of the number of days the commodity has been sitting on the shelf, which is calculated as follows:

$$\text{Stock days} = \frac{\text{Value of stock}}{\text{Average daily cost of sales}} \times 365$$

The ratio may be calculated for stocks in total and also for individual items of stock to highlight slow-moving items.

Cash management

Cash held by a business will be present in a variety of forms and may well include cash paid by customers, floats, cheques received, cheques paid but not sent and cash held in bank accounts. It is essential, therefore, that internal controls are maintained to minimize losses as follows:

- **separation of duties:** this imposes checks on the individual where tasks are shared and individuals will need to collude in order to misappropriate funds
- **management authorization to** raise payment for suppliers' invoices, employee expense claims or cash advance requisitions
- **surprise checks**, where cash is unexpectedly counted.

No system of control can be perfect, but internal checks can assist in preventing fraud and can reduce the likelihood of temptation.

Cash-flow forecasts

A business needs to have cash available to meet day-to-day expenditure such as payment to suppliers and staff, but it should also not be holding too much cash as this is an inefficient use of funds. Forecast cash-flow statements are essential for identifying peaks and troughs in cash requirements and may be produced with a simple receipts and payments approach or alternatively using a balance-sheet approach as recommended by FRS 1, an example of which is included in Chapter 3.

Summary
The availability of working capital is essential for business survival. Too little in the form of stocks and cash will mean that the business will seize up. Too much will mean that extra costs will be incurred in holding too high a level of stock, cash and debtors. Creditors provide a valuable form of short-term finance and a balance needs to be struck to ensure that creditors are maximized while maintaining flexibility in supplier relationships.

Questions

1 The cash operating cycle

The Carmen Hotel has a bistro style restaurant which, owing to growing demand, has recently been extended. A summary of the current-year results for the bistro is shown below:

	Food (£)	%	Beverage (£)	%
Sales revenue	150,000	100	100,000	100
Cost of sales	45,000	30	25,000	25
Gross profit	105,000	70	75,000	75

With the extension now complete, the following forecasts have been made for the coming year:

(i) Sales of food and beverage will increase to £200,000 and £150,000, respectively.

(ii) The amount of stock to be held will be:

Food: 10 days on average

Beverage: 25 days on average.

(iii) Of the total sales of food and beverage, 20% will be on credit and the debtors will be on average 45 days.

(iv) Food suppliers will give 30 days' credit and beverage suppliers 45 days.

(v) Advance booking deposits from parties will amount to 5% of 4 weeks' food sales.

You are required to:

(a) Prepare a statement analysing the average working capital requirements necessary to fund the business during the coming year compared with the previous year.

(b) Give illustrated examples of six key ratios that could be used to monitor the effectiveness of a restaurant operation.

Source: British Association of Hospitality Accountants, Stage 3 Paper, July 2001

2 The cash cycle

The West Hotels Group Ltd has been concerned with its liquidity position in recent months.

The most recent profit and loss account and balance sheet of the company are as follows.

Profit and loss account for the year ended 31 December 2004

	(£000)
Sales	10,125
Cost of sales	2,997
Gross profit	7,128
Departmental expenses	1,767
Undistributed operating expenses	2,367
Profit before fixed charges	2,994
Fixed charges	957
Net profit	2,037

Balance sheet as at 31 December 2004

	(£000)	(£000)	(£000)
Fixed assets (net):			
Freehold property			17,600
Equipment and furniture			4,100
			21,700
Current assets:			
Stocks of food and beverages			1,750
Debtors			2,250
Cash at bank			10
			4,010

Less creditors:
(Amounts due within 1 year)

Creditors	500
Taxation	1,300
Proposed dividend	1,100
Bank overdraft	1,500
	4,400

Net current assets/(liabilities)	(390)
	21,310

Less creditors:
(Amounts due in more than 1 year)

10% mortgage debentures 2006	8,400
	12,910

Financed by:

Ordinary share capital	6,910
Retained profits	6,000
	12,910

You are required to:

(a) Explain why West Hotels Group Ltd is concerned with its liquidity position.

(b) Explain the term 'operating cash cycle' and discuss why this concept is important for a business.

(c) Calculate the cash operating cycle for West Hotels Group Ltd based on the information in the statements above. Assume a 365-day year.

(d) Discuss the strategies that can be followed to improve the cash operating cycle.

Source: British Association of Hospitality Accountants, Stage 3 Paper, February 2005

3 The economic order quantity

The Roasta Coffee Shop sells a particular brand of coffee and has the following characteristics:

Sales	10 cases per week
Ordering costs	£10 per order
Holding costs	30% per year
Item cost	£80 per case

You are required to calculate:

(a) How many cases should be ordered at a time?

(b) How often should the coffee be ordered?

(c) What is the annual cost of ordering and holding coffee?

(d) What factors may cause the coffee shop to order a larger or smaller amount than the EOQ?

4 The role of the credit manager

(a) Explain the role of a credit manager within a business.

(b) Discuss the major factors that a credit manager would consider when assessing the credit worthiness of a particular customer.

5 Business liquidity

The following ratios are available for the Sands Hotel for 3 years of performance:

	2001	2002	2003
Current ratio	1.7	1.9	2.0
Acid-test ratio	1.3	1.4	1.5
Debtor days	35	38	40
Stock days	10	11	11

Use each of the above ratios to comment on the liquidity of the Sands Hotel from 2001 to 2003. What other information and ratios would be useful to give you full insight into the liquidity of the business and help you to interpret these values?

6 Managing inventory levels

A hotel is reviewing its stock ordering policy and has the following options available for the purchase of an item of cleaning materials used in housekeeping:

(a) purchase 100 cases of stock twice monthly

(b) purchase 200 cases per month

(c) purchase 600 cases every 3 months

(d) purchase 1200 cases every 6 months

(e) purchase 2400 cases once per year.

The purchase price for deliveries up to 400 cases is £10 per case. A discount of 5% is offered by the supplier for deliveries of 401–1000 cases. For orders in excess of 1000 cases a total discount of 20% is available. Each order incurs administration costs of £25. Costs of holding the stock are estimated to be £2 per case.

Analyse the above information and give advice on the optimum order size. Consider what other factors should be taken into account when making this decision.

7 Economic order quantity

The Alpha Food Service Company sells a particular brand of tea in all of its outlets. The tea is ordered centrally and then distributed to the outlets to gain the maximum discount from the supplier. The following data applies to the year 2003. Assume 52 weeks per year.

Sales	20 cases per week
Ordering costs	£20 per order
Holding costs (storage cost)	10%
Cost per case	£100

You are required to:

(a) Calculate how many cases should be ordered at a time.

(b) Calculate how often tea should be ordered.

(c) Calculate the annual cost of ordering and holding tea.

(d) What factors may cause the company to order a larger or smaller amount than the EOQ?

(e) How useful do you believe the application of the EOQ model to be in the hospitality industry? Give examples of where its usage would be most appropriate and least appropriate.

8 Working capital

(a) Explain what you understand by the term working capital.

(b) List the reasons why it is important to manage the level of working capital in a business.

(c) What factors influence the level of cash that should be available to the business?

British Association of Hospitality Accountants, Stage 3 Paper, January 2004

9 Controlling debtors

Seaside Hotels plc currently require payment from their customers by the month end after the month of checkout. On average it takes them 60 days to pay. Credit sales amount to £1 million per year and bad debts are 4% of sales per year.

It is planned to offer customers a cash discount of 2% for payment within 30 days. It is estimated that 40% of customers will accept this facility, but that the remaining customers, who tend to be slow payers, will not pay until 70 days after the stay. At present the company has a partly used overdraft facility costing 10% per annum. If the plan goes ahead bad debts will be reduced to 3% per annum and there will be savings in credit administration expenses of £3000 per annum.

You are required to:

(a) Advise Seaside Hotels plc on the viability of offering the new credit terms to the customers. You should support your answer with any calculations and explanations that you consider necessary. (Work to the nearest pound.)

(b) Describe the costs incurred in offering credit to customers and recommend a code of practice to ensure effective debtor management.

10

(a) Explain the term overtrading and describe the possible consequences arising from this condition.

(b) What are the main causes of overtrading in the hospitality, tourism and leisure industry?

(c) What financial ratios are useful for detecting signs of overtrading occurring?

Further reading

Atkinson, H., Berry, A. and Jarvis, R. (1995) *Business Accounting for Hospitality and Tourism*, London: Chapman and Hall.

Coltman, M. (2002) *Hospitality Management Accounting*, New York: John Wiley.

Edwards, B. (2004) *Credit Management Handbook*, London: Ashgate Publishing.

Harris, P. (1995) *Accounting and Finance for the International Hospitality Industry*, Oxford: Butterworth Heinemann.

Huston, T. and Butterworth, J. (1974) *Management of Trade Credit*, London: Gower.

Useful websites

http://partners.financenter.com/southtrust/learn/guides/smbizcashflow/importance.fcs
  Focuses on small business, but the principles apply whatever the size of business
www.toolkit.cch.com/text/P06_4001.asp   Hints and tips for business
www.planware.org/cashflow.htm   Check out the ways to improve cash flow
http://media.wiley.com/product_data/excerpt/57/07879538/0787953857.pdf   Chapter on cash-flow management techniques
www.acca.org.uk/publications/studentaccountant/57707   ACCA advice on working capital management; note the link to ROCE
www.investopedia.com/articles/fundamental/03/061803.asp   Includes interesting case studies

8 | Performance measurement

About this chapter

Tools and techniques for assessing business performance are essential elements of the manager's skills for controlling and directing a business. Organizational structure plays a key part in determining the nature and structure of internal reports. This chapter reviews the different likely forms of organizational structure and provides guidance on current practice in terms of both financial and non-financial performance measures.

Learning objectives On completion of this chapter you should be able to:

- understand and apply the range of operational measures used in the hospitality and tourism industries
- understand and apply performance measures for assessing profitability, liquidity, asset usage and share performance
- explain the factors to be considered when designing performance measurement systems
- describe the application of the balanced scorecard methodology to the hospitality and tourism industries.

Introduction

The measurement of performance is central to control in both profit-making and non-profit-making service organizations. It is essential for the manager to know what has happened, **why** it has happened and **what** can be done now to improve future performance. To be successful, systems for control should support all the organizational objectives as well as the competitive strategies of the business, and yet all too often the focus of performance measurement is centred on easily quantifiable aspects of performance where relationships between measurable quantities are compared with previous performance or standard benchmarks. For many service-orientated businesses the use of non-financial measures can provide a valuable additional dimension by providing information that attempts to quantify the competitive positioning of the business and as a result many operations now try to use a mix of financial and non-financial measures where intangibles such as quality and flexibility can be measured along with more traditional measures such as profitability and return on investment. The structure and size of the organization clearly have implications for the scale and range of measures that are appropriate, with particular problems arising as organizations increase in size and change in structure.

Case study: Four Seasons Hotels and Resorts Annual Report 2004, page 26

Our key financial and growth objectives over the long term are:

- Maintain and enhance our RevPAR growth and the operating profits of the hotels and resorts that we manage.
- Achieve growth of the Four Seasons portfolio through the addition of new hotels and resorts and selected luxury branded residential projects.
- Achieve an average return on capital employed of at least 10% over our long-term cost of capital.
- Achieve, on average, compounded earnings per share growth of 20% per annum over the long term.
- Generate at least 90% of our earnings from our management business.
- Maintain a strong balance sheet and a low cost of capital.
- Deploy the majority of our annual operating cash flow to obtain and enhance management opportunities that expand the Four Seasons brand.
- Identify and pursue opportunities that allow us to maintain high profit margins in our management operations.
- Maintain tax efficiency.
- Divest equity investments or advances when appropriate opportunities arise, to allow previously committed capital to be made available for investments related to new or enhanced management or royalty opportunities.
- Maintain a prudent risk profile on the investment of cash and cash equivalents.

Source: www.fourseasons.com/investor_information/annual_reports.html

The structure of the organization

The role of performance measurement is linked directly to the development of the structure of the organization. A relatively small business functioning with one or two key members of staff who also happen to be the owners will still require accurate information in terms of sales and costs. However, much of the information will be carried in the heads of the people involved in terms of costs and sales figures, which are easily remembered as each sales order and purchase invoice will have been processed personally. Many businesses start in this way, progressing as highly focused, owner-managed organizations with a restricted range of products and services serving a well-defined market. As the business grows more sophisticated systems for passing information are required and this information may be summarized in the form of performance measures. At this stage of growth a purely functional structure may be considered to be appropriate, with the justification being that by concentrating similar resources in one area of the business, the greatest possible level of economies of scale can be achieved. Evidence suggests that the larger the organization becomes the more elaborate its structure, requiring the specialization of tasks and the greater need for planning and control to ensure integration. As size increases, individual areas of activity

Figure 8.1 (a) Functional and (b) divisionalized organizational structure
IC = investment centre; CC = cost centre; RC = revenue centre.
Source: Adapted with permission from Drury (2005) *Management Accounting for Business*, p. 375.

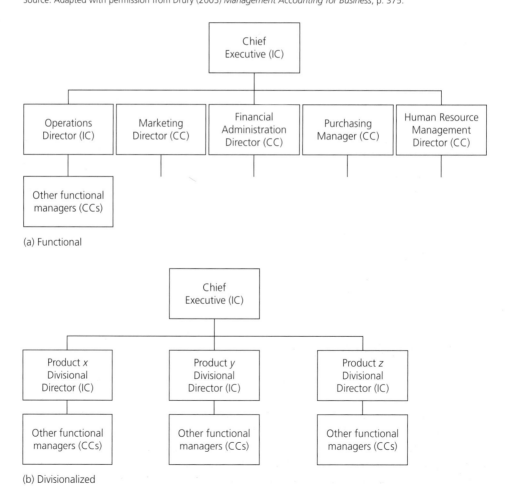

may become larger and increase in number and, in general, the behaviour of the organization becomes more formal. Consequently, within larger organizations the trend has been to move towards divisionalized structures where individual divisions are given greater autonomy and are responsible for short- and medium-term operating decisions, with only strategic decisions made centrally. Figure 8.1 illustrates the changing structures that can arise as an organization grows in size.

The functional organization is divided into the key activities of the organization such as operations and purchasing, along with the support activities such as marketing, finance and human resource management. The essential feature of this type of organization is that the operating areas share the services of the central support activities. This differs from divisionalized structures where the support activities are dedicated to each operating area. A division should be a natural grouping within the organization, such as a group of similar operations that share common operating practices, markets and possibly operate in a common environment. However, the completely divisionalized structure is often unable to achieve the same degree of economies of scale as a functional structure, particularly when each division is made effectively to stand alone, and as a result a combined structure can evolve that tries to obtain the benefits of both formats. This is illustrated in Figure 8.2.

Figure 8.2 Mixed organizational structure

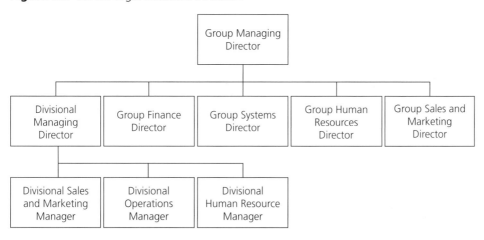

The needs of single-focus businesses

A single-focus business can be described as one operating with basically the same range of products and markets throughout. The key issue for single-focus businesses is the changing financial controls required as the business matures. Following the stages of the product life cycle, in the initial stages of development and launch the emphasis is logically on market research and product development requiring capital spend. During the growth stage, a key area of importance will be the levels of marketing spend. In addition to monitoring this spend and the subsequent market penetration, this is the time to evaluate how alternative barriers to entry may be erected so as to prevent a flood of competitors entering the marketplace. At this time the management accounting function needs to focus on ensuring that resource levels are available for significant marketing expenditure and for increasing investment in fixed assets without losing sight of cost control in other areas. The growth phase ends as the market moves into maturity. The business should now be concentrating on achieving a financial return to justify the earlier periods of investment. The management accounting system should be focusing on cost control and competitor analysis to improve and identify opportunities for developing a competitive cost advantage. Once the business is in decline the management accounting process should be evaluating the alternative opportunities for leaving the industry. However, this stage may be avoided if action is taken at the maturity stage to prolong the life of the product through product changes or market expansion or both.

The needs of divisionalized structures

Systems for performance measurement should be tailored to suit the operational needs of divisionalized structures and may also need to be linked to incentive and reward programmes. As a result, the development of suitable performance measures requires careful planning. Many organizational activities are complex and performance cannot be reduced to a single measure that is meant to serve as a summary of overall performance. The multidivisional structure (M form) is suited to organizations with a focus on traditional limiting factors such as finance, land and labour, and is suitable for organizations utilizing a management philosophy based on command, control, contract and compliance. However, Brander Brown and Atkinson (2001) suggest that many hospitality and tourism organizations should consider reverting to an N-form approach, which treats front-line managers as the entrepreneurs with responsibility for strategy and decision making. As a consequence, performance measurement systems need to be based on a balanced range of performance indicators.

Standards for performance measurement

There are generally five standards against which performance is normally measured:

- same unit or department in previous periods
- performance of similar units or departments, both internal and external to the organization
- estimates of expected performance in the form of budgets and forecasts
- estimates of what might have been achieved, set after the event
- performance necessary to achieve desired goals.

The problem with setting standard targets for performance is that the process assumes that the environment remains the same throughout the period. In practice, changes in trading conditions may render the process of comparison useless.

As a consequence, a system of this type is often perceived by managers as not being fair. In addition, the process can fail to take into account what is achievable, with standards being set based on best performance rather than average performance. This, coupled with the multiple nature of the objectives set, can lead to obsessive behaviour on the part of the manager as he or she attempts to meet all of the targets, many of which are in conflict with each other.

To summarize, to develop effective processes for performance measurement it is important to consider the following major issues:

- Organizational objectives can be complex and cannot easily be summarized with a single measure of performance such as the return on capital employed measure.
- Some aspects of performance such as service levels are difficult to measure in quantitative terms.
- Many organizational activities are interdependent and require co-operation between divisions, units or departments, and as a result performance measures should be tailored to the requirements of the organization.
- The evaluation of performance must also involve the exercise of judgement.

In the hospitality and tourism industry divisionalized structures are common. There are many examples of vertically integrated organizations, that is those that have expanded through the value chain into buyers and suppliers, and these can suffer from performance measurement problems arising from transfer pricing when products and services are sold internally.

The problem of transfer pricing

Transfer pricing situations occur when an organization structures itself into divisions that make independent decisions. A transfer price is needed when profit-making divisions within the organization sell products to each other. The transfer price may be defined as the cost of buying the product or service in the buying division and as sales revenue in the selling division. Consequently, the level of the transfer price will affect the profitability of each division and will, therefore, have serious implications for the process of performance measurement. The alternatives available for setting a price are to use cost price, but this will undermine the profitability of the selling division, to use a marginal cost figure, but this can be difficult to agree, or to use a market price. This final option can be achieved easily where there is a highly competitive market outside the organization. The price is set using the outside market and the two divisions can be allowed to deal with each other or not. In either case, total organizational profits will be achieved. The problem becomes far more acute when the outside market is non-existent or non-competitive. In this case the marginal cost may be used, but this means that the selling division is making no profit on the transfer, which is not appropriate for a division classified as a profit centre where performance measurement will be based on profit-related measures.

Additional problems occur with price setting where capacity constraints exist, and in this case it may be appropriate to use the opportunity cost, that is, the value in the next best use, but this is difficult to calculate in practice.

A suggested approach to overcome some of these problems is to set the price using a process of negotiation. If managers are placed in the position where they have to negotiate with each other to arrive at acceptable transfer prices, it is felt by behaviourists that they grow to understand each other's problems and that this is good for the organization as a whole. The process is less effective, however, where the two parties have unequal power. The remainder of this chapter will focus on the range of performance measures available to the hospitality and tourism industry.

Non-financial measures of performance

There is a range of non-financial measures appropriate to service industries, both quantitative and qualitative, which may be used as part of control process where actual results are compared with plans, budgets, standards and targets. In the past 50 years experts in management have attempted to identify performance criteria to cover all aspects of business performance. Drucker (1953) identified seven generic criteria set by organizations for each performance area, and these should be supported by appropriate measures that could be used continually to monitor and control performance against objectives. Sink (1985) developed Drucker's framework and redefined his own set of performance criteria:

- profitability
- productivity
- quality
- innovation
- effectiveness
- efficiency
- delivery performance
- flexibility.

More recently, the work of Fitzgerald et al. (1991) has focused specifically on service operations, classifying the business along a continuum based on numbers of customers processed per day and the level of services received by those customers. The research is based on operations drawn from this classification and has produced six dimensions against which measurement of business performance can take place. The research also suggests that every service organization will need to develop its own set of performance measures to help them gain and retain competitive advantage. The six criteria are summarized in Table 8.1.

The extent to which this comprehensive range of measures may be used will depend on the nature of the service business. Fitzgerald et al. reviewed performance measures used in a major international hotel chain with three- and four-star accommodation. The guidelines illustrated in Table 8.2 have been adapted from their work and others to illustrate how a range of measures may be used to assess performance in a hotel operation.

Each sector of the hospitality, tourism and leisure industries has its own range of operating ratios for measuring performance. The case study on page 181 draws data from the easyJet accounts for 2003 and 2004.

Table 8.1 Business performance criteria identified by Fitzgerald *et al.*

Financial performance Profitability Liquidity Capital structure Market ratios
Competitiveness Relative market share and position Sales growth Measures of the customer base
Resource utilization Productivity (input:output) Efficiency (resources planned:consumed) Utilization (resources available:consumed)
Quality of service Overall service indicators Measures of the 12 determinants of service quality: reliability, responsiveness, aesthetics, cleanliness, comfort, friendliness, communication, courtesy, competence, access, availability, security
Innovation Proportion of new to old products and services New products and service sales levels
Flexibility Product/service introduction flexibility Product/service mix flexibility Volume flexibility Delivery flexibility

Source: Fitzgerald *et al. Performance Measurement in Service Businesses* (1991).

Financial measures of performance

Single ratio analysis, sometimes referred to as univariate analysis, is based on the calculation of individual ratios using data from the trading accounts and the balance sheet. These ratios may then be used for comparison with previous trends, budgets or other similar operations. An alternative and less widely known technique is multidiscriminant analysis (MDA) or Z-scoring. This technique has attracted much attention in accounting circles in recent years. Broadly speaking, the methodology is based on a series of traditional ratios such as return on investment and working capital measures, and combines them to produce a single

Table 8.2 Measures to assess performance in a hotel operation

Financial performance	
• Profit and loss (P/L) account	Weekly/monthly report to management team
	Costs and revenue broken down by department
• Average spends	Accommodation, food, beverage
• Budget variance analysis	Each month general managers have to submit with
	their P/L account explanations for the largest variances
• Breakdown of pay-roll costs, days' absence, overtime, etc.	Reported by each hotel every week
• Working capital measures	Debtors, creditors, stock, cash holdings
Measures of competitiveness	
• Market share (number of rooms occupied out of total number of rooms available in the local market)	Weekly/monthly report to management team
• Number and percentage of rooms occupied for each of the top six local competitors	Weekly/monthly report to management team
• Average room rates charged by top six local competitors	Weekly/monthly report to management team
• Number of rooms sold by customer type	Weekly/monthly report to management team
• Customer loyalty: number of repeat bookings	Data available from computerized reservations
Resource utilization	
• Percentage of rooms occupied out of total rooms available	Weekly/monthly report to management team
• Percentage of beds occupied out of total beds available	Weekly/monthly report to management team
• Food and beverage sales per staying guest	Weekly/monthly report to management team
Service quality measures	
• Customer satisfaction with overall service levels	Guest questionnaires with data compiled into statistics
• Likelihood of repeat custom	Guest questionnaires
• Staff turnover by avoidable/unavoidable reasons for transfer	Monthly report to management committee.
• Number of training days per employee	Occasional report
• Complaints per 1000 customers	Occasional report
Innovation measures	
• Average age of menus	Occasional report
Flexibility measures	
• Average time to respond to a customer's request	Relevant in various areas

weighted statistic. This statistic may then be used within specific guidelines to assess the potential for success or failure for individual companies. The method was initially devised to overcome the key problem associated with single ratios, where some ratios move in the opposite direction to all the others, thus making interpretation difficult.

Case study: Selected consolidated operating data for easyJet plc

(Unaudited) Year ended 30 September	2004	2003
Number of aircraft owned/leased at end of year	92	74
Average number of aircraft owned/leased during year	85.0	67.8
Number of aircraft operated at end of year	90	71
Average number of aircraft operated during year	79.9	66.0
Number of routes operated at end of year	153	105
Number of airports served at end of year	44	38
Owned/leased aircraft utilisation (hours per day)	10.5	11.1
Operated aircraft utilisation (hours per day)	11.2	11.4
Available seat kilometres ('ASK') (millions)	25,448	21,024
Passengers (millions)	24.3	20.3
Load factor	84.5%	84.1%
Revenue passenger kilometres ('RPK') (millions)	21,566	17,735
Average internet sales percentage during the year	95.7%	93.8%
Internet sales % during final month of financial year	96.9%	96.3%
Average fare (£)	42.28	43.28

Source: easyJet website (www.easyjet.com)

Ratios by type

Traditionally, financial ratios may be classified into five groups:

- profitability and operating ratios
- asset utilization
- liquidity (control of cash and other working capital items)
- capital gearing ratios
- shareholders' investment ratios.

The constituent ratios for each of these groupings are shown in more detail in Table 8.3. Many of these are standard ratios used throughout many types of industry, where benchmarks and guidelines for ratios are commonly cited: however, care should be taken as the magnitude of the ratios can vary considerably from one industry to another. The following section aims to provide some guidance for the calculation and interpretation of these ratios when attempting to analyse company performance. It is worth remembering that ratio analysis is not an exact science and quite often a variety of methodologies is quoted for the calculation of one particular ratio.

Profitability and operating ratios

A range of measures is used across a range of business sectors to assess business performance. The return on capital employed (ROCE) ratio is widely used for comparing the return generated with the investment. However, there are several

Table 8.3 Financial ratios for measuring performance by category

Profitability and operating ratios Return on net assets Gross profit margin Net profit margin
Asset utilization Net asset turnover Stock-holding period Debtor collection period Creditor payment period
Capital gearing ratios Debt to equity ratio Number of times interest earned
Liquidity ratios Current ratio Quick assets ratio
Shareholders' investment ratios Return on shareholders funds Earnings per share Price/earnings ratio Dividend yield Dividend cover

methods for calculating this ratio and individual organizations should select the methodology most suited to their needs. The following examples represent the most typical approaches.

Return on net assets (return on capital employed)

$$= \frac{\text{Net profit before long-term interest and tax}}{\text{Total assets less creditors due within 1 year (net assets)}} \times 100\%$$

This version of the ratio uses profit before interest and taxes due and the net assets. The usual level of profit to use with this ratio is operating profit or profit before interest and tax, which then gives the profit available to both lenders and shareholders. By using the profit figure at this level in the profit and loss account the effects of taxation are avoided.

Alternatively, the following version of the ratio is sometimes used:

Return on net assets (return on capital employed)

$$= \frac{\text{Net profit after long-term interest and tax}}{\text{Total assets less creditors due within 1 year}} \times 100\%$$

The ratio should produce a value that is as high as possible without undermining the long-term success of the business. A short-term view will mean that earnings are increased through reducing expenditure in a number of areas such as training and maintenance and capital expenditure is reduced, but both of these policies will adversely affect the long-term viability of the business.

It is important to note that other alternative forms are sometimes used, such as return on total assets (fixed assets and current assets) and this will produce a quite different value. Consequently, it is important to be clear as to the basis of the ratio being used.

The ROCE or return on investment (ROI) ratio is the most widely used financial measure of divisional performance and is closely related to the accounting rate of return (ARR) investment appraisal technique described in Chapter 10.

The gross profit margin ratio considers the proportion of sales revenue remaining after the expense of making the product is taken into account. The ratio is calculated as:

$$\text{Gross profit margin} = \frac{\text{Gross profit}}{\text{Sales}} \times 100\%$$

This level of profit is a very important measure in the hospitality industry. The proportion of gross profit will depend on the pricing strategy of the firm. High volumes may be achieved with low prices, or low volumes may be supported by higher average spends and consequently higher gross profit cash values. The other important factor associated with gross profit margin is sales mix. The combination of the products and services sold will impact on the average gross profit margin achieved.

Example

Use the following data to compute the cost of sales and the gross profit percentage.

Opening stock 1 April	£22,184.00
April purchases:	
Meats	£11,501.00
Dairy	£6,300.00
Fruit and vegetables	£9,641.00
Other foods	£32,384.00
Closing stock at 30 April	£23,942.00
Sales	£193,560.00

The consumption is calculated using the formula:

$$\text{Opening stock} + \text{Purchases} - \text{Closing stock} = \text{Cost of sales}$$
$$22,184 + 59,826 - 23,942 = 58,068$$
$$\text{Cost of sales \%} = \frac{58,068}{193,560}$$
$$= 30\%$$
$$\text{Gross profit \%} = 70\%$$

The next level of profit is described as net margin.

$$\text{Net margin} = \frac{\text{Gross profit less salary and wage costs}}{\text{Sales}} \times 100\%$$

Staff and labour costs are a significant expense in the hospitality, tourism and leisure industry and this ratio reflects the importance of wage costs. The net margin ratio cannot usually be calculated from published figures, but can be very useful for internal reporting. For many businesses this cost uses a significant proportion of revenue.

$$\text{Net profit margin} = \frac{\text{Net profit before long-term interest and tax}}{\text{Sales}} \times 100\%$$

This ratio shows what is left of sales revenue after all the expenses of running the business. The value should be as high as possible provided that the business is not earning high profits at the expense of some other aspect. A short-termist attitude to maximizing profit may mean that expenditure on maintenance and replacements is cut, undermining the future potential of the business. The expected value of this ratio will differ quite considerably from one business to the next.

Asset utilization ratios

These ratios are used to assess the effectiveness of the business in using its assets. This includes both long- and short-term assets. The first of these is the net asset turnover ratio, which focuses on net assets in total:

$$\text{Net asset turnover} = \frac{\text{Sales}}{\text{Total assets less current liabilities}} \times 100\%$$

The net asset turnover ratio enables judgement to be made on the extent to which the business has generated sales. The size of the ratio will be dependent on the nature of the business and a high ratio does not necessarily indicate profitability, but generally speaking the higher the better.

The stock or inventory ratio can be calculated in a number of ways, which are dependent on the information available. When internal information is available it is possible to calculate a stock-holding day's value for every individual product line.

$$\text{Stock-holding period} = \frac{\text{Average stock held}}{\text{Stock consumption}} \times 365 \text{ days}$$

The ratio indicates the average number of days for which stock remains in the firm before it is sold. The stock turnover ratio is the reciprocal of this, that is, stock used divided by stock held. It is not possible to provide a standard figure as the days held will depend on the nature of the stock and the mix between fresh and dry goods. However, to maximize the use of working capital the figure should be as low as possible without a shortage arising. Another current asset requiring control is debtors, which are those customers who have yet to pay for goods and services received. Ideally, the debtors' ratio should be calculated using credit sales, but for analysis using published figures normally only the total sales are disclosed.

$$\text{Debtor collection period} = \frac{\text{Trade debtors}}{\text{Credit sales}} \times 365 \text{ days}$$

This ratio shows how long, on average, trade debtors take to pay. The figure should be as low as possible and ideally it would be better to allow no credit sales. However, the provision of credit is essential for many business operations in the hospitality and tourism industry. Every effort should be made to ensure the bills are paid up promptly and in full.

$$\text{Creditor payment period} = \frac{\text{Trade creditors}}{\text{Credit purchases}} \times 365 \text{ days}$$

This ratio indicates the average length of time the firm takes to pay its debts, after a purchase on credit. A good credit policy will ensure that the business will take as much 'free credit' as possible without losing the goodwill of suppliers.

Liquidity ratios

These ratios are used to assess how well a business is using its working capital. The following ratio provides a measure of the business's ability to meet its short-term liabilities by matching short-term assets with short-term liabilities.

$$\text{Current ratio} = \frac{\text{Current assets}}{\text{Creditors falling due within 1 year}}$$

A standard for the current ratio is often quoted as 1.5:2, which ensures that current liabilities are covered at least 1.5 times by current assets. However, companies in the hospitality sector have survived with ratios which are considerably less than 1, where current liabilities have exceeded current assets. The leisure sector in particular is typical, where sales are predominantly made for cash, stocks and cash holdings are kept at minimal levels, and purchases are bought on credit. Consequently, a consistent ratio of 0.5:1 can be expected. This ratio can be adapted to highlight liquid current assets.

$$\text{Quick assets or acid-test ratio} = \frac{\text{Liquid assets}}{\text{Creditors falling due within 1 year}}$$

Liquid assets are normally taken to be cash and debtors excluding stock. However, in some cases the stock may be more liquid than the debtors. Again, the often quoted benchmark is 1:1, but the value depends very much on the nature of the business.

Capital gearing ratios

Capital gearing is concerned with the level of funding provided by shareholders and loan providers. Loan financing in practice tends to be cheaper than equity, but loan funding exposes the shareholders to greater risk through the obligation to pay interest and the possibility of changing rates. The recommended value for this ratio changes from industry to industry and the assessment as to whether the value is high or low should be made in relation to industry values.

$$\text{Debt to equity} = \frac{\text{Borrowings (long term and short term)}}{\text{Total equity (shares plus reserves)}} \times 100\%$$

A measure of what is considered to be high risk should be based within the context of the nature of the industry. Typically hotel ventures, for example, require substantial investment at the start and a new operation with investment funding could initially be highly geared, possibly with debt exceeding equity in the early stages. As retained earnings increase, the ratio is likely to change, with equity becoming the dominant form of finance.

The gearing ratio is usually quoted with the following ratio, which measures the ability to service the loan finance:

$$\text{Number of times interest earned} = \frac{\text{Net profit before long-term interest and tax}}{\text{Interest payable}}$$

This ratio considers the profitability of the company from the viewpoint of the lender and assesses the ease with which interest is payable. A multiple factor of four times profit to interest is often suggested as a 'safe' value, although there is little evidence to support this.

Case study: Enterprise ups dividend as profits surge

Enterprise Inns reported a 53 per cent increase in profits for the first half of its financial year, boosted by acquisitions, and announced a 56 per cent increase in its interim dividend to 5.6p.

The pub operator made a pre-tax profit before exceptional items of £143.6 million, up from £93.7 million, on turnover of £453.9 million, up from £240.3 million.

The results were slightly ahead of City expectations. Shares in Enterprise Inns rose 11p to 733.5p in early trade.

The company, which rents out its 8,644 pubs to tenants, said the integration of the Unique pubs business, bought in March 2004, has now been completed. Enterprise said savings of some £27 million would be achieved, largely during the current year.

Chief executive Ted Tuppen said the first half results reflected the integration of Unique in a competitive environment.

'Against a background where some are talking of a downturn in consumer discretionary spending, our top quality pub estate continues to trade well', he said.

He added that future dividend policy and the potential for additional cash returns was being reviewed. The outcome of this review will be published with the preliminary results for the full year, which the group said it expects to announce in November.

Mr Tuppen also said the board continues to review acquisition opportunities that may become available in the market, evaluating these against stringent quality, return on capital and earnings enhancement criteria.

Enterprise shares had lost nearly 10 per cent of their value in the past three weeks, since Whitbread, the rival leisure group, said consumers were spending less at its health clubs and pub-restaurants.

Enterprise added that it is currently preparing for the implementation of International Finance Reporting Standards rules. It said it anticipated only minor adjustments to earnings. There will be no impact on cash flows in the business or on the company's debt covenants.

In summary, the board said performance since the period end reinforces the board's expectation of being *able to report* another year of solid progress.

'We are continuing our drive for increased profitability through improvements in all aspects of our business and will further enhance shareholder value through the optimal use of the strong cash flows which are generated.'

Source: *The Times Online*, 17 May 2005
Questions based on this report can be found on page 198.

Shareholders' investment ratios

These ratios consider the performance of the business from the viewpoint of the shareholder. Shareholders purchase shares to receive a regular income in the form of dividends and also, hopefully, to achieve capital growth when the share price increases.

$$\text{Return on equity (Return on shareholders' funds)}$$

$$= \frac{\text{Net profit after long-term interest and tax}}{\text{Share capital and reserves}} \times 100\%$$

This ratio considers return on capital specifically from the shareholder's point of view by considering the relationship between those profits that are attributable to the shareholder and their total funds invested. The following ratio, the earnings per share, is considered to be an important measure of corporate performance:

$$\text{Earnings per share} = \frac{\text{Profit after interest and tax}}{\text{Number of ordinary shares in issue}}$$

This is the profit attributable to each share. The profit generated by the firm belongs to the shareholders whether it is paid out as dividend or not. The more equity increases, the greater the dilution of the earnings per share. This would indicate that funding from loan sources would serve to improve the resulting value. Although this is true it should be remembered that loan finance carries its own risks associated with the commitment to pay interest and repay the capital sum. Earnings per share is normally linked with the price/earnings ratio:

$$\text{Price/earnings} = \frac{\text{Current market price per share}}{\text{Earnings per share}}$$

This ratio can be seen as the number of years that it would take, at the current share price and rate of earnings, for the earnings from the share to cover the price of the share. The ratio indicates how much an investor is prepared to pay for the business earnings. The value of the ratio depends not only on the business itself, but also on the industry in general. The following ratio is a measure of the return the investor is receiving on the current value of the investment:

$$\text{Dividend yield} = \frac{\text{Dividend per share (grossed up for tax)}}{\text{Current market price per share}} \times 100\%$$

This measure enables investments to be compared with each other and enables the investor to seek out those investments that outperform the market in general. The ability to pay the dividend is measured by the following ratio, dividend cover:

$$\text{Dividend cover} = \frac{\text{Earnings per share}}{\text{Dividend per share}}$$

This ratio indicates how comfortably the firm can meet the dividend out of current profits. A public limited company is under some pressure to provide a consistent dividend to maintain share price. However, failure to reinvest in the business can undermine the long-term viability of the operations.

To conclude, shareholder investment ratios are important for the manager of a business because of the power of the market in determining the fortunes of the business in the long term.

Operating statistics

Ratios need not be derived exclusively from the accounting reports. Specific operating statistics focusing on resource utilization are well used in the hospitality and tourism industry and these may be usefully classified into two categories, those that focus on sales activity and those that focus on cost reduction. Table 8.4 includes several key ratios highlighted in the Uniform System of Accounts for Hotels. Most of these measures are self explanatory, but it is worth noting the use of the key measures for assessing accommodation sales performance: the RevPAR and the yield statistic.

RevPAR is calculated as follows:

$$\text{RevPAR} = \frac{\text{Revenue achieved}}{\text{Rooms available for sale}}$$

Table 8.4. Ratios used in the Uniform System of Accounts for the Lodging Industry

Sales-related ratios	Cost-related ratios
Rooms division	
Room occupancy percentage	Labour costs in relation to sales
Double room occupancy percentage	Laundry costs in relation to sales
Bed occupancy percentage	Servicing cost per room
Maximum rooms revenue	Cost per available room (CostPAR)
Average room rate per room occupied	
Average room rate per guest	
Room sales per front desk clerk	
Total average spend of each guest	
Revenue per available room (RevPAR)	
Sales-mix ratio	
Yield percentage	
Number of room services per employee	
Food and beverage operations	
Restaurant occupancy by meal or by day	Wages in relation to sales
Average spend per cover	Material costs in relation to sales
Sales revenue per employee	Stock turnover
Percentage of beverage to food revenue	Stock days
Percentage of food/beverage to rooms revenue	Expenses in relation to sales
Seat turnover	
Seat turnover (measure of seat usage in restaurants)	

This measure assesses the overall earning power of the rooms available for sale and is a key measure for evaluating the usage of accommodation letting space. The yield statistic is the ratio of the actual revenue (generated by the number of rooms sold) to potential revenue (the amount that would be received from the sales of rooms in the hotel at a rack rate) and is expressed as:

$$\text{Yield statistic} = \frac{\text{Actual revenue}}{\text{Potential revenue}}$$

This measure is discussed in more detail in Chapter 5 in relation to pricing strategies. A cost reduction approach may bring increases in profitability, but only increases in revenue can bring about an increase in cash flows into the business, and for high fixed cost industries increases in sales bring about substantial increases in profitability.

Problems with using ratios

The use of ratios can be confusing when differing advice is offered as to how the ratios can be calculated. The choice of ratios used, the exact definition of the ratio and the conclusions drawn are very much based on personal judgement. Weaknesses in the use of ratios can also stem from the nature of the accounting information used in the analysis. There is a tendency for the profit and loss account to overstate the profit levels and a tendency for the balance sheet to misstate the value of capital tied up in the business.

The balance-sheet figures represent the position at a single point in time and the figures may not be representative of the business in general. This creates problems for the interpretation of ratios, particularly where ratios are calculated using profit statement and balance-sheet figures combined. Figures from the profit and loss account represent a series of transactions over a period of time, whereas balance-sheet figures do not. Finally, the process of dividing one figure by another means that information is lost: therefore, the most useful way to analyse performance is to use the ratios with the original statements, with an enquiring and critical approach.

Problems with specific ratios and performance measurement

The most common form of measuring business performance is to use some form of profit in the context of the investment needed to generate that profit; that is, the return on capital employed or return on net assets. One particular problem with this ratio when it is used to compare managers' performance arises when managers attempt to 'manage' the ratio by reducing the level of investment rather than attempting to increase profit. Consequently, it may be useful to use a related concept, called residual income (RI). Residual income is defined as controllable contribution or profit less a cost of capital charge on the investment controlled by the manager. In this case the group makes a notional charge for interest to the divisions for any funds used. The level of interest may be varied from division to division to reflect the perceived risk associated with the division and its related assets. The resulting figure is an absolute measure.

Economic value added

The term residual income was redefined by the consultants Stern Stewart during the 1990s as economic value added (EVA), and they advocate that it is the financial performance measure that comes closer than any other to capturing the true economic profit of a business. The EVA is calculated as follows:

EVA = Net operating profit after taxes (NOPAT) − (Capital × Cost of capital)

Research has suggested that a focus on EVA provides companies with a long-term strategic approach to performance measurement, although the measure is not widely applied in the hospitality and tourism industries.

Using key performance indicators

Given the plethora of performance measures available it can be difficult to identify the key measures for performance in an organization. Many businesses, particularly those with public shareholders, are driven to focus on return on capital employed and shareholder measures. However, the results used in these measures are driven by a range of operational measures, as the pyramid of measures illustrated in Figure 8.3 demonstrates.

Figure 8.3 Pyramid of key performance indicators (KPIs). ROCE: return on capital employed; EPS: earnings per share; COS: cost of sales

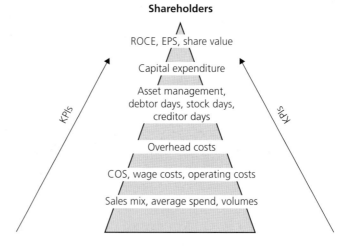

Using accounting ratios to predict failure

The calculation of a series of individual ratios using data taken from the company accounts for performance measurement was first used in the 1930s. The technique is now widely used as a monitoring device, but there are serious problems associated with using ratios. This is based on the fact that published accounts are historical and by the time the results have been published it may be too late to take evasive action. The practice of 'creative accounting', often introduced by failing companies, may also serve to render the process of ratio analysis useless where values in the accounts have been manipulated to mask poor results. Finally, there is the problem of interpretation. One ratio on its own is virtually useless. Instead, a group of ratios should be calculated to obtain the overall picture.

Much research has been carried out to establish whether ratios are capable of predicting failure. Ratios focusing on cash flow are generally recognized as being important indicators of performance and Beaver (1968), in a general study, determined that the ratio measuring cash flow to total debt correctly classified firms as failed or non-failed at least 76% of the time, with the ratio profit to capital employed being the next best indicator. In each of the cases the predictions were for 1–5 years prior to failure. In a study specifically on restaurant failure in America, Olsen, Bellas and Kish (1983) found the ratios in Table 8.5 to be the best indicators of impending failure over the time spans indicated.

To use single ratio analysis effectively as a monitoring device, a variety of ratios should be calculated regularly, taking care to ensure that a standard formula is always used with similar data from the trading accounts to ensure comparability. The predictive power is derived by the process of comparison, where ratios are compared over time for the same business to establish whether the situation is improving or declining, and to compare ratios between similar businesses to see whether the company in question is performing better or worse than the average industry result. Intrafirm comparison, although useful to potential investors, industry observers and participants, does have several inherent dangers, the most significant being the validity of the resulting averages calculated by leading industry consultants using a diverse sample of companies from the hospitality industry. The details of the individual companies within the sample are withheld by the consultants to protect the individual organizations, but the observer is unable to ensure that comparability is valid.

Table 8.5 Ratios used to predict failure

Ratio	Months prior
Current assets/Current liabilities	5–9 months
Working capital/Total assets	6–9 months
Earnings before interest and taxes/Total assets	16–18 months
Earnings before interest and taxes/Revenue	12–18 months
Total assets/Revenue	11–19 months
Working capital/Revenue	7–11 months

Source: Olsen *et al.* (1983) *International Journal of Hospitality Management* 2(4): 187–93.

Multidiscriminant analysis

The volume of information provided from traditional ratio analysis methods has led many writers and analysts to be critical of accounting ratios as a sound monitoring device. It can be argued that traditional ratios do not work as they have failed to change and adapt with changes in the business environment and, in reality, businesses have continued to fail despite the use of the technique as a monitoring device. In 1968, an American named Altman proposed, in a leading article, that the prediction of corporate solvency or failure could be measured by a single value or Z-score. The Z-score model was refined by Altman, and subsequent predictive models in use in the UK and USA are all based on the statistical technique multidiscriminant analysis (MDA). In general, MDA models contain a number of predetermined ratios (five in Altman's version), each with its own weighting, such that the sum of the products of the individual ratios and individual weights yields a Z-score. Guidelines are then provided from research for the interpretation of the score. Several models have been produced by different researchers following Altman's first publication. Altman has revised his model, releasing a later Zeta model, but details for this are not available to the outside user. In the UK, Taffler's model is perhaps the most well known, but the full details of the model structure and coefficients are not publicly available. The models used by Altman and Taffler are illustrated in Figure 8.4.

Figure 8.4 Z-score models developed by Altman (1968,1983) and Taffler and Tisshaw (1977)

Altman's model (1968):
$$Z = 1.2\,X_1 + 1.4\,X_2 + 3.3\,X_3 + 0.6\,X_4 + 1.0\,X_5$$
where

X_1 = working capital/total assets
X_2 = retained earning since inception/total assets
X_3 = earnings before taxes and interest/total assets
X_4 = market value of equity/book value of debt
X_5 = sales/total assets

Altman's revised model (1983):
$$Z = 0.717\,X_1 + 0.847\,X_2 + 3.107\,X_3 + 0.420\,X_4 + 0.998\,X_5$$
where

X_4 = book value of equity/book value of debt

Taffler's model (1977):
$$Z = 0.53\,X_1 + 0.13\,X_2 + 0.18\,X_3 + 0.16\,X_4$$
where

X_1 = profit before taxation/current liabilities
X_2 = current assets/total liabilities, i.e. total debt
X_3 = current liabilities/total assets
X_4 = the 'no credit interval'

The 'no-credit interval' is defined as:

$$\frac{\text{Immediate assets} - \text{Current liabilities}}{\text{Operating costs} - \text{Depreciation}}$$

Problems in the use of multidiscriminant models

Controversy has continually surrounded the use of the models, and leading writers in the field of accounting continue to disagree on the effectiveness of the models as a means for predicting corporate failure. However, what is certain is that the models cannot, in their present form, be considered to be 100% successful. In addition, the authors have issued different and conflicting guidelines for the use of these models over the period since their initial release. The essential criticisms are that almost all models handle failing companies successfully, but are less accurate in respect of surviving companies. Inaccuracies may be due to the difficulty in establishing whether the model may be used to transcend industry groups, and particularly whether a model developed for the manufacturing industry may legitimately be used for service industries. Although there is no clear evidence to indicate the importance of industry type, common sense would indicate that specific industries have specific requirements in terms of prediction models and that the ideal solution would be for each industry type to have its own model. Further, the methodology in developing the original model is complex and consequently a model cannot be easily altered in terms of constituents or cut-off points to meet different needs. For example, Altman's original model included a ratio based on the market value of equity and many researchers, including Altman, assumed that the book value could be substituted. This has since been shown to produce spurious results and Altman has revised the model, as described earlier.

Balanced scorecard and performance measurement

The balanced scorecard concept was first launched by Robert Kaplan and David Norton in 1992. Kaplan and Norton's approach recommended broadening the scope of traditional financial measures such as return on capital employed and profit to sales ratios by including four key areas in the performance measurement process:

- financial performance (How do we look to shareholders?)
- customer knowledge (How do customers see us?)
- internal business processes (What must we excel at?)
- learning and growth (Can we continue to improve and create value?).

This approach not only attempts to monitor how the business is performing now, but also tries to assess the potential for the future. In recent years Kaplan and Norton's approach has been refocused beyond performance measurement, but now includes the broader remit of performance management. Kaplan and Norton (1996) explain that companies are using the balanced scorecard concept to achieve the following critical management processes:

- clarifying and translating vision and strategy into specific objectives and identifying the critical drives of strategic objectives
- communicating and linking strategic objectives and measures
- planning and setting targets in line with strategic initiatives
- enhancing strategic feedback and learning.

Many companies in the hospitality and tourism sector have adopted variations of the balanced scorecard approach as a means for evaluating and presenting business performance.

Summary This chapter has reviewed a variety of performance measures and where possible has attempted to use the measures to assess company performance. Single ratio analysis continues to be the most widely used technique for monitoring company performance, but many companies in the service sector are supplementing this with operational measures based on non-financial criteria. To be effective, ratio analysis requires standardization of the definitions used in the process to ensure success and, consequently, the alternative approaches to items such as the revaluation of assets, the capitalization of interest and the misuse of extraordinary items can seriously undermine the effectiveness of the technique for monitoring performance.

Questions   **1**   Shareholder ratios

You have received the following data with regard to a public limited company operating in the hospitality sector for the year 2004:

(a) The company has an issued share capital of 1,000,000 ordinary shares of £1 each nominal value. There are no preference shares.

(b) The market price of the shares is currently £18.80.

(c) The net profit after taxation for the year was £800,000.

(d) The Directors are proposing a dividend of 80p per share for the financial year ended 31 December 2004.

You are required to calculate:

(i) dividend yield

(ii) dividend cover

(iii) earnings per share

(iv) price/earnings ratio.

(v) Comment on the results you have calculated.

Stage 3 BAHA Education and Training Programme, Examination Paper, February 2005

2   The return on capital employed ratio is often the preferred measure for assessing the profitability of a business. Discuss the advantages and disadvantages of this particular measure and contrast this approach with that offered by the balanced scorecard approach.

Stage 3 BAHA Education and Training Programme, Examination Paper, February 2005

3   'All businesses seek to "profit maximise".' Comment on the validity of this statement with particular reference to key performance measures and other possible business objectives. Give examples of non-financial measures that are used in the hospitality industry to measure performance.

4 Below are the financial results of the Skyway Hotel for the years 2004 and 2005. The hotel has been operating since 1980 and its main activity is room letting.

Balance sheets as at 31 December

	2004		2005	
	£000	£000	£000	£000
Fixed assets (net)				
Land and buildings		640		780
Equipment and furniture		140		200
		780		980
Current assets				
Stock of food and beverages	40		150	
Debtors		24		100
Cash	106	170	4	254
Current liabilities				
Creditors	16		30	
Taxation		80		120
Proposed dividend	50		60	
Overdraft	4	150	24	234
Net total assets		800		1000
Financed by				
Ordinary share capital		500		640
Retained profits		180		240
		680		880
10% debenture (secured on property: 2010)		120		120
		800		1000

Profit and loss accounts for year ending 31 December

	2004	2005
	£000	£000
Sales	1000	1400
Less cost of sales	200	280
Gross profit	800	1120
Operating costs	640	880
Net profit before tax	160	240
Less		
Corporation tax (50%)	80	120
Net profit after tax	80	120

Less

Proposed ordinary share dividend	50	60
Retained profits for the year	30	60

Note: 50% of total sales are on credit.

You are required to:

(i) Calculate ten key accounting ratios for 2004 and 2005 to show liquidity profitability and gearing.

(ii) Comment on the strengths and weaknesses revealed by the ratios and any other information you consider relevant.

5 (a) Review the statements below and prepare:

  (i) A comparative analysis of the two years of performance.

  (ii) A range of ratio calculations to evaluate profitability, liquidity and asset utilization.

(b) Using the calculations you have prepared, comment on the business performance and give recommendations for future courses of action.

Avon Hotels plc has been operating since 1960 and its main activity is room letting. The actual results for 2002 and 2003 are shown below:

Profit and loss accounts for year ending 31 December

	2002		2003	
	£000	£000	£000	£000
Sales		3000		3800
Less: Cost of sales		600		790
Gross profit		2400		3010
Less: Labour	750		1050	
Depreciation	70		100	
Other expenses	1050		1450	
		1870		2600
Net profit before tax		530		410

Note: Other expenses includes interest.

Analysis of sales

	2002	2003
Accommodation	1450	1900
Food	800	1100
Beverage	600	600
Other	150	200
Total	3000	3800

Analysis of cost of sales

	2002	2003
Food	240	340
Beverage	150	160
Other	210	290
Total	600	790

Balance sheets as at 31 December

	2002			2003		
	£000	£000	£000	£000	£000	£000
Fixed assets (net)						
Freehold property			2450			2670
Equipment and furniture			280			400
			2730			3070
Current assets						
Stocks of food and beverages		120			150	
Debtors		450			650	
Cash at bank					45	
		570			845	
Less creditors						
(amounts due within 1 year)						
Creditors	75			90		
Taxation	80			85		
Proposed dividend	100			120		
Bank overdraft	85					
		340			295	
Net assets			2960			3620
Less creditors						
(amounts due in more than 1 year)						
10% mortgage debentures 2005			340			340
			2620			3280
Financed by						
Share capital						
Ordinary shares of 10p each			2260			2690
Reserves						
Retained profits			360			590
			2620			3280

Notes:
(1) 50% of sales are on credit, 50% for cash.
(2) The debentures were issued in 1995.
(3) The current share price is £5.00.

Stage 3 BAHA Education and Training Programme, Examination Paper, January 2004

6   Explain the purpose and difficulties of using ratio analysis. Suggest a range of non-financial measures that could be used to monitor a hospitality business using examples drawn from both your study and your experience.

7 Discuss the advantages that may be claimed for Kaplan and Norton's balanced scorecard as a basis for performance measurement over traditional management accounting views of performance measurement. Your answer should include specific examples of measures for each aspect of the balanced scorecard.

8 You have received the following data with regard to a public limited company operating in the hospitality sector for the year 2002:

(a) The company has an issued share capital of 1,000,000 ordinary shares of £1 each nominal value. There are no preference shares.

(b) The market price of the shares is currently £18.80.

(c) The net profit after taxation for the year was £800,000.

(d) The directors are proposing a dividend of 80p per share for the financial year ended 31 December 2004.

    You are required to calculate:

    (i) dividend yield

    (ii) dividend cover

    (iii) earnings per share

    (iv) price/earnings ratio.

    (v) Comment on the results you have calculated.

9 You are asked to write a succinct report to a potential investor who is taking a keen interest in the management and performance of two companies in the hospitality and tourism sector. You are required to select two appropriate companies to consider. Research the results for each company for the last 2 years and the trends for the last 5 years, comparing these with the particular sector norms.

   You should include an interpretation of the key financial statements with reference to aspects such as:

(a) long-term cash flows

(b) working capital controls

(c) growth and profitability

(d) asset utilization

(e) risk

using a range of methods for analysis.

   Your report should contain recommendations advising the potential investor on the merits and weaknesses of each company and the prospects for return on investment.

   Return to page 186 and reread the report on Enterprise Inns before answering the following questions.

Questions based on Enterprise Inns

1 What do you think are the key measures of performance for Enterprise Inns?

2 Devise a series of financial and non-financial measures that could be used to assess performance.

Discussion questions

1 What is the balanced scorecard?

2 Provide examples of performance measures for each of the four perspectives of the balanced scorecard.

Further reading

Atkinson, H., Berry, A. and Jarvis, R. (1995) *Business Accounting for Hospitality and Tourism*, London: International Thomson Business Press.

Boardman, R. D. (1991) *Hotel and Catering Accounts*, Oxford: Butterworth Heinemann.

Chin, J., Barney, W. and O'Sullivan, H. (1995) *Hotels: Financial Management and Reporting: An Industry Accounting and Auditing Guide*, London: Accounting Books.

Owen, G. (1998) *Accounting for Hospitality, Tourism and Leisure*, Harlow: Longman.

Useful websites

www.imgservers.com/inv/pdf/pe_ratio.pdf   A tutorial on the price earnings ratio
http://www.balancedscorecard.org
http://www.evanomics.com/
http://www.Som.cranfield.ac.uk/som/cbp/pma/index.htm
http://www.quickmba.com
www.skymark.com/resources/methods/balancedscorecard.asp
www.bscol.com/
http://cbe.unn.ac.uk/PALS/PDFs/The%20Balanced%20Scorecard%20-%20The%20Theory.pdf
www.portfoliomgt.org/ForumItem.asp?itemID=1012
www.articles911.com/Performance_Management/Balanced_Scorecard/
www.balancedscorecard.biz/articles.html
www.themanager.org/Knowledgebase/Management/BSC.htm
http://whitepapers.informationweek.com/rlist/term/Balanced-Scorecard-Methodology.html
www.valuebasedmanagement.net/methods_strategy_maps_strategic_communication.html
www.cio.com/archive/110103/strategy.html?printversion=yes
www.valuebasedmanagement.net/

References

Altman, E. I. (1968) Financial ratios, discriminant analysis and the prediction of corporate bankruptcy, *Journal of Finance* 23: 589–609.

Altman, E. I., Haldeman, R. G. and Narayanan, P. (1977) Zeta analysis: a new model to identify bankruptcy risk of corporations, *Journal of Banking and Finance*, 1: 29–54.

Atkinson, H. and Brander Brown, J. (2001) Budgeting in the information age: a fresh approach. *International Journal of Contemporary Hospitality Management* 13(3): 136–43.

Beaver, W. H. (1968) Alternative accounting measures as predictions of failure, *Accounting Review*, 43: 113–22.

Drucker, P. (1953) *The Practice of Management*, New York: Harper Brothers.

Drury, C. (2005) *Management Accounting for Business*, London: Thomson Learning.

Fitzgerald, L., Johnston, R., Brignall, T. J., Silvestro, R. and Voss, C. (1991) *Performance Measurement in Service Businesses*, London: CIMA.

Kaplan, R. and Norton, D. (1992) The balanced scorecard – measures that drive performance, *Harvard Business Review* Jan–Feb, 71–9.

Kaplan, R. and Norton, D. (1996) Using the balanced scorecard as a strategic management system, *Harvard Business Review* Jan–Feb, 75–8.

Olsen, M., Bellas, C. and Kish, L. V. (1983) Improving the prediction of restaurant failure through ratio analysis, *International Journal of Hospitality Management* 2(4): 187–93.

Sink, D. S. (1985) *Productivity Management: Planning Measurement and Evaluation, Control and Improvement*, New York: John Wiley.

Taffler, R. (1982) Forecasting company failure in the UK using discriminant analysis and financial ratio data, *Journal of the Royal Statistical Society*, 145(Part 3): 342–58.

Taffler, R. and Tisshaw, H. (1977) Going, going, gone – four factors which predict? *Accountancy* 88: 50–4.

Ward, K. (1992) *Strategic Management Accounting*, Oxford: Butterworth Heinemann.

IV Strategic options

Developing the future strategy for an organization is often the most important part of the strategic planning process because it is at this stage that the long-term future directions for the business are determined. The strategic direction taken will depend on the existing position of the organization and the current level of success in meeting the organizational key goals. Having established where the organization is currently placed in terms of resources, efficiency and competitiveness, the process of formulating the future strategy can follow. The first step is normally to decide on a fundamental strategy for the organization and the nature of this can be summarized by the following five simple terms: conservative growth, high growth, neutral, recovery and reduction. Each of these terms is developed in more detail in Chapter 9.

A business can grow through either internal expansion by increasing sales or external acquisition by operating at more and more sites. One of the tasks of senior managers is to identify and evaluate potential investment opportunities and to proceed with those that should be successful. In this section the chapters are devoted to considering the sources of long-term funds, the financial tools available to help evaluate projects, and a consideration of the merits, disadvantages and practicalities of each. The first step in evaluating a strategic decision is to perform a feasibility study.

Feasibility studies

A decision involving capital investment will require supporting information in the form of an in-depth analysis of the financial feasibility of the project. The nature of the investment may range from a decision to purchase new equipment to a major new property development. Research by Collier and Gregory (1994) identified the following types of decision as being typical for major hotel companies:

- new builds: to include new hotels, extensions to existing hotels and facility additions
- acquisition of existing hotels
- disposal of existing hotels
- equity stakes in new hotels, existing hotels and projects involving management contracts
- refurbishment and replacement programmes.

Typically, a feasibility study for a new operation should include an economic overview of the location, a site evaluation, an assessment of the competition and market research to estimate the demand for the facilities offered. The financial content of the feasibility study is of paramount importance and should address the following issues:

- calculation of capital investment required and financing plan: this will include fixed assets, preopening expenses and working capital requirements

- the expected useful economic life and an estimate of the residual value: a complication arises with investment decisions relating to businesses such as hotels and restaurants, in that the project does not have a finite life. Unlike a piece of equipment that may be depreciated to zero book value, a business operation will be at least holding its value. The problem can be solved by attempting to place a valuation on the business at a point in time when the business can be realistically assessed to be stable. This typically involves considering a 5-year or 10-year time horizon
- preparation of forecast trading statements for a 5-year period based on expected revenues and costs
- preparation of cash flows to show income from trading, capital spend and repayments of debt. In the case of a hotel, this involves an assessment of room occupancy, room rates, food, beverage and other sales, wage costs and other cash expenses. From these cash flows are deducted management fees, property taxes and insurance
- sensitivity analysis to show the likely effect of price-level changes for each cost and revenue component
- taxation effects
- the anticipated cost of capital associated with the financing of the project
- evaluation of the project using capital budgeting methods.

Several of the aspects described above are now given detailed consideration in the following chapters.

Reference

Collier, P. and Gregory, A. (1994) Strategic management accounting: a UK hotel sector case study. *International Journal of Contemporary Hospitality Management* 7(1): 18–23.

9 | Funding growth

About this chapter

This chapter reviews the alternative forms of finance available either from equity sources or from borrowing for funding the development and expansion of businesses in the hospitality and tourism sectors. Each form of funding is considered in terms of the advantages and disadvantages. The hospitality, tourism and leisure industries are able to take advantage of a range of alternative approaches for funding investment based on the separation of ownership from control, including approaches such as franchising and management contracts, and the merits and implications of these will also be considered. Selecting which options to pursue and how to fund those options is an important aspect of the strategic process, and this chapter and the following chapters focus on the issues relating to effective implementation of strategic developments.

Case study: Joint £1 bn deal set to secure Méridien's future

The future of Le Méridien Hotels and Resorts, the debt-laden hotel company, looked more certain yesterday after Lehman Brothers and Starwood Capital announced an estimated £1 billion deal to buy the company.

In a complex transaction, Lehman, the investment bank, which effectively controls Méridien through its £750 million of debt, has set up a joint venture with Starwood Capital, a US investment firm, to acquire the 36 hotels that are owned and leased by Méridien.

At the same time, Starwood Hotels and Resorts, the US hotel group, which shares the same chairman as Starwood Capital, is to buy the Méridien brand together with the management and franchise business. It will also assume the management of the owned and leased hotels.

The financial terms of the back-to-back deals, which are expected to be completed in the third quarter of this year, have not been disclosed. It is thought that together they are worth about £1 billion.

It is understood that Lehman and Starwood Capital will inject as much as £300 million of new equity into the business to rebuild its balance sheet. Lehman is expected to reduce its exposure by refinancing the debt with other banks. The proceeds of the brand sale will be used to repay debt.

Méridien, which has a total of 135 hotels, mostly managed or franchised, in 56 countries, will become a division of Starwood Hotels alongside the Sheraton and Westin brands. Starwood said it would continue to run all the hotels under the Méridien badge.

The Times, 29 April 2005

Questions relating to this news story may be found on page 222.

Learning objectives On completion of this chapter you should be able to:

- list the main sources of financing a business
- appreciate the factors to be taken into account when selecting long-term funds
- list benefits and disadvantages of each type of financing
- list the alternative approaches for funding expansion available to the hospitality, tourism and leisure sectors.

Introduction

The strategic direction of a business can take a variety of formats, as shown in Table 9.1. A business selecting a strategy based on expansion will certainly need to consider additional sources of finance. The various sources of finance are shown in Table 9.2.

Table 9.1 Fundamental strategy goals and approach

Fundamental strategy	Goals and approach
Conservative growth	An approach to increase sales, profits, etc., through the same or related businesses. This is achieved through the development of new products and/or new markets in the existing business
High growth	An approach to increase sales significantly by acquiring further existing or new products to be sold in existing or new markets. This approach is typified by a strategy of acquisition of companies with similar or unrelated products or by buying 'supplying' or 'buying' companies
Neutral	An approach to maintain the status quo holding sales and profit at historical levels of performance
Recovery	The purpose of this strategy is simply to survive. This may involve reducing assets, reducing costs and attempting to increase sales
Reduction	This approach is to maximize the value of a declining business by salvaging remaining assets and liquidating the business. Alternative approaches may be to sell, negotiate management buyouts or franchise

Table 9.2 Sources of finance

Short term	Medium term	Long term
Trade credit	Bank loans	Debentures
Bank overdrafts	Credit loans	Other types of loans
Factoring	Hire purchase	Shares
Bills of exchange	Leasing	

There is a variety of sources that a business may wish to consider and the choice very much depends on a range of factors, including:

- the cost of raising the finance
- the cost of servicing the finance
- the obligation to pay a return on the capital
- the obligation to repay the finance
- the tax effects
- the effect on the levels of ownership and control.

Risk and return

For many new businesses a variety of sources of investment is required to raise the necessary funds to purchase the required fixed assets and provide for working capital. The hotel sector within the hospitality and tourism industries is traditionally heavily fixed asset based and often considerable sums of investment are required just to get started. Each of the possible sources of funds will have its own cost, that is the return required by the provider of the source of funds, and the size of cost is normally related to the size of the risk as perceived by the lender. In general, research in this area has indicated that investors expect and normally achieve higher returns in return for accepting increased risk.

For the small business just starting out, the proportions of borrowings to equity can be crucial to survival in the early years of trading. In the past it has been relatively easy to borrow 70% or even 80% against assets from the banks, but this presents the business with enormous debt-servicing costs in the form of interest payments. Experience has indicated that levels of 50–60% borrowing against assets can provide a workable level of debt without causing cash-flow problems later. The other crucial factor to consider when raising finance is the maximum cost of the finance. In the case of long-term borrowing, such as loans, the cost of servicing the finance is determined by interest rates and the amount of interest to be paid. Alternatively, equity funds are serviced by the payment of dividends, which are often flexible in payment and size. However, despite this flexibility, experience indicates that equity investors, who are company shareholders, expect the highest returns in return for being subject to the highest risk. The relationship between risk and return is summarized in Figure 9.1.

The merits and disadvantages of each type of finance will now be considered in detail.

Figure 9.1 Relationship between risk and return

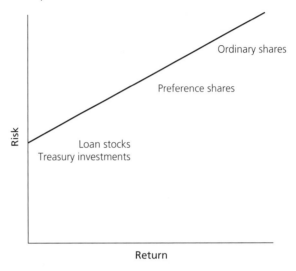

Equity capital

Equity capital comprises three possible components:

- ordinary shares
- preference shares
- reserves.

Ordinary shares

When the business is first established, a decision is made to establish how much equity finance can be raised and the number of shares available to do this. The Articles of Association will specify the number of authorized ordinary shares available for issue. When ordinary shares are first issued they are given a value known as the **par value** or the **nominal value** and this is usually about £1 in value. Once the company has become established its shares usually trade above the basic price. This requires setting a price per share by which the total number of shares can be multiplied to calculate the total capital to be raised. A company wanting to issue new shares will do so at **market price** and the difference between market price and the nominal price is known as the **share premium**.

Preference shares

This category of shares forms part of the shareholders' funds, although in practice they are hybrids that fall between pure equity and pure debt. The issue costs are similar to those to be incurred when issuing new shares, while the servicing costs tend to be lower than for ordinary shares and are directly related to the nominal value of the share. There is no obligation to pay preference dividends, but where a dividend is to be paid the preference shareholders have priority over ordinary shareholders. Some preference shares are redeemable and this fact needs to be built into the cash flow. In general, preference shareholders have no voting rights, so the balance of control within the business remains unaltered. In practice, the issue of ordinary shares remains by far the most common form of raising equity finance.

Reserves

It is a common mistake to assume that the reserves shown in the balance sheet are the cash balances. The reserves can comprise a range of items, including the share premium account and retained earnings. The retained earnings represent the profits earned by the business in previous years and set the limit for the amount of dividend that can be declared and be paid out. Retained profit is an effective source of funds as there are no issue costs. However, it is not true to say that this is a free source of finance. Retained earnings are the property of the shareholders and as a consequence there is an opportunity cost incurred by reinvesting in the existing business. The business has, therefore, an obligation to ensure that the retained earnings produce a satisfactory return for the shareholders. Retained earnings represent the most effective method for funding expansion for most companies in terms of cost, and the distribution of control remains unaffected. However, projects that require an injection of finance over a period of years face uncertainty using this method of finance as the level of retained profits from year to year depends on the trading success of the business. The **revaluation reserve** is created when the revaluation of the business assets such as fixed assets reveals a surplus over the stated book value.

Gaining a listing

For quoted companies (that is, companies with a stock exchange listing) there are three main markets for raising equity:

- the primary capital market
- the secondary capital market
- the alternative investment market (AIM).

The primary market is used for providing new finance in the form of new equity issues to the public at large. There are a number of stock exchanges around the world, including the International Stock Exchange, and normally a business will choose to raise funds in the country in which they predominantly operate. The UK stock market is the London Stock Exchange's Main Market. According to the London School of Economics (LSE), this is the world's most active international equity market, with companies from a range of sectors participating including retailing, technology, finance and manufacturing. More than 2000 companies, including more than 500 overseas companies, have securities that are quoted on this market.

The secondary market is used for the buying and selling of existing shares.

The Alternative Investment Market (AIM), which opened in 1995, was especially created to meet the needs of smaller and growing companies and is more lightly regulated than the main market. This market replaces the Unlisted Securities Market and more than 1200 companies are traded on AIM, representing a variety of industries, including information technology, leisure and hotels, healthcare and biotechnology stocks. The benefits offered by this market are targeted at the ease of access. There are no qualifying restrictions in terms of capital value, length of trading record or percentage of shares in public hands. There are, however, several conditions to be met and advice should be sought on meeting these.

Case study: Is the AIM bubble set to burst? The high number of directors selling shares is worrying investors in the junior market

As the Alternative Investment Market (AIM) prepares to celebrate its tenth anniversary next month, figures show that its shares have surged by 76% over the past two years.

London's junior stock market for small and growing businesses has left the main indexes in its wake during the recovery from the lows of March 2003. The FTSE Small Cap, the bottom 4% of the All-Share index, has climbed 43%; the FTSE Mid 250 has risen 49%; the FTSE 100 of Britain's biggest stocks is up only 23%.

Firms have been rushing to float on AIM to take advantage of the boom, making it the most successful market for fledgling enterprises. In June 1995 AIM was served up to a sceptical public with just 10 companies worth £82 m. Now 1181 firms have quotes on the market, including household names such as Monsoon, Majestic Wine and Domino's Pizza. Together they are worth more than £35 billion.

A sign of its growing credibility are plans by the FTSE Group to launch three new indexes tomorrow – the AIM 50, AIM 100 and AIM All-Share – to monitor its shares.

But as the market approaches its tenth anniversary there are worrying signs that the party may be over, for the time being at least.

Company bosses have been cashing in their shareholdings after the strong run. Directors have in-depth knowledge of their businesses, so investors track their moves closely as a sign of future trends.

There are a host of reasons why bosses might sell, other than a negative view of business conditions. They might cash in for tax reasons or because they want to pass wealth to family members. But when selling increases it is often a sign that share prices have peaked.

Over the past three months, directors of AIM firms have sold £34.5 m of shares – nearly four times the £9.3 m they bought.

Times Online, 15 May 2005

Raising equity finance

Financing from equity is principally the most important source of finance in the UK, being the largest source of capital and attracting both private and institutional investors. The ordinary shareholders are principally the owners of the business who through their voting rights have control over the business. As owners they carry the greatest risk, being the first to suffer if the business collapses. However, in the successful business the shareholders are the principal beneficiaries as their return in the form of dividends and capital growth is directly related to business success. Access to funding depends on whether a company is quoted on the stock exchange, as a listing opens up far greater access to capital. The UK Stock Exchange has more than 2,800 companies listed, with a market capitalization of over £3,500 bn (May 2005). Normally a limited company starts off as a private company. As the company becomes larger the need to raise additional finance increases beyond what is available from retained profits and loans and a stock exchange listing is sought. There are three main approaches to obtaining a quotation:

- **Offer for sale by prospectus:** shares are sold to an issuing house and then offered at a fixed price to the general public including institutions.
- **Via a placing:** shares are placed with institutional investors by a merchant bank acting for the company.
- **Offer by tender.**

When a company chooses to sell shares via a prospectus the issue costs are much higher because of the volume of information that needs to be prepared, regardless of which approach is used. The issue price is crucial to ensure that the maximum number of shares is sold for the maximum price. When fixing the price of shares it is usual to consider the key shareholder measures such as the price/earnings ratio, dividend yield and dividend cover. These ratios were considered in detail in Chapter 8. There are two ways in which the problem of price setting can be reduced. The first is to have the shares underwritten by a broker, but this process incurs additional costs. The second approach is to offer the shares for sale by tender. This is demonstrated by the following example.

Example

A business wishes to issue 5 million shares by tender. After publishing an advertisement to attract potential buyers the following offers are received:

1 m shares at £5.00 each
1 m shares at £4.50 each
1 m shares at £4.00 each
2 m shares at £3.00 each
2 m shares at £2.00 each
5 m shares at £1.00 each

The share issue will be successful if priced at £3.00 per share as there are offers for £5 million shares at £3.00 and above. All the shares will be offered at this price.

The final consideration is the change in control that is likely to occur by inviting further parties to purchase shares.

Rights issues

A rights issue is one where existing shareholders are given the opportunity to purchase additional shares, often at favourable rates. The number of new shares available to each shareholder is usually dependent on their current level of ownership and does not, therefore, dilute their current level of control. The price is often set at about 20% below the market price for the period just before the issue. This ensures that the shareholder takes up the offer or sells the offer to avoid being disadvantaged in the future. The effect of the share issue will be to dilute the value of the share as more shares come into circulation. The price immediately after the share issue is called the 'ex-rights' price. This effect is demonstrated by the following example.

Example

Given a balance-sheet extract (£000):

Total net assets		5,000
Funded by:		
Share capital	Authorized	Issued
Ordinary shares of £1 each	6,000	3,000
Reserves		
Retained profit		2,000
		5,000

When the market price of the share is 150p the company is said to have a market capitalization value of

$$3,000 \text{ shares at } 150p = £4,500$$

If a rights issue is made on a 1 for 3 basis at a price of 120p when the market price is 150p, a 20% discount on market price has been given. The effect is that 1,000,000 new shares are issued, raising £1,200,000 in cash if all the shares are taken up. This is shown in the balance sheet as £1,000,000 at nominal value and £200,000 as share premium.

The likely new share price after the share issue is theoretically

$$\frac{£4,500,000 + £1,200,000}{4,000,000} = 142.5p$$

The value of the rights is calculated as being 150p less 142.5p, that is 7.5p per share. The effect on the balance sheet is as follows:

		(£000)
Total net assets		6,200
Funded by:		
Share capital	Authorized	Issued
Ordinary shares of £1 each	6,000	4,000
Reserves		
Share premium account		200
Retained profit		2,000
		2,200
		6,200

If a shareholder does not wish to take up the entitlement to purchase shares at a discount the rights may then be sold to someone else irrespective of whether they are an existing shareholder or not. However, for the majority of existing shareholders it is not financially viable to ignore the share offer, even if this means buying the rights to sell on immediately. This ensures that most rights issues are successful in terms of all the shares being sold and the required amount of capital subsequently being raised.

Costs associated with equity capital

The costs associated with this form of finance include the issue costs and the servicing costs. The issue costs vary depending on the type of shares issued and can range from virtually zero up to about 15% of the value of the new finance raised. Such costs include legal and underwriting costs and, for the introduction of new shareholders, advertising and prospectus costs.

Servicing costs occur in the form of capital appreciation of the value of the share and in the size of the dividend. The size of the dividend is at the discretion of the directors, who have the right to withhold payment if they wish. However, this is often not the case as shareholders will soon display their displeasure by selling shares, causing the market price per share to drop, which in the majority of cases is undesirable. A drop in share price downvalues the company and creates opportunities for predator companies to engineer a takeover bid while the price is lower.

Equity finance offers the benefit of no obligation to repay the investment, unless the firm is to be liquidated. However, a disadvantage lies in the fact that dividend payments are not deductible for corporation tax. This tends to make dividend payments more expensive than loan interest repayments, which fall above taxation in the profit and loss account and are, therefore, tax deductible. A higher level of equity funding can increase the overall cost of capital for a business, and this will be discussed in more detail in Chapter 12.

During the 1990s a large number of hospitality and tourism businesses became listed on the stock exchange as more and more firms expanded in size and looked to the public markets to raise additional funds. However, in the early years of the twenty-first century there has been an increasing trend for UK hospitality businesses to return to private status. Wallace and Cosser attribute this trend for businesses such as Jarvis Hotels, Macdonald Hotels, Thistle Hotels and Hanover International to return to private status as being due to:

- the effects of terrorism and SARS
- loss of confidence in the sector
- falls in share prices valuing businesses below their net asset value.

Long-term borrowing

There are basically two types of long-term borrowing:

- loan stocks or debentures issued via the money markets
- term loans via the banks.

The first of these are described as securities or bonds and are issued through the capital markets with a fixed interest rate (the coupon rate) and a prestated repayment date to individual investors. When the securities are raised the loan may be secured on the assets of the business (debenture) or be simply based on a contract. The issue costs tend to be relatively low and the service costs in the form of interest are lower than those returns often expected by shareholders. Holders of loan stocks have the right to enforce payment of interest and also the repayment of the loan itself, and this can present a sizeable commitment to the business, particularly during periods of poor trading.

Convertible loan stocks bridge the gap between loan stocks and ordinary shares, being securities that are essentially loan stocks which, at a prestated date, may be converted by the holders into ordinary shares. This can represent a cheap way to issue shares as the costs of issuing loan stock are lower than for shares. From the investor's point of view this represents a simple way of diversifying risk in that loan stocks may be purchased during the early life of the company, minimizing risk, and these then convert to ordinary shares later with the potential for higher return when the company has become more established. The interest rate tends to be higher than for debenture stock because of the higher risk. A business that issues convertibles increases its gearing ratio. This form of funding is particularly suited to a business with relatively high business risk but with strong potential for growth.

A term loan is a single loan negotiated from a bank or financial institution. These differ from loan stocks in that a single sum is received from one lender and is not passed from lender to lender, nor may it be traded in the capital markets. The usual source of this type of finance is a recognized financial institution and investment seekers should be beware of non-legitimate sources of borrowing. An offer of finance advertised in a quality newspaper is no guarantee that the finance is genuine. The fund should be checked out with associations such as the National Association of Commercial Finance Brokers as early as possible. Funds offered below existing market rates should be avoided, as these are often not viable.

The remaining part of this chapter will consider what may be considered as less traditional sources of funds, but in practice represent effective routes to securing funds for expansion.

Franchising

Franchising represents an alternative approach to growth strategy by enabling a business to expand by forming strategic alliances. The process may be defined as an arrangement whereby a manufacturer or marketer of a product or service grants exclusive rights to local, independent entrepreneurs to conduct business in a pre-scribed manner in a certain place over a specified period.

The origins of franchising can be traced back to the Middle Ages, when King John of England granted franchises to tax collectors. However, the use of franchis-ing as a business strategy gained prominence in the early twentieth century, when manufacturers attempted to establish links with retailers. Today franchis-ing is used in many different business sectors as a means to achieving rapid expansion.

Franchising in the hospitality and tourism industries has long been associated with high-street restaurant chains and hotel operators, where it has been mostly highly successful. The restaurant chain probably most often associated with fran-chising is MacDonald's, where the majority of outlets worldwide are franchised rather than company owned. In the early 1990s it was estimated that as many as 20% of all hotel and restaurant units were operating under franchise arrange-ments. Steve Rushmore, in his *Hotel Investments Handbook*, describes one of the first franchise arrangements in the hotel industry, which occurred in 1907 when Caesar Ritz allowed his name to be used on hotels in New York City, Montreal, Boston, Lisbon and Barcelona.

Types of franchise strategy

Franchising is a form of strategic alliance and, compared with other forms of alliances, it is low in risk. In terms of cost, it has been found to be more expensive than licensing, but cheaper than operating a joint venture. Franchises appear in three general forms:

- product tradename
- business format
- business conversion.

Product tradename franchising refers to alliances where the franchisee distrib-utes a franchisor's products, such as the Body Shop stores. Business format franchising, also known as package franchising, provides the franchisee with a product or service, trade name, methods of operation and continuous guidance for aspects such as marketing, administration and staff training in return for a fee. This type of franchising is used most regularly in the hospitality industry.

In addition to the benefits arising from the support activities already described, the franchisor may offer access to centralized reservation systems, yield management systems and property management systems.

Conversion franchising describes the development of a network of operations by attracting independent operators and persuading them to work together under a brand name, to attract customers and achieve cost savings through bulk purchasing power. This arrangement is best illustrated by consortia arrangements such as Best Western Hotels. Often membership requires meeting strict targets in terms of quality, as illustrated by the Leading Hotels of the World brand.

Advantages of franchising

For the corporate franchisor, the franchising arrangement offers considerable advantages, primarily allowing a company to expand without using its own capital, thus incurring lower costs than with many other approaches to expansion. There are also fewer administrative problems as the individual franchisee takes over the workload. Many franchisors also own hotels or operate properties under management contracts and franchising provides the opportunity to spread fixed operating costs over a range of properties. Finally, the franchisor can obtain greater purchase discounts from suppliers when individual outlets are tied to one supplier as part of the franchise agreement. There are, however, drawbacks for franchisors when loss of operational control over franchisees can sometimes harm the overall company image if standards start to drop. In general terms, hospitality businesses with high-quality facilities are less likely to franchise than those offering a more basic service. Franchise chains try to implement operational controls by regularly inspecting franchised units and specifying guidelines for operational standards. Franchisors can also be limited by the restriction imposed by franchises with regard to future developments, as restrictions may be imposed limiting further expansion of similar units in the same region.

Benefits to the franchisees include the advantage of starting up with a proven name and a tried and tested concept. This reduces start-up costs as the franchisor often provides management assistance in the areas of business location, facilities design, operating procedures, purchasing and promotion. This enables new units to gain a regular business clientele more quickly from target market segments. These factors offer substantial benefits to the new operator, as research has shown that the failure rate among new franchised businesses is much lower than among new small independent businesses. In return, a fee is required often with an ongoing royalty, and franchisees may also be tied to the company's nominated suppliers. It is critical for the potential franchisee to choose the correct type of franchise to suit local markets and trading conditions.

When franchise relationships fail, deteriorating relationships between franchisor and franchisee are usually cited as the key cause. Often the franchisee resents the royalty imposed by the franchisor and finds it difficult to assess the benefits being received in return. One way to overcome such problems is to expand with partly franchised units and partly wholly owned units. This enables new products, equipment and management techniques to be evaluated and provides an example of 'best practice' for the franchisees.

Managing and controlling franchises

It is commonly believed that the average length of a franchise is about 20 years. During this time the link between franchisor and franchisee can be highly intensive, with continual flows of information, funds, products and services, supplies, operations technology and administrative activity. Links between franchisees are also encouraged in some organizations such as McDonald's, Wendy's and Best Western Hotels, where franchisees face similar market conditions and can then co-operate on promotions and share costs. The co-ordination between franchisee and franchisor is based on legal documentation, but also on trust. The franchisor can foster this by offering, in addition to start-up training, ongoing programmes to encourage the development of a culture of trust and shared values. This activity also ensures that standardization is maintained throughout.

Case study: InterContinental Hotels

InterContinental hotels group acquires Candlewood Suites brand, growing hotel portfolio to six brands

InterContinental Hotels Group (IHG) announced that as of December 31, 2003, it had acquired the Candlewood Suites brand, through its affiliate Six Continents Hotels, Inc., and increased its management portfolio by more than 40% in the Americas. This addition brought the total number of IHG brands to six, and the number of owned, managed, leased and franchised properties (through various affiliates) to more than 3400 hotels and 527,500 guest rooms in nearly 100 countries and territories around the world. A spokesman from IHG was quoted as saying:

'We are very pleased with this acquisition because it is consistent with our long-term strategy to prove and deliver winning brand concepts, while reducing our capital exposure in real estate assets and growing our revenue stream from management and franchise fees.'

Source: InterContinental press release, 2 January 2004 (www.ihgplc.com)

Franchise fees

These vary from group to group depending on the nature of the contract. In the case of hotels the basic fee is often around 4–6% of rooms revenue. In addition to this there may be a requirement for the franchisee to pay joining fees, royalties, reservation commissions and specific fees for other services provided by the franchisor. Lashley and Morrison (2000) explain that franchisors can derive income from eight principal sources:

- **Initial franchise fee:** this is paid when a franchisee starts up in business.

- **Management service fee:** the franchisor typically receives 4–10% of the franchisee's gross sales.
- **Fixed management service fee:** a franchisor may choose to set a fixed management service fee regardless of business activity.
- **Markup on goods supplied:** the franchisor may compel the franchisee to buy goods from the franchisor and the mark-up on the goods represents the franchise service fee.
- **Advertising fee:** a further percentage of sales may be taken to cover central sales and marketing costs.
- **Administration fee for leasing premises:** a rental administration fee may be incurred where the lease for buildings is held by the franchisor.
- **Renewal fees:** fees may be incurred at the end of the initial period of the franchise arrangement.
- **Other sources of income:** the start-up package may include other add-on services.

Clearly, franchisors need to be fairly large to generate significant profits, but with careful planning the process of franchising can provide the route for considerable expansion. Economies of scale ensure that for the larger franchisor the conversion of franchise revenue into profit may be as high as 95%.

Management contracts

This method of hotel operation separates ownership from management. The management contractor not only offers a licence for the use of its brand name and reservation system, but is also responsible for the day-to-day running of the operation and its performance. Many international hotel chains now include a number of managed hotels in their portfolio of total operations, including Bass, Forte, Four Seasons, Hilton Hotels Corporation, InterContinental, Ladbroke and Marriott. The providers of equity for the investment range from individuals to governments, financial institutions and property developers.

De Haast (2004) suggests that to maximize the return from a management contract the asset manager needs to consider the following criteria:

- **Market positioning:** the market segment must be clearly defined and the asset must match the market positioning.
- **Brand name development:** the value of operating with a brand name is well recognized in the hospitality and tourism sectors.
- **Marketing:** the recognized brand name will normally bring with it the opportunity to take advantage of a variety of marketing programmes, including customer loyalty programmes.
- **Supporting systems:** a key factor in selecting an operator will be the extent of support systems to manage day-to-day operations.

- **Terms and conditions:** the unit owner pays a fee to the operator based on the level of experience, shared risk and predicted future cash flows.

Lease contracts for land and buildings

This is another approach to expansion, again based on the separation of ownership and control. CIMA Management Accounting Official Terminology defines a lease as 'a contract between a lessor and a lessee for the hire of a specific asset. The lessor retains ownership of the asset but conveys the right to the use of the asset to the lessee for an agreed period in return for the payment of specified rentals.'

The key difference between a management contract and a leasing arrangement is that whereas with a management contract a fee is paid to the managing company, with a lease the managing company pays a rent to the owners and the remainder of the profits remain with the managing company. A lease is normally long term, with the owner receiving rent on an annual basis. The most effective form of lease arrangement for the operator is one with a rental charge based on a proportion of turnover. This arrangement enables operators to build up the business without the commitment to fixed levels of rent. Fixed rental payments tend to be based on providing the owner with a target return on capital and could, in periods of recession, be more than the profit made for the period.

Sale and leaseback

This approach to funding is based on the sale of assets to a financial institution, which are then leased back. This form of funding is particularly popular during periods of high asset values and interest rates. At one time it could also be used as a form of off-balance sheet financing, whereby the asset itself was not required by accounting convention to be shown on the balance sheet. This served to improve return on capital calculations and reduce gearing ratios. Accounting conventions have now changed following the requirements of FRS 5, where assets sold and leased back are now required to be shown on the balance sheet as an asset and as a liability. This approach enables a business to raise funds, but the disadvantage is the loss of capital appreciation.

Case study: Thistle Hotel Group

In 2005 the Singapore owner of the Thistle Hotel group, BIL International, sold six UK hotels to an unknown buyer for a combined value of £185 m (US $352.5 m, € 272 m) in a sale-and-leaseback deal.

The net profit from the sale has been calculated at approximately £46.7 m (US $89 m, € 68.7 m). Following the sales all the hotels were leased back to Thistle for a 30-year period.

▶

In a press release a spokesman for Thistle explained that:

'We will continue to grow our hotel brands through product and service enhancements and new hotel openings. At an operational level, our focus will remain on revenue growth, cost efficiencies and cost reductions. The sale proceeds will be utilized for debt reduction and new investments.'

Thistle's hotel portfolio comprises more than 10,800 bedrooms and includes 50 full-service owned, leased and managed sites. Flagship owned hotels of the group include the Thistle Tower and Marble Arch.

Source: Adapted from the Leisure Property Report, 9 May 2005 (**www.leisureproperty.com**)

Alternatives to purchasing equipment

If the resources are available, buying a piece of equipment outright is often the most cost-effective approach and gives the freedom to make a purchase from a wide range of choices. However, if cash flow does not permit immediate purchase or uncertainty exists over the purchasing decision, then other alternatives may be more suitable.

The principle of free-on-loan is widely used in the hot beverages market, where dispensers are provided free of charge and will need to be filled with ingredients from the supplier of the machine. This may mean that a business is able to have access to equipment of a standard that it could not normally afford and be able to benefit from free upgrades as well. Renting the equipment presents an alternative option. These agreements are often fixed, being unchanged by changes in interest rates, for example, and are fully deductible for tax purposes.

Leasing arrangements can be confusing when it comes to ownership and tax implications. With lease rental agreements where the leasing company retains ownership at the end of the lease, all payments are fully tax deductible. However, with any financing agreement there is usually a premium to pay for saving money now and paying later.

Leasing equipment

Leases may be divided into two types:

- operating leases
- financial leases.

Operating leases equate simply to hiring the use of an asset. The ownership remains with the lessor, who carries out any necessary maintenance. Financial leases are effectively loans with the capital repayable in instalments. As described earlier, these used to be popular because, although the effect is basically a loan, neither the asset nor the obligation needed to appear on the balance sheet. Changes in accounting practice now ensure that both the asset and the obligation appear on the balance sheet, ending the practice of off-balance sheet financing. Another important feature of leasing is the tax efficiency that may arise. Lease payments are shown as an expense in the profit and loss account and are, therefore, fully deductible for corporation tax.

Despite accounting changes in the approach to leasing, this approach to funding remains popular as the implied interest rate in the leasing contract is often lower than that which the business would have to pay if it bought the asset itself.

The leasing decision

When the business is considering the purchase of an asset, the usual procedure is to assess the net benefit of owning the asset in terms of incoming cash flows and then to discount those cash flows using an appropriate discount rate that reflects the level of risk in the project. When the resulting net present value is positive, the project is worth pursuing. The decision to invest or not is a completely different decision to that regarding the source of finance. This is illustrated by the following example.

Example

A hotel has decided to purchase new equipment at a cost of £100,000. The decision to make the purchase has already been made on the basis of the expected savings to be gained. However, the subsequent decision is how to fund the purchase. The asset may be purchased outright with a loan costing 12% per annum or alternatively the company could enter into a lease agreement. The terms of the lease are £20,000 to be paid starting at the date of the acquisition and for the next 4 years. After that date the lease may be extended by paying a nominal charge of £100 per year for a further 5 years. The differences in the financing should be assessed based on the fact that leasing incurs a timing difference in the cash outflows. This timing difference is assessed using discounted cash-flow tables. (The principles of discounted cash flows are explained in more detail in Chapter 10.) The future payments on the lease should be discounted using the cost of borrowing as a discount rate.

The net present value of the lease is calculated as follows:

Year	£000	Discount factor	Present value
0	20.0	1.00	20.00
1	20.0	0.89	17.80
2	20.0	0.80	16.00
3	20.0	0.71	14.20
4	20.0	0.64	12.80
5	0.1	0.57	0.057
6	0.1	0.51	0.051
7	0.1	0.45	0.045
8	0.1	0.40	0.040
9	0.1	0.36	0.036
Net present value			81.029

The lease option is worth pursuing, as the net present value of the payments equates to £81,029, which is less than paying £100,000 now.

Taxation issues

Cash flows associated with taxation also need to be included in the project analysis and these will vary depending on the project and the nature of the taxation relief attracted. Capital allowances are forms of relief set against taxable profit, based on the type of asset purchased, and are intended to stimulate certain types of investment. It is beyond the scope of this book to go into further detail, apart from to note that there are generally two types of capital allowance available for the hospitality sector in the UK. These are industrial building allowances (IBAs) and plant and machinery allowances (PMAs) in the form of first-year allowances and annual writing-down allowances. There are also specific hotel allowances that relate to hotel buildings provided they are used as 'qualifying hotels'. For a hotel to be classed as a qualifying hotel several criteria must be met, including:

- it is open for at least 4 months between April and October
- it has ten or more letting bedrooms used wholly or mainly for letting
- the services provided normally include provision of breakfast and an evening meal.

Taxation affects cash flows from investments and further advice should be sought from specialized sources.

Real estate investment trusts

These are essentially a US phenomenon and comprise a real estate mutual fund that permits small investors to participate in large, professionally managed real estate projects. According to www.investinreits.com (2005), there are approximately 180 publicly traded real estate investment trusts (REITs) in the USA today, with assets totalling $375 billion. REITs are classified in the following categories:

- Equity REITs own and operate revenue generating assets.
- Mortgage REITs lend money directly to asset owners and their operators, or indirectly through the acquisition of loans or mortgage-backed securities.
- Hybrid REITs are companies that both own properties and make loans to owners and operators.

REITs have been in existence in the USA since the 1960s, but have been slow to be used as an investment vehicle in other regions of the world. In the UK the 2005 budget confirmed the UK government's commitment to the introduction of the REIT concept. However, at the time of writing it remains unclear whether this form of funding will be available as a source of funds for the hotel sector.

Summary The purpose of this chapter has been to review the various forms of long-term finance available for expansion and to consider these in terms of the merits and disadvantages of each. Equity finance, which provides the vast majority of finance used by hospitality and tourism organizations, offers the benefits of low gearing, although it should be remembered that the cost of servicing equity finance is often higher than that required for loan finance. Issues relating to cost of capital and gearing will be discussed in detail in Chapter 12.

Questions

1 List three sources of the following:

   (a) short-term finance

   (b) medium-term finance

   (c) long-term finance.

2 Describe the alternative forms of financing available for funding a hotel asset and comment on the effects on the way the hotel is operated.

3 A large hotel and catering company is planning extensive expansion plans overseas. Describe the various forms of investment strategy available to a multinational business with access to the capital markets.

4 Rights issue

   On 5 April 2003 the Riviera Hotels plc's shares were listed on the London Stock Exchange at £1.00 each. There were 25 million 25p shares in issue. On 6 April Riviera Hotels announced to the press that it intended to purchase a smaller hotel group and the price of its shares rose to £1.20. On 1 May the company announced that it was intending to raise £4 million to fund the purchase of the hotel group by means of a rights issue priced at 80p.

   (a) Calculate the market capitalization of the business at 5 April 2003.

   (b) How many shares will be issued to raise £4 million?

   (c) Why do listed companies normally make rights issues for new equity capital rather than public shares?

   (d) What factors can cause a movement in a company's share price?

5 Rights issues: theoretical ex-rights price

   In 2006 Sunshine Holiday Parks plc plans to acquire several new sites to expand the group. The new sites are expected to cost £52 million. The group's existing performance can be judged from:

Profit and loss account for the year ended 31 December 2005

	2005
	£000,000
Sales	96.8
Gross profit	79.0
Less: operating costs	
Staff costs	34.8
External charges	25.4
Depreciation	4.8
	65.0

Trading profit	14.0
Less: interest	4.0
Profit before tax	10.0
Less: corporation tax	3.0
Profit after tax	7.0
Less: dividends	2.0
Retained profit for the year	5.0

At present, 80 million shares have been issued and are currently valued at 160p each on the Stock Exchange.

The directors aim to issue new shares to finance exactly the purchase of the new hotels (issue costs can be ignored). They propose to do this with a rights issue to be offered at 140p per share.

You are required to:

(a) Calculate the theoretical ex-rights price per share.

(b) Calculate the value of the rights per existing share.

(c) Calculate the market value of each share after the rights issue, on the assumption that the new hotels produce an increase in profit after tax of £5.0 million and that the current price/earnings ratio is maintained.

(d) Discuss the advantages and disadvantages of a rights issue over a public share issue.

6 **News story questions**
Do you recall the news story at the beginning of this chapter? Now return to that story and reread it before answering the following questions.

(a) Describe the issues that can arise when reconciling the strategic objectives of owners and operators.

(b) What performance measures do you think will be the most useful for the owners, financiers, brand owner and managers?

Further reading
Field, H. (1995) Financial management implications of hotel management contracts: a UK perspective, in P. Harris (ed.) *Accounting and Finance for the International Hospitality Industry*, Oxford: Butterworth Heinemann.
Hoffman, R. and Preble, J. (1991) Franchising: selecting a strategy for rapid growth, *Long Range Planning* 24(4): 74–85.
Pike, R. and Neale, B. (2003) *Corporate Finance and Investment Decisions and Strategies*, London: Prentice Hall.
Seltz, D. (1982) *The Complete Handbook of Franchising*, Reading, MA: Addison Wesley.
Wallace, L. and Cossar, A. (2004) Going private: public-to-private transactions in the hotel sector in the UK, *Journal of Retail and Leisure Property* 4(1).

Useful websites

http://www.hvsinternational.com/Library/   A useful selection of articles from HVS International

http://www.hvsinternational.com/emails/rushletter/2004-11-02.htm   Hotel investments: a guide for lenders and owners

References

De Haast, A. (2004) Asset management, in J. Ransley and H. Ingram (eds) *Developing Hospitality Properties and Facilities*, Oxford: Butterworth Heinemann.

Lashley, C. and Morrison, A. (2000) *Franchising Hospitality Services*, Oxford: Butterworth Heinemann.

10 | Capital budgeting

About this chapter

Many of the options being considered in the strategic decision-making process will require an assessment of the viability of a capital spend. CIMA Management Accounting Official Terminology (2000) defines capital investment appraisal as 'the application of a set of methodologies (generally based on the discounting of cash flows) whose purpose is to give guidance to managers with respect to decisions as to how best to commit long term investment funds'. This chapter reviews the range of methods available for assessing the viability of a capital project.

Case study: Whitbread

Leisure sector takes a tumble as downturn hits Whitbread

Whitbread sent a chill wind through the leisure sector yesterday after sounding a cautious note over the impact of faltering consumer confidence and mounting costs on its pub restaurants and health clubs.

Shares of Whitbread, which touched a six-year high of 965p last month after it announced plans to sell its Marriott hotel arm, fell by 44½p to close at 873½p after the company revealed that its Brewer's Fayre, Brewsters and David Lloyd Leisure brands had all seen a downturn.

The news sent share prices across the pub sector tumbling, with Wolverhampton & Dudley Breweries falling 35p to close at £10.40 and Greene King off 35p at £12.30. Mitchells & Butlers dropped 15¼p to 314¾p.

Alan Parker, the chief executive, pointed out that rivals had given a similar assessment of trading, including LA Fitness, Greene King and Spirit Group, the pub operator.

He added: 'I don't see any signs of the consumer picture getting better in the next few months. We have an election looming and it would be a rash man who predicted there would be no impact, though what it will be I don't know.'

Analysts shaved about 5% from their 2005–06 profit forecasts, although Mr Parker insisted: 'We are confident of being able to grow our sales and profits during this year and of being able to grow all our brands organically.'

In the year to March 3, Whitbread reported a 9.4% rise in profits before tax and exceptionals to £263.5 million, from turnover up 6.8% to £2.11 billion.

Adjusted earnings per share reached 64.08p (58.22p) and the final dividend of 18.35p makes a total of 25.25p, up 13.6%. Whitbread's Premier Travel Inn, Costa and Pizza Hut brands all delivered strong growth. However, its pub-restaurant division saw a 7% fall in profits as the consumer slow-down exacerbated disruption from the conversion of its Brewsters chain to the Brewer's Fayre brand and the updating of the Beefeater concept.

David Lloyd had a poor year, with its mature clubs ending up with 10,000 fewer members. While its tennis-based clubs proved resilient, its 12 health and fitness clubs struggled to attract new members amid stiff competition.

Christopher Rogers, Whitbread's new finance director, said that its pub-restaurants and health clubs had continued to experience slow trading in the first few weeks of the current year, with like-for-like sales growth across the group slowing from 2.6% to about 1%.

As a result, the company has reined back its David Lloyd and pub-restaurant opening programmes, focusing its capital expenditure on Premier Travel Inn and Costa.

The Times, 27 April 2005

Questions relating to this news story may be found on page 245.

Learning objectives On completion of this chapter you should be able to:

- explain the concept of discounted cash flows
- apply the techniques of net present value (NPV), internal rate of return (IRR), payback, profitability index (PI) and accounting rate of return (ARR)
- explain the advantages and limitations of each method.

Introduction

Capital investment appraisal is concerned with long-term decisions based on major investments that will affect the future strategic direction of the organization. The process includes planning the capital expenditure, evaluating and selecting projects, and finally controlling capital expenditures that will generate future cash flows. Planning capital expenditure involves ensuring that the alternative projects selected by the organization yield maximum returns while minimizing or maintaining a certain level of risk. In general, the basis for selecting the potential investment should be that only those projects that meet the objectives of the business should be considered and the expected rate of return should exceed the financing cost for the project to be worthwhile. Selecting which investment proposal to pursue and which to avoid is crucial to the business because of the large sums of finance often involved and the long-term nature of the commitment. Therefore, a long-term financial investment decision needs to fit with the strategic direction of the business and be financially justified by evaluating all the relevant costs and resulting cash inflows associated with the project. A number of factors need to be taken into account, including:

- the size of the investment
- the economic life of the project
- the certainty of the returns
- the strategic importance to the company.

In the hospitality and tourism industries a capital investment could include expenditure on assets such as:

- equipment
- furniture and fixtures
- building extensions
- new strategic business units or groups of units.

As a guideline, capital expenditure is spend that is likely to have benefit to more than one accounting period. If a business wishes to survive and grow it will need to invest continually in capital projects.

There are several standard approaches to capital investment appraisal and these will now be considered in detail, including:

- accounting rate of return (ARR)
- payback period (which may also be discounted)
- net present value (NPV)
- internal rate of return (IRR).

Accounting rate of return

This method, also known as the return on investment (ROI), compares the average annual profits over the life of the project with the initial investment, expressing the outcome as a percentage.

$$\text{ARR} = \frac{\text{Average annual net profit before interest and taxation}}{\text{Initial capital employed on the project}} \times 100$$

This is the only method to be considered that uses profits rather than cash flows as the basis of the calculation. The profit after straight-line depreciation is averaged for the estimated life of the project and the resulting percentage is then compared with some predetermined rate. Competing projects can then be compared with each other, and the project with the higher accounting rate of return is determined as being the more worthwhile, as the following example demonstrates.

Example

Two projects are being considered, both with a 6-year life and both with an original investment of £120,000. This value is to be depreciated in full over the life of the project using straight-line depreciation (see Chapter 3 for more details on this). The anticipated profits for the projects are as follows:

	Project 1 (£)	Project 2 (£)
Year 1	20,000	4,000
Year 2	16,000	6,000
Year 3	10,000	8,000
Year 4	6,000	10,000
Year 5	4,000	16,000
Year 6	2,000	18,000
Total	58,000	62,000

The average net profit over the life of each project is £9,667 for project 1 and £10,333 for project 2. The return on the original investment is:

Project 1:
$$\frac{9,667}{120,000} \times 100\% = 8.06\%$$

Project 2:
$$\frac{10,333}{120,000} \times 100\% = 8.61\%$$

Using the ARR, project 2 is marginally better than project 1.

The ARR can also be calculated using the average capital employed, as follows:

$$ARR = \frac{\text{Average annual net profit before interest and taxation}}{\text{Average annual capital employed}} \times 100$$

The average annual capital employed is calculated using:

$$\frac{\text{Initial capital employed} + \text{Residual value}}{2}$$

Using the previous example,

Project 1:
$$\frac{9,667}{60,000} \times 100\% = 16.11\%$$

Project 2:
$$\frac{10,333}{60,000} \times 100\% = 17.22\%$$

The benefits of the ARR approach can be summarized as follows:

- The technique is easy to calculate and use.
- The result is easy to understand by non-financial managers.
- The principle is based on a widely used performance statistic, the return on capital employed.

The disadvantages are that the method is based on profit rather than cash flows, the latter now being recognized as a clearer indicator of company health. As a result, the method ignores the timing of the cash flows and hence the financing cost. The term profit can be subject to different definitions and it is not always clear whether the original value of the investment or the average should be used. The use of residual value in the average method means that the higher the residual value the lower the ARR. Returning to the above example where the timing of the profits is quite different for each project, project 2 is favoured despite the fact that the majority of the profits are forecast to occur at the end of the 6-year period and are subject to far greater uncertainty.

Where just one project is to be evaluated, the decision is made on the basis of a comparison of the resulting ARR with the prevailing cost of borrowing, with targets often set 5–10% in excess of these rates. The ARR approach is acceptable as long as the meaning of the result is understood throughout.

Payback method

This technique is based on an assessment of how long it will take for the investment to pay for itself out of the cash inflows generated by the project. A project will only be selected if it pays for itself within a certain period; alternatively competing projects will be selected on the basis of the project that pays for itself first. To use this method the following information is necessary:

- the total value of the investment
- the amount of the cash flows to be generated by the project
- the accounting periods in which the cash flows will fall.

This approach is very easy to use and interpret, although the basis of the decision is fairly simplistic. Setting suitable payback periods is a somewhat arbitrary decision and too much emphasis on this aspect will ensure that only short-term decisions are made. However, the acceptability of the payback approach can be improved by discounting the cash flows to take account of the changing value of the inflows over time, although this still tends to emphasize cash flows before payback rather than those occurring in the long term. Cash flow is defined as the profit before interest and tax plus any non-cash items that have been deducted to arrive at the profit figure, which is principally depreciation. The method is illustrated using data from the previous example.

Example

The anticipated profits for the projects are as follows:

	Project 1 (£)	Project 2 (£)
Year 1	20,000	4,000
Year 2	16,000	6,000
Year 3	10,000	8,000
Year 4	6,000	10,000
Year 5	4,000	16,000
Year 6	2,000	18,000
Total	58,000	62,000

The straight-line depreciation based on the write-off of £120,000 over 6 years with zero residual value will be £20,000 per year. Therefore, the anticipated cash flows are:

	Project 1 (£)	Project 2 (£)
Year 1	40,000	24,000
Year 2	36,000	26,000
Year 3	30,000	28,000
Year 4	26,000	30,000
Year 5	24,000	36,000
Year 6	22,000	38,000
Total	178,000	182,000

These cash flows can be used to identify the point when the original investment will be repaid. For project 1 the payback period will fall between year 3 and year 4 and for project 2 at some point between year 4 and year 5. On this basis project 1 would be favoured despite the fact that project 2 provides the greater cash inflow.

Note that this result is opposite to that recommended by the ARR method. The payback method is a relatively easy concept to understand and calculate, but it has a number of disadvantages as a technique for assessing the viability of projects. In particular, it is difficult to assess exactly when cash flows will be received and the overall total amount of the cash inflows is ignored. The focus on payback means that the overall profitability of a project is also ignored. Finally, the timing of the cash flows is not taken into account; for example, £1 received now is preferable to £1 received in 3 years' time. However, this disadvantage can be overcome by discounting the cash flows. Despite the disadvantages of the method it is widely used in the hospitality industry to assess both refurbishment and new investment decisions.

Discounted cash flows

Capital investment appraisal is based on an assessment of future returns forecast to be generated by a project. The earlier the funds are made available the sooner they can be used to make a further contribution to profit. The discounted cash flow attempts to analyse the timing and size of future cash flows. However, the difficulty lies in comparing £1 of cash inflows received today with £1 received in the future, as they cannot be equal to each other. There are three reasons for this:

- interest lost
- inflation effects
- risk.

First, there is the interest forgone if the £1 were to be invested over the period and this represents an opportunity cost. So £1 invested for 1 year at 10% will be worth £1.10 at the end of this period. Secondly, inflation undermines the purchasing power of the £1, so that the same amount will not buy the equivalent value of goods and services in 1 year's time. Finally, risk needs to be considered, because £1 received today has more certainty attached to it than the possibility of £1 being received in 1 year's time.

The process of discounting the cash flows aims to take into account the timing of the cash flows based on the interest forgone. Levels of inflation and anticipated risk are less easy to determine, although a premium may be built into the discount rate used to compensate for these. Issues surrounding these aspects will be considered in Chapter 11. The procedure for discounting cash flows includes:

- Calculate the future cash flows to be generated by the project.
- Estimate an appropriate rate of interest based on the cost of capital.
- Multiply the net cash flows by a discount rate.

A table of discount rates is included in Appendix 1 of this text.

Discounted payback

This is a variation of the technique described earlier and is based on an assessment of how long it will take for the investment to pay for itself using discounted cash flows. The example below uses data from the earlier example.

Example

Two projects are being considered, both with a 6-year life and both with an original investment of £120,000.

The anticipated cash flows are discounted at 10% to give the present values (PVs).

	Discount rate	Project 1 (£)	PV (£)	Project 2 (£)	PV (£)
Year 1	0.909	40,000	36,360	24,000	21,816
Year 2	0.826	36,000	29,736	26,000	21,476
Year 3	0.751	30,000	22,530	28,000	21,028
Year 4	0.683	26,000	17,758	30,000	20,490
Year 5	0.621	24,000	14,904	36,000	22,356
Year 6	0.564	22,000	12,408	38,000	21,432
Total		178,000	133,696	182,000	128,598

Project 1 pays back between years 4 and 5 and project 2 pays back between years 5 and 6. Therefore, project 1 would be preferred. Discounted payback has the advantage that it takes into account the changing value of money and will be based on more of the cash flows, since the discounted payback period will always be longer than the simple payback method. However, the other disadvantages given for the simple payback method still apply.

Net present value

This technique for assessing capital projects is based on an assessment of future cash flows discounted to take account of the opportunity cost of the interest forgone. If one were simply to compare investing £10 m held today at 10% for 1 year with an investment that is expected to be worth £12 m to be received in 1 year's time, this would mean that the future cash inflow represents a better return than could be achieved with the present £10 m invested at 10%. Alternatively, one could compare how much (I) would need to be invested now to achieve a return of £12 m in 1 year's time at an interest rate of 10%:

$$£12\,m = I \times 1.10$$

I can be deduced to equal £10.9 m and is called the present value. The present value of the future cash flows forms the basis of the capital appraisal technique known as net present value (NPV). Where the sum of the future discounted cash flows exceeds the initial investment, the project is deemed to be acceptable and is described as having a positive NPV. Where more than one project is to be assessed, the one with the highest NPV is deemed to be the most acceptable. The discount factor is calculated from the interest rate, where it is assumed that the cost of borrowing equals the cost of lending. After 1 year the discount factor at 10% will be

$$\frac{1}{1.10} = 0.909$$

To take account of several years, the discount rate needs to be compounded and although this can be done simply arithmetically it is usual practice to make use of published tables giving discount factors for a range of interest rates over a number of years. These are published as an appendix in most accounting textbooks and can be found in Appendix 1 of this text.

To calculate the NPV of a project the following steps are required:

1   Forecast the cash flows to be generated over the life of the project.
2   Select an appropriate discount rate (how to do this will be discussed in Chapter 12).
3   Use tables to find the appropriate discount rates for multiplication with the annual cash flows.
4   Sum the discounted cash flows.
5   Compare the sum of the discounted cash inflows with the sum of the discounted cash outflows (cash flows in year 0 are discounted by a factor of 1).
6   Consider whether the NPV is positive or negative.

This approach is demonstrated by the following example.

Example

A hotel owner decides to invest in renting an adjacent building to run as a restaurant. His initial feasibility study shows that it will cost £1,000,000 to prepare and equip the site for trading. The projected cash flows derived from net profit after tax with depreciation added back, for the next 5 years, are as follows:

	£
Year 1	230,000
Year 2	235,000
Year 3	240,000
Year 4	250,000
Year 5	255,000
Total	1,210,000

The depreciated value of the furnishings at the end of this period is anticipated to be £120,000. Given these values, the hotel owner appears to be gaining by investing in the new site. However, a more accurate picture emerges when the time value of money is taken into account. The future cash flows discounted at 12% are as follows:

$$\text{Year 1: } 230,000 \times 0.893 = 205,390$$
$$\text{Year 2: } 235,000 \times 0.797 = 187,295$$
$$\text{Year 3: } 240,000 \times 0.712 = 170,880$$
$$\text{Year 4: } 250,000 \times 0.636 = 159,000$$
$$\text{Year 5: } 255,000 \times 0.567 = 144,585$$

Plus residual value of the investment:

$$120,000 \times 0.567 = 68,040$$

Total value of cash inflows = 935,190

Note that the residual value of the investment is also termed as a cash inflow and should be discounted at an appropriate rate. The cash inflows are less than the initial cash outflow and this creates a negative NPV to the value of £64,810. On this basis the project should be rejected because the investment is failing to achieve a 12% return.

With the use of discounted cash flows it is possible to identify for any project the present value for all future cash flows over the life of the project. The present value of the investment, when taken away from the present value of the cash inflows, produces the NPV, which indicates the financial benefit of going into the project in today's cash terms. The higher the present value the more attractive the project. The NPV approach is a logical method for assessing potential investments because the calculation takes into account the timing of the cash flows and the cost of financing the project, as well as being practical and easy to use. Despite these benefits the method is not always widely used, with many businesses preferring to use the other approaches.

The discount factor

The discount value applied to the calculations is obviously of critical importance. The higher the discount factors the lower the resulting NPV. If the factor chosen is too high there is the danger that profitable projects will be rejected, whereas using a factor that is too low will result in loss-making projects being pursued. Normally, the factor is chosen by considering the cost of the funds being used for the project with additional premiums built in for risk as required. The calculation of the discount factor is considered in further detail in Chapter 12.

Cash flows

When discounting cash flows several assumptions are made. The first is based on when the cash flows actually occur. The discount tables assume that the cash flow is received in its entirety on the last day of the year. This is not likely to be the case, but to simplify the workings the last-day principle is used, which means that the cash flows are always slightly understated in terms of value. Selecting which cash flows to put into a forecast can cause difficulty, particularly when the project is based on existing assets. In general, it is essential to determine the relevant cash flows, that is the future likely cash flows, and ignore past or sunk costs. Opportunity cost cash flows are cash flows that are not actually paid out, but instead represent the benefit forgone by taking one particular course of action.

Internal rate of return

An alternative approach using discounted cash flows is the method known as the internal rate of return (IRR). This approach assesses the rate of return required by the project to balance cash inflows and outflows. CIMA Management Accounting Official Terminology defines the IRR as the 'annual percentage return achieved by a project, at which the sum of the discounted cash flows over the life of the project is equal to the sum of the discounted cash outflows'.

Solving the value of IRR is not easy and a process of trial and error is required. To assess a project only those with an IRR above a predetermined level are accepted, or if competing projects are being assessed the one with the highest value is the one to be accepted. Using the data given for the NPV calculation the following workings demonstrate the IRR method.

Example

The future cash flows were discounted at 12% as follows:

Year 1: 230,000 × 0.893 = 205,390
Year 2: 235,000 × 0.797 = 187,295
Year 3: 240,000 × 0.712 = 170,880
Year 4: 250,000 × 0.636 = 159,000
Year 5: 255,000 × 0.567 = 144,585

Plus residual value of the investment:

120,000 × 0.567 = 68,040

Total value of cash inflows = 935,190

The cash inflows are less than the initial cash outflow and this creates a negative NPV to the value of £64,810. On this basis the project should be rejected because the investment is failing to achieve a 12% return. To find the IRR it is necessary to discount the cash flows a second time to provide the basis for finding the discount rate, which will give an NPV of zero.

The future cash flows are now discounted at 8% as follows:

Year 1: 230,000 × 0.926 = 212,980
Year 2: 235,000 × 0.857 = 201,395
Year 3: 240,000 × 0.794 = 190,560
Year 4: 250,000 × 0.735 = 183,750
Year 5: 255,000 × 0.681 = 173,655

Plus residual value of the investment:

120,000 × 0.681 = 81,720

Total value of cash inflows = 1,044,060
NPV = 44,060

Therefore, the IRR must fall between 8% and 12%. The exact value can be pinpointed as follows. A factor of 12% gives a negative NPV, whereas a discount factor of 8% gives a positive NPV. Therefore, an NPV of zero will fall between the two positions:

(64,810)---------------------0-------------------+44,060
  12%   ?%   8%

A change of 4% represents NPV of 108,870. The distance from 64,810 to 0 is:

$$\frac{64,810}{108,870} \times 4\% = 2.38$$

Therefore, the IRR is 8% + 2.38% = 10.38%

The advantages of the IRR method are that the timing of the cash flows is taken into account and the method gives a clear percentage return on investment. However, in practice it is not an easy concept to understand and the method only gives an approximate rate of return. To identify the IRR it is necessary to apply alternative rates of discount to pinpoint the exact value and this can be time consuming. However, the disadvantage can now be easily overcome with the use of computer software, and electronic spreadsheets such as Excel contain the function to calculate IRR automatically.

More importantly, several conceptual shortcomings associated with the IRR method should be noted. First, it is possible for there to be more than one IRR associated with a project. This occurs when the cash flows are a combination of positive and negative values throughout the life of the project. Under these circumstances it is not easy to identify the real IRR and the method should be avoided. Secondly, although IRR is closely related to the NPV approach the two methods can sometimes give conflicting signals. This occurs when the two projects have different levels of investment, because IRR is based solely on percentage returns rather than the cash value of the return. As a result, when considering a project one may have a return of, say, 10% and another of 13%, but the 10% project may yield the higher NPV in cash terms and would therefore be preferable. Finally, IRR cannot cope with differing required rates of return. With NPV calculations it is possible to use different discount factors throughout the life of the project as the cost of capital changes, whereas IRR can only provide an average rate of return.

Despite these major shortcomings IRR continues to be a popular approach to capital investment appraisal. Managers seem to prefer the calculation of a percentage value that can then be compared to a hurdle rate, rather than the comparison of cash values for choosing between projects.

Comparing results from NPV with IRR

The NPV method tends to be the preferred method because the result is more easily understood: it indicates the amount by which the value of the company has increased. However, IRR has the benefit in that it provides a single percentage as the result, which is useful for comparison to a target or hurdle rate. It is always useful to use a range of capital investment appraisal techniques to ensure that all aspects of a project have been considered. The NPV and IRR methods should both normally give the same result: if the NPV using the discount factor of the cost of capital is positive, then the IRR for the same project must be above the cost of capital. However, decisions become difficult to make when results provided by IRR and NPV are in conflict with each other.

Example

For example, a leisure company has received two quotations for computer systems. The first will cost £12,000 and will save annual costs of £3,500 for 5 years. The alternative is a system that will cost £6,500, where the annual cost savings are £2,000 for 5 years. The cost of capital for both is 10% p.a.

Option 1

	Cash flow	Discount rate 10%	Discounted cash flow	Discount rate 20%	Discounted cash flow
Year 0	(12,000)	1,000	(12,000)	1.000	(12,000)
Year 1	3,500	0.9091	3,182	0.8333	2,917
Year 2	3,500	0.8264	2,892	0.6944	2,430
Year 3	3,500	0.7513	2,630	0.5187	2,025
Year 4	3,500	0.6830	2,392	0.4823	1,688
Year 5	3,500	0.6209	2,173	0.4019	1,407
Total			1,268		(1,533)

To calculate the IRR:

$$10\% \longleftrightarrow 20\%$$
$$(1,268) \qquad (1,533)$$

$$\frac{1,268}{2,801} \times 10\% = 4.53$$

$$IRR = 10 + 4.53$$
$$= 14.53\%$$

Option 2

	Cash flow	Discount rate 10%	Discounted cash flow	Discount rate 20%	Discounted cash flow
Year 0	(6,500)	1.000	(6,500)	1.000	(6,500)
Year 1	2,000	0.9091	1,818	0.8333	1,666
Year 2	2,000	0.8264	1,653	0.6944	1,389
Year 3	2,000	0.7513	1,503	0.5187	1,157
Year 4	2,000	0.6830	1,366	0.4823	965
Year 5	2,000	0.6209	1,242	0.4019	804
Total			1,082		(519)

To calculate the IRR:

$$10\% \xleftrightarrow{\hspace{4cm}} 20\%$$
$$1,082 \hspace{5cm} (519)$$

$$\frac{1,082}{1,601} \times 10 = 6.76$$

$$IRR = 10 + 6.76$$
$$= 16.76\%$$

According to the NPVs the first alternative should be selected, but the IRR results suggest that the second alternative should be selected. This conflict arises because of the differing sizes of the alternatives.

Profitability index

The final method to consider is the profitability index (PI), which relates the NPV to the size of the investment. It can be used to rank projects, with the highest ratios being given the highest priority, in capital rationing situations. To calculate the PI, divide the present value of cash inflows by the initial investment.

Case study: Demonstration of capital investment appraisal techniques

The Advent Hotel Group plc is planning to build a 100-bedroom hotel operation in a city centre location in the UK. The feasibility study has included forecasts for:

- room rate, room occupancy and yield
- contribution to cash flows from food and beverage departments
- contribution to cash flows for other income such as telephone and leisure sales
- hurdle rate for the IRR at 20%
- cost of capital at 10%: the project is to be financed using 60% equity and 40% loans.

The cash flows to be generated have been calculated using gross operating profit less taxation, insurance, rentals, management fee and any other costs before financing costs. A capital expenditure reserve has also been deducted, representing 3% of the investment value. The total cost of the investment includes a forecast for additional working capital (£1 m) and capitalization of the interest and preopening costs. The total investment amounts to £100,000 per room, i.e. £10,000,000, and the residual value at the end of 5 years is estimated to be ten times the cash earnings for that year. The cash flows to be generated are:

Year	Cash flow (£000)
1	800
2	800
3	1,000
4	1,000
5	1,000

The viability of the project is calculated as follows:

Year	Cash flow (£000)	Discount factor 10%	Discounted value	Discount factor 15%	Discounted value
1	800	0.9091	727.28	0.8333	666.64
2	800	0.8264	661.12	0.6944	555.52
3	1,000	0.7513	751.30	0.5787	578.70
4	1,000	0.6830	683.00	0.4823	482.30
5	1,000	0.6209	620.90	0.4019	401.90
Residual value	11,000	0.6209	6,829.90	0.4019	4,420.90
Total inflows			10,273.50		7,105.96
Original investment			10,000.00		10,000.00
NPV			273.50		−2,894.04

The results indicate that, although the discounted cash flows exceed the cost of capital, the project does not make the target return of 20%. The difference between the two NPVs is 3,167.54, which represents 10%. The IRR is therefore, slightly less than 11%. This can be proven by discounting at 11% as follows:

Year	Cash flow (£000)	Discount factor 11%	Discounted cash flows
1	800	0.9009	720.72
2	800	0.8116	649.28
3	1,000	0.7312	731.20
4	1,000	0.6587	658.70
5	1,000	0.5935	593.50
Residual value	11,000	0.5935	6,528.50
Total inflows			9,881.90
Original investment			10,000.00
NPV			−118.10

From this, it can be concluded that the project makes a return slightly in excess of the cost of capital, but falls short of the target return of 20%.

Appraisal methods and hospitality organizations

All of the methods discussed here, along with hybrid versions, are successfully used in the hospitality industry. It is not unusual to see capital expenditure decisions in larger groups being split into two types: those associated with refurbishment, which are assessed locally and are not subject to formal analysis, and those associated with development, where considerably larger sums of investment are required and a range of capital investment appraisal techniques may feature in the feasibility study. Table 10.1 summarizes the relative benefits of the four investment techniques.

Research based on the hotel industry carried out by Collier and Gregory (1995) suggests that a range of methods is used for capital investment appraisal, with the NPV approach being the least popular, although a number of businesses use the IRR.

Table 10.1 Summary of the relative benefits of the appraisal techniques

	ARR	PBP	NPV	IRR
Directly related to wealth maximization	No	No	Yes	No
Accounts for timing of cash flows	No	No	Yes	Yes
Uses all relevant information	Yes	No	Yes	Yes
Easy to use and understand	Yes	Yes	Yes	No
Comparison to WACC	Yes	No	Yes	Yes
Takes account of risk	Yes	Yes	Yes	Yes

WACC: weighted average cost of capital.

Capital investment control

The control and evaluation of capital investment projects is essentially concerned with ensuring that the achieved cash flows match the forecast values and that the anticipated level of NPV will be achieved. Failure to achieve the forecast NPV is primarily due to actual cash flows falling short of target and/or the discount rate used for discounting the cash flows being lower than that actually required.

A shortfall in cash flows may be due to the trading environment being less favourable than was originally forecast or the organization's internal costs associated with the project being higher than originally anticipated.

An increase in the required discount rate can come about following either an increase in prevailing interest rates or an increase in the company's own cost of capital percentage. Finally, the initial spend on the investment may be considerably more than first anticipated and this will also reduce the forecast NPV.

Consequently, the monitoring and control of capital projects is as important as the initial evaluation. The process of monitoring occasionally identifies that a project is no longer worth continuing with and a decision needs to be taken as to whether the project should be abandoned. The final decision should be based on an NPV analysis of the relevant costs and the benefits of continuation relative to those associated with abandonment. Postcompletion auditing is the process of reviewing the project once it has reached its conclusion to ensure that any errors in the investment decision process are not repeated. This process is less appropriate in the hospitality industry, where investments tend to have a long life.

Case study: The Ship Inn Company

This case study examines the position of a fictitious company based in the south of England. The Ship Inn Company is a small business comprising three sites that could be described as public houses with additional facilities. The company is jointly owned by two businessmen who have equal shares in the business.

The case is divided into the following sections and appendices:

1 Background to The Ship Inn Company

2 Personnel

3 Administration

4 The case problem

5 Forecast projections

Appendix A Profit and loss account 2001/02

Appendix B Balance sheet at year end 2001/02.

Background to The Ship Inn Company

The Ship Inn Company was formed in 1982, when two businessmen invested their savings in their first public house, the Marie Rose I. One of the partners, Michael Donnelly, had previously worked in the licensed trade in the East End of London and was considered by those who had worked for him to be a tough but fair operator. The other partner, Peter Williams, had, in the past, been involved in a variety of business interests in a number of different areas. He saw himself as a shrewd businessman with the ability to adapt to the needs of any business that appeared to be viable. He had already bought and sold several businesses, usually in the retail or computer industries, and always for a good profit. This business, The Ship Inn Company, was their first venture together in partnership and they formed an uneasy but successful liaison. Each had clear roles, Donnelly looking after the operational aspects, working long hours travelling from one unit to the other, and Williams dealing with the administrative details and investigating other possible acquisitions to develop the partnership. A further two operations, Marie Rose II and Marie Rose III, were purchased from a large brewery in 1984, but no further acquisitions have been made since.

Personnel

Each operation has its own bar manager, bar staff and cleaners. The workforce is generally made up of young, part-time staff who have low levels of training, and staff turnover in all outlets is high. The managers are normally college trained with a supervisory qualification and are individually responsible for cellar control and bar supervision. At Head Office there is one assistant, Betty Jones, who acts as secretary, administrator and book-keeper.

Administration

Where possible, all administration is performed centrally, enabling managers at each site to concentrate on the practical aspects of running the business. The manager of each outlet may order their own stocks using the nominated suppliers and the invoices are received and paid for centrally. Prices from suppliers are negotiated by Donnelly who, as a result, decides which brands should be sold.

The case problem

Peter Williams has recently located a new potential site for an additional outlet and is particularly excited about its possibilities. The location appears to be perfect for an operation in the style of Marie Roses I and II, although the purchase will involve buying an existing city centre unit currently trading as a music store. This is not considered to be a problem, as The Ship Inn Company will then commence the transformation to a bar and club, resulting in a tailor-made operation. Williams feels that it is reasonable to forecast that the new outlet will open for trading within 6 months from purchase. Williams has also produced some financial projections and these are illustrated below. Given these forecasts, Williams feels confident that the venture will return a satisfactory level of profit. However, Donnelly has some reservations about the new acquisition as he feels that the partnership may be overstretched both financially and operationally by the introduction of a fourth unit. He has consequently asked Williams to prepare some detailed financial projections for them both to discuss and consider. The details relating to the project are given below.

Forecast projections

Williams has conducted a market survey costing £150,000 which has yet to be paid. The initial capital expenditure is subject to straight-line depreciation and requires additional working capital to support the project.

The project is to be evaluated over 6 years and requires capital expenditure of £6,000,000. At the end of year 6 the residual value of the capital expenditure is forecast to be £1,000,000. The working capital requirements are forecast to be:

Stocks	£250,000
Cash	£50,000
Creditors	£50,000

The best forecasts for sales over the life of the project are:

Year 1	£6,000,000
Year 2	£6,000,000
Year 3	£8,000,000
Year 4	£8,000,000
Year 5	£8,000,000
Year 6	£10,000,000

The variable costs are estimated to be 60% of sales.

Fixed costs are estimated to be £2,500,000, which includes an apportionment of the total business overheads of £500,000. The actual additional overheads to be incurred by this project are £300,000. The estimate for fixed costs also includes a charge for depreciation.

The directors are uncertain as to how to fund the project. One approach would be to fund the project partly from reserves and partly with a loan of £6,000,000 repayable in full at the end of the 6 years. Donnelly favours this option because he argues that using loans is cheaper than raising additional equity. Williams argues that equity funds are less risky and would therefore be preferable. The business weighted average cost of capital is estimated to be 12% p.a. and it has a marginal borrowing rate of 8% p.a. It uses 20% p.a. as an initial target return.

Williams has approached a variety of lenders requesting a loan for £6,000,000.

Appendix A

Profit and loss account

	2001 £m	2002 £m
Sales	200	280
Less: Cost of sales	40	56
Gross profit	160	224
Less: Wages and staff costs	56	80
Operating profit	104	144
Less: Expenses	65	86
Less: Depreciation	7	10
Trading profit	32	48
Less: Corporation tax	11.2	16.8
Profit after tax	20.8	31.2
Less: Dividend	10.0	12.0
Retained profit	10.8	19.2

Appendix B

Balance sheet: 31 December

Fixed assets (net)	2001 £m	2002 £m
Freehold property, at cost	128.0	156.0
Equipment and furniture, at cost	28.0	30.0
	156.0	186.0
Current assets		
Stock	8.0	10.0
Debtors	20.8	20.0
Bank balance	6.4	2.8
	35.2	32.8

Less: Creditors – Amounts due in less than 1 year		
Creditors	5.2	6.0
Dividend (proposed)	10.0	12.0
Taxation	11.2	16.8
	26.4	34.8
Net current assets	8.8	(2.0)
Total net assets	164.8	184.0
Capital and reserves		
	£m	£m
Share capital		
Ordinary shares	100.0	100.0
Reserve		
Profit and loss account – retained profit	64.8	84.0
Capital employed	**164.8**	**184.0**

Summary This chapter describes the various theoretical approaches to assessing investment opportunities. In practice it is the accountants in the business who will select the methodologies to be used for evaluating a project, but managers need to understand the methodologies if they are to put forward projects for successful appraisal. Academically the net present value approach is considered to be the most accurate as it takes account of a range of factors, including the changing value of money, future cash-flow expectations and risk. Despite this, a range of methods is used in practice and it is not uncommon in the hospitality and tourism industries for emphasis to be placed on the accounting rate of return and the payback period. To use investment appraisal techniques successfully it is essential that other practical considerations are addressed, such as taxation, inflation, risk and sensitivity analysis, and these will be discussed in the following chapter.

Questions

1 Describe the payback method of capital investment appraisal. List the advantages and disadvantages.

2 What is discounting in the context of capital investment appraisal?

3 List the advantages and disadvantages of net present value approaches to capital investment appraisal.

4 **Calculating net present value and the internal rate of return**

The Exclusive Club is considering adding fresh home-baked breads to its menu. However, an oven that costs £30,000 will have to be purchased. It has an estimated 7-year life and the owners have calculated that the club will sell £20,000 of breads annually, with a food cost of 30% and a labour cost of 35%. The residual value of the machine at the end of 7 years is forecast to be £5000.

The target return is 15% per annum.

You are required to:

(a) Calculate the net present value for this investment.

(b) Calculate the internal rate of return.

(c) Comment on your findings. Do you think the machine should be purchased?

(d) Describe the different capital investment appraisal techniques available and give the strengths and weaknesses of each. Which method do you feel is the most effective and why?

Stage 3 BAHA Education and Training Programme, Examination Paper, July 2001

5 Using capital investment appraisal methods
Fairview Productions is considering the purchase of new food production equipment. The introduction of the automated equipment will save labour costs. The business is considering two types of pieces of equipment and the following data are forecast:

	Equipment A (£000)	Equipment B (£000)
Initial cost	400	260
Estimated life	6 years	5 years
Residual value	150	120
Working capital	None required	None required

Annual labour cost savings arising from purchase (equivalent to cash flows generated):

	Equipment A (£000)	Equipment B (£000)
Year 1	120	90
Year 2	120	90
Year 3	120	60
Year 4	50	60
Year 5	50	60
Year 6	50	N/A

The weighted average cost of capital is 10%. The target rate of return for investment is 20%.

You are required to:

(a) Calculate the viability of each piece of equipment assuming a purchase is made. The following capital investment methods should be used:

  (i) average accounting rate of return

  (ii) net present value

  (iii) internal rate of return.

(b) Write a report to the Director reviewing your findings. You should also include in your report comments to address the following issues:

  (i) A review of the advantages and disadvantages of the capital investment methods that could be used.

  (ii) Comment on how the risk associated with the project could be quantified and monitored.

  (iii) Your conclusion as to what action the business should take.

Stage 3 BAHA Education and Training Programme, Examination Paper, January 2004

6 News story questions

Do you recall the news story at the beginning of this chapter? Now return to that story and reread it before answering the following questions.

(a) What do you think will be the impact on the company's ability to attract more customers following the Whitbread strategy to cut back on capital expenditure in the declining business areas?

(b) What other reasons do you think Whitbread might have for halting capital expenditure?

Further reading

Arnold, G.C. and Hatzopoulos, P.D. (2000) The theory–practice gap in capital budgeting: evidence from the United Kingdom, *Journal of Business Finance and Accounting* 27(5/6): 603.

Atkinson, H., Berry, A. and Jarvis, R. (1995) *Business Accounting for Hospitality and Tourism*, London: International Thomson Business Press.

Drury, C. and Tayles, M. (1997) The misapplication of capital investment appraisal techniques, *Management Decision* 35(1/2): 86.

Owen, G. (1998) *Accounting for Hospitality, Tourism and Leisure*, Harlow: Longman.

Ransley, J. and Ingram, H. (2004) *Developing Hospitality Properties and Facilities*, Oxford: Butterworth Heinemann.

Useful websites

http://www.inlandrevenue.gov.uk/capital_allowances/investmentschemes.htm
http://www.egeneration.co.uk/centre/modules/sustainable_tourism/12_contacts.asp
www.greentourism.org.uk/GoingGreen3.pdf
www.eca.gov.uk
www.investopedia.com/terms/i/irr.asp

Reference

Collier, P. and Gregory, A. (1994) Strategic management accounting: a UK hotel sector case study, *International Journal of Contemporary Hospitality Management* 7(1): 18–23.

11 | Practical aspects of investment appraisal

About this chapter

The purpose of this chapter is to consider how capital investment appraisal techniques can actually be put into practice as part of the process for evaluating strategic options. A range of important issues is considered, including the practicalities for:

- forecasting accurate cash flows
- assessing the lifespan of a project
- calculating the residual value
- allowing for working capital requirements
- taxation and inflation effects
- measuring risk.

Case study: De Vere Group to take its first shot at foreign venture

De Vere Group, the hotel and leisure operator, will today announce its first move overseas with a 20-year contract to manage a hotel and golf complex in southern Spain.

The company, which was once part of the old Greenalls brewing and pub empire, is to run a 150-room hotel and spa with an 18-hole championship golf course and beach club near La Manga, in Murcia.

It will pay €2 million (£1.4 million) for a minority stake in the project, which is due to open in mid-2008 as the De Vere Roda. The contract includes the right to develop timeshare at the resort in partnership with the developer, Roda Golf and Beach Resort.

The group has also secured the right to manage a second golf resort in Murcia, at Corvera, which is expected to open in 2009.

The golf course at the Roda complex is designed by Dave Thomas. Mr Thomas also designed the Brabazon course at The De Vere Belfry, the Ryder Cup venue near Birmingham. De Vere recently announced a £186 million sale and leaseback of The Belfry.

Carl Leaver, De Vere's chief executive, said that the Roda contract did not include any guarantees for the owners, which was unusual. 'We were not prepared to take the kind of risk associated with a guarantee in a new market like Spain', he said.

Mr Leaver said that the resort would derive much of its business from British golfers. However, he would also try to develop new markets, which in turn would boost De Vere's UK hotels.

He hinted that he was in early stage discussions on potential golf-based hotel projects in other parts of the southern Mediterranean but declined to discuss any details.

The Times Online, 27 April 2005

Questions relating to this news story may be found on page 260.

Learning objectives On completion of this chapter you should be able to:

- understand how to forecast accurate cash flows
- appreciate the factors to consider when assessing the lifespan of a project
- understand the significance of working capital in investment appraisal
- appreciate the impact of taxation and inflation effects
- apply techniques for measuring risk.

Introduction

Several writers have commented on the misuse of capital investment appraisal techniques for assessing the viability of projects, with the effect that companies are underinvesting because they misapply or misinterpret discounted cash-flow techniques. Surveys have indicated (Drury and Tayles, 1997) that companies are regularly using conservative cash-flow forecasts, combined with incorrect treatment of inflation and excessive discount rates to evaluate projects.

Which methods are preferred?

Several studies based on the use of capital investment appraisal methods in organizations from the manufacturing sector conclude that the most frequently used method for capital investment appraisal is the payback method, although this is often used alongside other methods. Where discounted cash flow is used, the preferred method appears to be the internal rate of return (IRR) rather than the theoretically preferred net present value (NPV). The rate of return is also often used despite the problems associated with this method. Many organizations also attempt to analyse risk formally through the use of sensitivity analysis and incorporate estimates for inflation into the calculation. Research carried out in the hotel industry by Collier and Gregory (1995) indicates similar conclusions. Table 11.1 is a summary of their findings in this area.

In view of the arguments against the use of the IRR approach described in the previous chapter it is perhaps surprising that the use of the method is so widespread. This may be due to the fact that the workings provide a percentage result, which is easier to interpret than the NPV result. IRR also provides a ranking of projects of different size and timescales without the need for a predetermined discount rate as is required by the NPV method. The availability of computer software in the form of a simple spreadsheet greatly assists in the calculation of this method and this has also probably led to an increase in usage.

Table 11.1 Nature of capital investment appraisal in the hospitality industry

Nature of industry	Management style	Investment technique	IRR	Cost of capital
Hotel and leisure	Centralized	Profit payback	No	NA
Hotel and leisure	Centralized	ARR/payback	Partly	Loan rate
Travel	Decentralized	IRR	Yes	1.5 × loan rate
Conglomerate	Decentralized	Cover interest (year 1)	No	NA
Brewing	Decentralized	ARR/IRR	Yes	Business specific rate
Brewing	Decentralized	IRR	Yes	Corporate WACC

Source: Collier and Gregory (1995) *Management Accounting in Hotel Groups.*
WACC: weighted average cost of capital.

The value of accurate forecasting

In order for capital investment appraisal to be successfully carried out it is essential that the forecast data be as accurate possible. In practice, this means reliance on management experience and standard relationships unique to the hospitality industry. Collier and Gregory (1995) support this view, commenting that the considerable bank of past experience available to many hospitality organizations enables the investment decision to be fairly standard, with rules of thumb such as 'build cost per room' for a given star rating often being quoted along with expected room occupancy figures. This information can then be usefully supported with data drawn from sensitivity analysis and computer simulations. The fundamental factor in investment appraisal is the accurate estimate of the annual cash flows from the project. Mills and Stiles provide three key groupings for analysing all the relevant factors likely to affect the cash-flow forecast. These are:

- financial factors
- marketing factors
- operating factors.

Within these headings are included a number of relevant factors, as shown in Table 11.2.

It should also be noted that capital investment techniques assume that cash flows will occur at the year end for discounting purposes. Discount tables can be produced on a month-by-month basis, but the use of these would considerably increase the nature of the workings. As a result the year-end assumption means that cash flows are marginally overdiscounted and are, therefore, included in the calculation at a slightly lower value than would be the case in reality. The

Table 11.2 Factors likely to affect cash flow forecasts

Financial factors	*Marketing factors*	*Operating factors*
Inflation	Sales forecast	Operating costs
Risk	Product life	Material and supply costs
Taxation	Discount policy	Start-up costs
Residual value	Promotional policy	Shut-down costs
Working capital	Selling costs	Maintenance costs

Source: Adapted from Mills and Stiles (1994) *Finance for The General Manager.*

effect of this is to increase marginally the payback period and to understate the NPV and IRR.

Feasibility studies

To arrive at a set of accurate cash flows a feasibility study will be required. This may be carried out by the investing organization or an independent consultant. The aim is to ensure that all possible aspects of the suggested project have been considered and that the forecasts for sales, volumes and costs are as accurate as possible. The typical steps in a feasibility study are illustrated in Figure 11.1.

The first steps require a detailed knowledge of the business environment and current trends in order to forecast the likely sales volumes, average spends and sales mix. Knowledge of the cost structure in terms of fixed and variable costs is critical for ensuring that the profit and cash flow forecasts are practical. These aspects were considered in Part 2 of the text. The initial financial evaluation is then subject to a sensitivity analysis. CIMA Management Accounting Official Terminology (2000) defines sensitivity analysis as 'a modelling and risk assessment procedure in which changes are made to significant variable in order to determine the effect of these changes on the planned outcome.' With the financial forecasts agreed, the financing for the project can be confirmed and the detailed operational aspects of the project specified.

Lifespan of the project

The determination of lifespan for a project can prove awkward to forecast in the hospitality and tourism industries, where investments are considered to have an indeterminate life. A piece of equipment is normally considered to have a certain working life and is then depreciated on the basis of this. This type of investment is, therefore, simple to analyse in terms of initial spend, cash savings and residual

Figure 11.1 Typical stages in a feasibility study

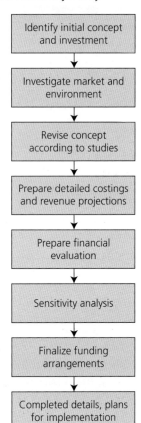

value. Projects involving long-term investments cannot be evaluated over an indefinite period as the value of the forecast cash flows becomes virtually meaningless. As a result, hospitality and tourism projects are normally evaluated over a 5–10-year period and the accuracy of the residual value at this point is of prime importance. The residual value may be in excess of the initial spend and the determination of this figure will require an understanding of valuation techniques.

Residual value or exit value

This is the value of the project at the end of the evaluation period. A simple approach to arriving at a valuation figure would be to revise the purchase or construction cost in line with the retail price index. Other valuation methods may be appropriate, such as the current market price or the depreciated replacement cost. However, considerable controversy has surrounded the valuation of hotel assets, for example, with several major groups facing substantial devaluation of fixed assets at some point in their history. As a result the British Association of

Hospitality Accountants (1993) produced a guide to recommended practice and advise that:

> *hotels should be valued by reference to their recent/current performance and future trading potential. This is achieved by the 'Income Capitalisation' approach which seeks to assess value by reference to projected net cash flows (reproduced from* Recommended Practice for the Valuation of Hotels, *published by the British Association of Hospitality Accountants, 1993).*

The income capitalization approach is achieved by using either discounted cash flows or a method called the 'earnings multiple'. The discounted cash-flow approach is based on the capitalization of the anticipated net cash flows for an operation by discounting at the appropriate discount rate. The earnings multiple approach requires the application of a multiplier to the maintainable earnings, which are defined as the adjusted cash flows, expressed in present values, that can be sustained over the foreseeable future.

Working capital

In addition to the capital investment, most projects will require an injection of working capital. This will normally be required throughout the life of the project to fund and maintain stock levels and to allow for credit sales while enabling the suppliers to be paid. It is fair to suppose that this part of the investment will be substantially released at the end of the project and should, therefore, be shown as a cash inflow in the final year. However, at the end of the project, its value will be considerably reduced owing to the changing value of money over time. Consequently, it is normal practice to discount the working capital released, with the discount factor rate prevailing at the conclusion of the project.

Taxation

The complexities surrounding taxation and capital appraisal are beyond the scope of this text. However, the basic principles will be discussed briefly and more detailed sources of information are supplied in the further reading suggested at the end of the chapter. Capital expenditure may attract tax relief for a business in the form of capital allowances and this should be reflected in the forecast cash flows. The capital allowance amounts to a reduction in the taxable profit to relieve expenditure on fixed assets, and acts as an incentive to industry to encourage investment. There are several categories of fixed asset, each with its own rules and level of capital allowance. However, the two most widely used categories are plant and machinery and industrial buildings.

The first of these, plant and machinery, includes a wide range of assets and a business may deduct 25% of the cost of the asset from the profit for the period during which the asset was acquired. In each subsequent year of ownership, 25% of the balance may be deducted.

The second group is that of industrial buildings, which includes buildings used directly or indirectly in manufacturing, the transport industry and other restricted purposes excluding shops and offices. Relief is given by allowing a business to deduct 4% of the cost from the taxable profit for each year the asset is in use. Other types of asset attract capital allowances and these include, in particular, hotels. The important aspects of taxation for the hospitality industry include:

- ensuring that all allowances are claimed for, particularly for plant and machinery, as this represents an important resource
- assessing the effect of taxation on the investment decision
- assessing the benefits to be derived from alternative methods of funding, for example, outright purchase versus rental.

Plant and machinery allowances

This allowance can be of significant importance to the hospitality and tourism industry, where there is substantial investment in this form of assets, and yet this is often an underutilized resource. The difficulty in gaining the maximum benefit from these allowances lies in the complexities of separating out those items that are allowable from those that are not. This is particularly difficult to achieve where contractors are involved to complete work, the value of which includes equipment costs as well as installation costs. The contractor may be unwilling to reveal the plant and machinery figures within the total cost and a separate valuation may be required. The definitions for plant and machinery eligible for capital allowances are often quite complex and specialist advice will ensure that the maximum benefit is achieved. The following example illustrates the calculation of capital allowances.

Example

A restaurant purchases a delivery van for £15,000. The capital allowances would be calculated as follows:

Year	Balance (£)	Capital allowance
2003	16,000	4,000 (25% of £16,000)
2004	12,000	3,000 (25% of £12,000)
2005	9,000	2,250 (25% of £9,000)
2006	6,750	1,688 (25% of £6,750)

This pattern is continued until the asset is scrapped or sold.

Taxation effects on the investment decision

A serious implication for capital investment appraisal occurs when taxation distorts the investment decision by converting a viable investment into a non-viable investment. This can occur when profits are different to cash flows generated by the project, which may be the case when equipment is purchased and capital allowances are set against the profit and loss account.

The level of distortion depends on the level of sophistication of the tax system. It is important to realize that when tax rules change, specialist advice should be sought to ensure that the current rates and benefits are being fully utilized.

The impact of inflation

The term inflation means the erosion of the purchasing power of currency owing to the increase in price of goods and services and is a condition that affects most economies of the world at some time. Even relatively low levels of inflation can affect purchasing power over long periods and therefore the implications need to be assessed in the capital investment appraisal workings. The use of discounted cash flows is not sufficient to take account of the full effect of inflation. The general principle is that cash flows stated in real terms, that is without adjusting for inflation, should be discounted with a rate that also excludes inflation in order for like to be compared with like. Where sales and costs have been adjusted for inflation, a rate incorporating an adjustment for inflation should be used.

The difficulty in forecasting for inflation lies in the fact that, in reality, the individual cash-flow elements such as sales, material costs, labour costs and others may not all be subject to the same degree of inflation.

Measuring risk in investment appraisal

Any project that is to be assessed over the long term must be subject to some risk or uncertainty. Risk describes the situation where it is possible to identify all the likely outcomes and possibly their likelihood of occurring without being absolutely sure what will actually occur. Uncertainty describes the situation where it is not possible to be sure of all the likely outcomes. All business decisions are subject to some uncertainty and risk, but it is really only the latter that can be identified and subsequently assessed.

There are many possible sources of risk that may cause actual revenues and costs to be different from those initially forecast, and these may be classified as:

- business risk
- operating risk
- financial risk.

The first of these, business risk, occurs as the result of changes in the economic and business environment, and all businesses will be subject to this. It can arise from a variety of sources such as changes in the nature of the competition, technological changes and innovation, and fluctuations in the national or world economy.

Operating risk arises from the cost structure of the operation and occurs when variable costs are substituted by fixed costs. Substantial fixed costs mean that a certain level of revenue is required simply to cover those costs. In times of good business conditions this can be an advantage, but losses will soon be incurred during periods of recession.

Financial risk arises from the method of financing used by the business and is reliant on the cost of servicing the debt. Sources of funds derived from borrowings incur an interest charge that must be paid regardless of the level of profit. The relationship between equity funds and interest-bearing funds is called gearing and is described in greater detail in Chapter 12. During periods of good trading conditions high gearing, that is where the majority of funds is provided from borrowing, can be beneficial. The interest charge is fixed and once this has been paid the remainder of the profits can be used for dividend payments or reinvestment. However, during periods of recession the fixed interest charge must be met regardless of the level of trading, which means possibly incurring an even greater loss as a result of paying interest.

It is vitally important to take account of risk, whatever the form, and this should be done on a formal basis for each investment project. The methods to be discussed in the remainder of this chapter are:

- sensitivity analysis
- probability and expected value.

Sensitivity analysis

Sensitivity analysis is used to evaluate the effect of a change on each of the factors contained in the forecast. In the capital investment appraisal calculation a variety of factors will need to be forecast. These include:

- the value of the initial investment
- the length of the project
- the sales projections based on volume
- the selling price and sales mix
- the cost projections
- the predicted discount rate.

All of the values are subject to change either individually or as a result of dependence on another variable. Simple calculations can easily be performed where just one variable changes and to determine the likely effect on the project. More complex relationships may require the use of computer simulations, and even a basic spreadsheet can be of assistance for modelling 'what if' situations. The following example illustrates a basic approach to sensitivity analysis where each variable changes independently of the others.

Example

The Riverside Hotel plc has the opportunity to invest in a new café to support its existing activities. The demand is estimated to be 10,000 covers per year for a minimum of 5 years. The following data relate to the decision:

- The restaurant is estimated to have no residual value and will cost £140,000 payable immediately.
- The average spend per cover is estimated to be £10.
- The variable costs are estimated to be £6 per cover (£3 for labour and £3 for materials).
- Overheads are not expected to be affected by the decision.
- The firm's cost of finance for such a project is estimated to be 10%.
- The project is not expected to require any additional working capital.
- The effects of taxation are to be ignored.
- All cash flows occur at the year end.

The annual cash flows will be:

$$10,000 \times £(10 - (3 + 3)) = £40,000 \text{ each year.}$$

Thus, the project's cash flows are forecast to be:

Year 0	(£140,000)
Year 1	£40,000
Year 2	£40,000
Year 3	£40,000
Year 4	£40,000
Year 5	£40,000

The discount factor is 10% and this can now be used to calculate the NPV of the project:

Year	Cash flows (£)	Discount factor	Present value/(£)
0	(140,000)	0	(140,000)
1	40,000	0.909	36,360
2	40,000	0.826	33,040
3	40,000	0.751	30,040
4	40,000	0.683	27,320
5	40,000	0.621	24,840
		3.791	11,600

The annuity factor for 5 years at 10% is 3.791 (see Appendix 2). The NPV is therefore:

$$-140,000 + (40,000 \times 3.791) = 11,600$$

The project has a positive NPV and is therefore favourable. The aim of sensitivity analysis is to assess the effect of a change in the input factor on the overall acceptability of the project. The factors used in the above example to calculate NPV are:

Original investment	I
Annual sales volume	V
Selling price per unit	S
Labour cost per unit	L
Material cost per unit	M
Cost of capital	C
Life of the project	n
Annuity factor	A

The above workings can be represented by a single equation:

$$-I + (V \times (S - (L + M))A = \text{NPV}$$

To carry out the sensitivity analysis each factor will be considered in terms of what change is required to reduce the NPV to zero, which is the point when the project would no longer be acceptable.

1 Original investment

$$-I + (10,000 \times £(10 - (3 + 3)))3.791 = 0$$
$$I = 151,640$$

2 Annual sales volume

$$-140,000 + (V \times £(10 - (3 + 3)))3.791 = 0$$
$$V = 9,232$$

3 Selling price per unit

$$-140,000 + (10,000 \times £(S - (3 + 3)))3.791 = 0$$
$$S = £9.69$$

4 Labour cost per unit

$$-140,000 + (10,000 \times £(10 - (L + 3)))3.791 = 0$$
$$L = £3.30$$

5 Material cost per unit

$$-140,000 + (10,000 \times £(10 - (3 + M)))3.791 = 0$$
$$M = £3.30$$

6 Cost of capital

$$-140,000 + (10,000 \times £(10 - (3 + 3)))A = 0$$
$$A = 3.5$$

Looking at tables, the annuity factor is closest to 13% for a project 5 years in length.

7 Life of the project

$$-140,000 + (10,000 \times £(10 - (3 + 3)))A = 0$$
$$A = 3.5$$

Looking at tables, the annuity factor is closest to 4½ years for a project with a 10% return.

The results are summarized as follows:

Factor	Original estimate	Value for zero NPV	% Difference
Original investment	£140,000	£151,640	8.3
Annual sales volume	10,000 units	9,232 units	7.7
Selling price per unit	£10	£9.69	3.1
Labour cost per unit	£3	£3.30	10.0
Material cost per unit	£3	£3.30	10.0
Cost of capital	10%	13%	30.0
Life of the project	5 years	4½ years	10.0

This highlights those factors that are the most sensitive and are most likely to undermine the profitability of the project, which in this case are selling price and sales volume.

The above example illustrates a simplistic view of sensitivity analysis, but even this level of analysis enables the decision maker to gain a grasp of the critical factors in the project.

Use of probabilities

The use of probabilities enables a whole range of possible outcomes for each factor to be considered, providing that it is possible to assess the probability of each outcome occurring. It is then possible to calculate a range of possible NPVs for the project. In practice this can be difficult to achieve, but as with sensitivity analysis the exercise offers the opportunity for the decision maker to become familiar with the key factors in the project.

Example

Using the above example it will be assumed all factors are known with certainty except for sales volume and the material costs. In practice, all factors should be assigned probabilities as none can be determined with certainty. However, this would produce a large volume of calculations which, in practice, would need to be calculated with the aid of a computer. Extensive market research indicates that annual demand will be:

(a) 11,000 covers (0.3 probable) or

(b) 10,000 covers (0.5 probable) or

(c) 9,000 covers (0.2 probable).

The possible outcomes are:

$$\text{NPV at 11,000 units} = -140{,}000 + 11{,}000(10 - 6)3.791$$
$$= 26{,}804$$

$$\text{NPV at 10,000 units} = -140{,}000 + 10{,}000(10 - 6)3.791$$
$$= 11{,}640$$

$$\text{NPV at 9,000 units} = -140{,}000 + 9{,}000(10 - 6)3.791$$
$$= (3{,}524)$$

This could then be combined with possible outcomes for a second factor. Independent of sales volume, the cost of materials will be:

(a)   £3 per cover (0.6 probable) or

(b)   £4 per cover (0.3 probable) or

(c)   £2 per cover (0.1 probable).

The situation now becomes more complicated because there are nine possible outcomes based on three alternatives for sales volume and three alternatives for material costs.
    The possible outcomes are:

(a) Material costs of £3 per cover

$$\text{A} \quad \text{NPV at 11,000 units} = -140{,}000 + 11{,}000 (10 - 6)3.791$$
$$= 26{,}804$$

$$\text{B} \quad \text{NPV at 10,000 units} = -140{,}000 + 10{,}000 (10 - 6)3.791$$
$$= 11{,}640$$

$$\text{C} \quad \text{NPV at 9,000 units} = -140{,}000 + 9{,}000 (10 - 6)3.791$$
$$= (3{,}524)$$

(b) Material costs at £4 per cover

D   NPV at 11,000 units $= -140{,}000 + 11{,}000 \,(10 - 7)3.791$
$= (14{,}897)$

E   NPV at 10,000 units $= -140{,}000 + 10{,}000 \,(10 - 7)3.791$
$= (26{,}270)$

F   NPV at 9,000 units $= -140{,}000 + 9{,}000 \,(10 - 7)3.791$
$= (37{,}643)$

(c) Material costs at £2 per cover

G   NPV at 11,000 units $= -140{,}000 + 11{,}000 \,(10 - 5)3.791$
$= 68{,}505$

H   NPV at 10,000 units $= -140{,}000 + 10{,}000 \,(10 - 5)3.791$
$= 49{,}550$

I   NPV at 9,000 units $= -140{,}000 + 9{,}000 \,(10 - 5)3.791$
$= 30{,}595$

To assess the probabilities of two events occurring the probabilities need to be combined, and this is achieved by multiplying the two values together. The following table indicates the possible outcome and probability.

Possible outcome	NPV	Probability
A	26,804	0.18
B	11,640	0.30
C	(3,524)	0.12
D	(14,897)	0.09
E	(26,270)	0.15
F	(37,643)	0.06
G	68,505	0.03
H	49,550	0.05
I	30,595	0.02
		1.00

Using the above data only one of the above options can occur. Only projects with a positive NPV should be accepted, and from the above data it is possible to conclude that there is a 58% chance of a positive NPV occurring.

Summary This chapter investigates the important practical issues that have to be considered when evaluating capital investment projects. The general manager needs to be aware of the implications of inflation, taxation and risk on the capital investment decision and how to assess the effect of these factors in practice. Specific issues such as taxation will need the input of specialist advice to determine the current implications for a particular organization. However, a major requirement of general management is to be able to assess and manage risk to ensure that exposure is minimized. It is important to be able to identify risk within the risk and there is a range of financial techniques available to assist in this. These include an analysis of key ratios and cash flows. The techniques described in this chapter can be effectively used and developed further with the use of computer software such as spreadsheets or more complex simulation packages.

Questions

1 Briefly discuss the techniques used by companies to analyse risk in capital budgeting.

2 Explain the distinction between business risk, financial risk and operational risk.

3 Select a business from the hospitality and tourism sectors and describe the types of risk associated with investment decisions. Suggest how the scales of these risks can be assessed in practice.

4 Your hotel company is an international player looking to expand its presence in Asia and is considering the suitability of an investment in the Islamic Republic of Iran. You have been asked to prepare a presentation outlining the full range of risks the investing company is likely to be exposed to with this investment. Use an appropriate range of risk management models to structure your analysis.

5 **News story questions.**

Do you recall the news story at the beginning of this chapter? Now return to that story and reread it before answering the following questions.

(a) What factors do you think De Vere will need to consider when performing a feasibility study for this new venture?

(b) Which of the capital investment appraisal methods will be the most appropriate and why?

Further reading

Arnold, G.C. and Hatzopoulos, P.D. (2000) The theory–practice gap in capital budgeting: evidence from the United Kingdom, *Journal of Business Finance and Accounting* 27(5/6): 603.

Atkinson, H. Berry, A. and Jarvis, R. (1995) *Business Accounting for Hospitality and Tourism*, London: International Thomson Business Press.

Collier, P. and Gregory, A. (1994) Strategic management accounting: a UK hotel sector case study, *International Journal of Contemporary Hospitality Management* 7(1): 18–23.

Owen G. (1998)*Accounting for Hospitality, Tourism and Leisure*, Harlow: Longman.

Ransley, J. and Ingram, H. (2004) *Developing Hospitality Properties and Facilities*, Oxford: Butterworth Heinemann.

Shimell, P. (2001) *The Universe of Risk: How Top Business Leaders Control Risk and Achieve Success*, London: FT Prentice Hall.

Waring, A. and Glendon, A. (1998) *Managing Risk: Critical Issues for Survival and Success into the 21st Century*, London: Thomson Learning.

Useful websites

www.inlandrevenue.gov.uk/capital_allowances/investmentschemes.htm
Hotels make room for risk management
   http://www.insurancejournal.com/magazines/midwest/2004/08/23/coverstory/45573.htm
Political risk and foreign investment decision of international hotel companies
   http://www.hotel-online.com/Neo/Trends/PanAmerProceedingsMay99/PolRiskInvestHotels.html
http://www.hotel-online.com/Trends/Aon/index.html
Have you protected your hotel from risk?
   http://www.hotel-online.com/Trends/Aon/Report/May2000_RiskProtected.html
Insurance premiums to rise in 2000: what can hotel owners do to minimize the impact?
   http://www.hotel-online.com/Trends/Aon/Report/Jan2000_InsPremiums.html
http://www.hotel-online.com/Trends/Aon/Report/Oct98_SafetyForum.html

References

Recommended Practice for the Valuation of Hotels. British Association of Hospitality Accountants (1993) BAHA.
Collier, P. and Gregory, A. (1995) *Management Accounting in Hotel Groups*, London: CIMA.
Drury, C. and Tayles, M. (1997) The misapplication of capital investment appraisal techniques, *Management Decision* 35(1/2): 86.
Mills, R. and Stiles, J. (1994) *Finance for the General Manager*, London: McGraw-Hill.

12 | The cost of funds

About this chapter

The purpose of this chapter is to illustrate the relationship between the cost of capital and gearing, and to demonstrate how the cost of capital can be calculated for each of the sources of funds. From this the overall value can be determined, reflecting the capital structure of the business. Establishing the cost of capital can be difficult in practice and the financial theories available are quite complex. The aim of this chapter is to provide a simple overview of the key issues surrounding the cost of capital calculation to enable the manager to understand the principles involved.

Learning objectives   On completion of this chapter you should be able to:

- understand the concept of gearing
- explain the meaning of the weighted average cost of capital (WACC)
- understand the relationship between WACC and the gearing ratio
- appreciate the factors that impact on the selection of capital for the financing of a business or capital expenditure.

Introduction

The potential sources of funds available to an organization have already been described in detail in Chapter 9. These can basically be divided into two main groupings, those classified as equity sources and those that can be termed borrowings or debt capital. Equity sources include:

- ordinary shares
- preference shares
- reserves.

Debt financing can include:

- debentures
- convertibles
- bonds
- mezzanine finance.

It has already been noted that equity sources can expect a varying level of return, whereas borrowed funds normally require a fixed return in the form of interest. In general, the providers of the finance expect a level of return that is directly linked to the perceived level of risk. The higher the risk, the greater the expected return. The advantages of debt financing include the cost of the funding, which is usually lower than equity financing. This is because:

- The pretax rate of interest is lower than that expected by shareholders because share capital is perceived to be more risky as the returns, i.e. the dividend, are not guaranteed.
- Debt interest falls above taxation in the profit and loss account, reducing the overall cost of the interest.
- The administrative costs of debt capital, such as the issuing costs, are normally lower than those required for issuing share capital.

Cost of capital

CIMA's Official Terminology defines the cost of capital as 'The minimum acceptable return on an investment, generally computed as a hurdle rate for use in investment appraisal exercises. The computation of the optimal cost of capital can be complex and many ways of determining this opportunity cost have been suggested.'

The cost of capital depends on the riskiness of projects being evaluated. Davies *et al.* (1999) define it as 'the weighted average of the costs of the various investments of which the company is made up', determined by the risk of the firm's investment opportunities. It consists of the combined costs of equity and debt.

If a company is to survive in the long term it must achieve a return in excess of the cost of the funds invested in that company. The total cost is dependent on the cost of funds from equity sources and on those from borrowings. The return on equity is made up of the returns paid to shareholders in the form of dividends and also the funds that belong to shareholders that have been retained within the company for reinvestment. The simplest approach to finding the cost of capital requires estimating the cost for each source of funds and combining these to provide a single value using a weighted average. However, there are other approaches that are considerably more complex and these will only be described briefly in this text.

The cost of equity

Equity comprises both the share capital and the retained profits invested in a business. Retained profits are often, mistakenly, considered to be a free source of finance. However, this is not the case, because there is an opportunity cost associated with using these funds. The calculations for the cost of equity should, therefore, reflect this fact. The cost of equity can be calculated in two ways. The first of these, the dividend growth model, provides the simplest approach to determining the cost of equity. The second approach, the capital asset pricing model (CAPM), is more complex and will only be considered briefly here. However, some of the issues surrounding the second approach are of importance and these merit further discussion.

The dividend growth model

This approach calculates the cost of equity from the annual dividend payment and the current market price of the share as quoted on the capital markets, this being the dividend yield ratio.

$$\text{Dividend yield per cent} = \frac{\text{Dividend}}{\text{Market price}}$$

This simple ratio only represents the cost of capital when the dividend remains the same for each following year and of course this is not always the case. In addition, the method faces difficulty with a dividend payout of zero.

The dividend growth model is an attempt to overcome this shortfall by building into the equation an estimate for future increases in dividend levels. The most common version is known as the Gordon's growth model, where:

$$\text{Cost of equity} = \frac{(d(1 + g) + g) \times 100}{M}$$

where d = the last dividend paid out, g = expected dividend growth rate in percentage terms where investors expect the dividend to grow at a constant rate into the future, and M = the market price of the share.

This formula is demonstrated with the following example.

Where a company pays a current dividend of 12p per share and the current market price of the share is 96p, if the anticipated growth rate is 4% the cost of equity (k_e) will be

$$k_e = \frac{(12(1 + 4\%) + 0.04) \times 100\%}{96}$$
$$= 16.5\%$$

This model provides a simple approach to finding the cost of capital, but the relationship should be used with care. In practice, it is difficult to establish a value for g, the growth rate, with any certainty. The model also assumes that g will be less than the cost of capital. This is proven by rearranging the formula to show the market price of the share, M:

$$M = \frac{D(1 + g)}{k_e - g}$$

If in the long run the growth rate is equal to the cost of capital, the formula solves to show the value of the company as infinite, which is clearly not practical.

The capital asset pricing model

This approach to estimating the cost of equity is based on the returns expected by the investor for buying the share. It assumes that the greater the risk, the greater the expected return. The level of risk is measured via a factor known as beta. This is combined with two other factors to determine the cost of equity. These are the risk-free rate and the market risk premium.

- **The risk-free rate of return** represents the most secure rate return that could be achieved and this is normally quoted as being the rate available from government stocks.
- **The market risk premium** represents the excess return above the risk-free rate that investors expect in order to compensate them for holding riskier investments.
- **Beta** is the measure of systematic risk, which is the riskiness implied by a business activity and the way in which it is financed.

Risk measured by beta is that part of the total risk that a business faces which cannot be diversified away because it is present in the general business environment and will affect all businesses in some form. The beta can be measured in a number of ways, but the most usual approach is to estimate it using standard regression techniques based on historical share prices. This is the approach adopted by the London Business School's Risk Measurement Service, which publishes beta values for industry use. The cost of equity is thus calculated with the following formula:

Cost of equity = Risk-free rate of return + (Beta × Market risk premium)

To apply this formula in practice requires knowing the beta factor for a particular business. Beta factors are published for companies, while estimates for the other two factors are freely available in the UK.

Example

A business financed 100% from equity has a beta of 0.8. The risk-free rate of interest is 4% and the expected rate of return on the market portfolio is 10%.

Cost of equity = Risk-free rate of return + (Beta × Market risk premium)
= 4% + 0.8 (10 − 4)
= 8.8%

This approach to calculating the cost of equity is also useful for unquoted companies where there is no available market price for the shares. In this case a beta factor for a similar company might be used to enable a cost of equity value to be calculated. The CAPM approach has generally become an acceptable approach to calculating the cost of capital. However, there are still some problems associated with this method. Evidence suggests that it is not always possible to summarize the market-related risk with a single indicator such as beta. The approach also assumes that the past is an accurate indicator of the future. This is not necessarily true in a changing economic environment. Despite these disadvantages CAPM remains a superior approach to the dividend growth model.

Cost of loan capital

A second element in the cost of capital calculation is the cost of borrowing. Loans can be classified into two types:

- **irredeemable**, where only interest is required
- **redeemable**, where both interest and capital repayments are required.

The true cost of loans can be calculated quite simply where the debt is irredeemable. In this case, the cost of debt is calculated using the following formula:

$$\text{Cost of debt} = \frac{\text{Interest}}{\text{Market value of the security}}$$

When the debt is redeemable or repayable in full the cost of capital is found by discounting the cash flows. The discount rate which equates the present value of the future cash flows to the current market value of the debt is the cost of capital for those borrowings. The following example illustrates this.

Example

Loan stock was originally issued at a par value of £100. The current market value is £93. The repayment of the original amount is due in 5 years' time and interest of 10% is due annually on the original amount. The cost of the loan stock is calculated by considering the cash flows over the next 5 years.

Year	Cash flow (£)	Discount factor	Present value (£)
0	(93)	1.000	(93)
1	10	0.909	9.09
2	10	0.826	8.26
3	10	0.751	7.51
4	10	0.683	6.83
5	110	0.621	68.31

At 10% discount factor a positive present value of £7 is achieved. If a discount factor of 12% is used the resulting NPV is almost zero and this, therefore, equates to the cost of debt. The drop in the value of the loan stock has occurred because the return of £10 or 10% must be below the market rate of interest. As a result, the perceived value of the stock fall belows the original value of £100.

Normally, businesses may have more than one source of debt finance. The overall cost of the debt can be calculated by taking a weighted average of the individual components.

Loan capital and tax relief

The interest payable on borrowings attracts corporation tax relief, so the true cost of loan capital should reflect the benefit derived from this. The true cost of the interest payment is calculated as follows:

$$\text{Cost} = i(1 - T)$$

where T is the corporation tax rate, and i is the interest rate.

Weighted average cost of capital (WACC)

Having calculated a cost of capital for each element of the capital structure the resulting cost of capital is calculated by combining these values as a weighted average, as shown in the following example.

Example

At present a company is funded by a combination of equity and debt capital. The equity shares were originally issued at £0.60 and have a current market price of £2.70. The current dividend is £0.10 per share and this has been growing at a rate of 5% per annum in recent years. The loan capital issued by the company is irredeemable and has a current market value of £95 against an original cost of £100. Interest is paid out at a rate of 12%. The company has 70% of its operations funded by equity, with the remainder funded by borrowings.

The WACC is calculated from the cost of the two sources of funds. The cost of equity is found using the dividend growth model:

$$\text{Cost of equity} = \frac{10p(1 + 0.05) + 5\%}{270p}$$
$$= 8.9\%$$

The cost of the borrowings is found as follows:

$$\text{Cost of debt} = \frac{12}{95p}$$
$$= 12.6\%$$

The weighted average cost is found from

$$(70\% \times 8.9\%) + (30\% \times 12.6\%) = 10.01\%$$

Effect of gearing on the cost of capital

A very large proportion of businesses have some level of gearing. It is important, therefore, to consider the relationship between gearing and cost of capital. The most common approach is known as the traditional view and is based on the assumption that as gearing increases the perceived risk increases and equity investors and lenders will require a higher return. It is suggested that at lower levels of gearing neither investor group requires greatly increased returns, and as loan sources tend to be cheaper than equity sources the WACC will decrease.

At higher levels of gearing risk becomes more important to investors and the WACC starts to increase significantly. As a result there is a point where the WACC is at a minimum and this is described as the optimum level of gearing. This effect is shown in Figure 12.1.

This approach was questioned in the 1950s by Miller and Modigliani (MM) who published what is now considered to be an extremely significant article questioning the basis of the traditionalists' view. MM argued that it is not possible for a business to borrow additional funds and by so doing reduce its weighted average cost of capital. Their view is that when additional cheap loan finance is introduced the WACC is not affected because there is a corresponding increase in the cost of equity. The effect is illustrated in Figure 12.2.

As a result, MM conclude that there is no optimum level of gearing. Since MM proposed their theories there has been much debate by academics on the issue of cost of capital and gearing. It has since been shown that some of the assumptions underlying the MM approach are incorrect, although there is some logic in the MM theory. As a result a compromise position is recommended, whereby WACC is likely to fall as gearing increases, but this trend will change when equity holders and lenders become increasingly conscious of risk.

Figure 12.1 Weighted average cost of capital (WACC): traditional view

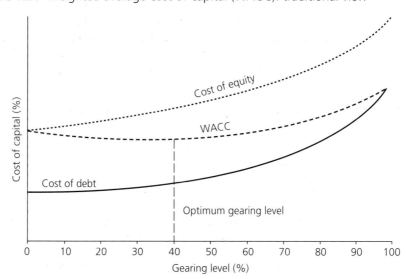

Figure 12.2 Cost of capital for varying levels of gearing: the MM (pretax) view

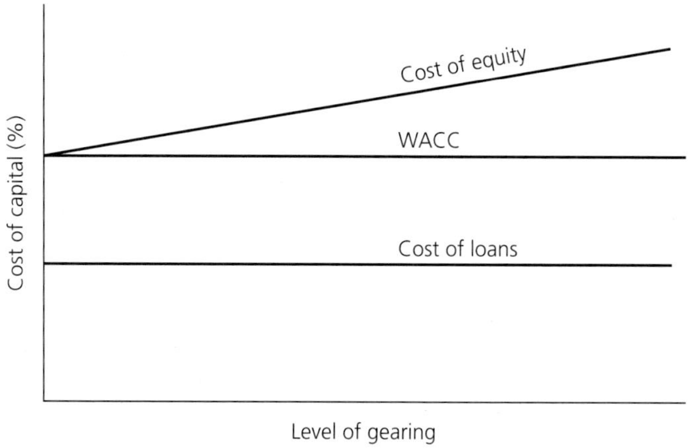

Summary The cost of capital is an important concept to be understood in all types of organization. All sources of funds have a cost of servicing associated with them in the form of either variable or fixed charges. Accurate determination of the cost of capital is vital as this figure represents the discount rate used in capital investment decisions. If a figure is calculated that is higher than the actual level this may result in profitable projects being rejected. Conversely, an estimate that is too low means that unprofitable projects will be accepted. There are different approaches to the calculation of the cost of capital value and each of these has its inherent difficulties. The level of gearing in a company is thought to affect the cost of capital of the component sources of finance based on the perception of risk. It is generally believed that increased gearing up to a certain level reduces WACC; however, Modgliani and Miller have proposed that gearing makes no difference to the cost of capital. The theories remain unproven and consequently the general consensus is that gearing does have some bearing on the resultant cost of capital.

Questions 1 Calculate the cost of equity in the following case:

(a) Share price is £2.70

(b) Past dividend growth is 5%

(c) EPS is £0.24

(d) Dividend cover is 4 times.

2 The directors of Venus Hotels plc are considering opening a new resort facility. The finance director has provided the following information:

Initial capital investment   £2,750,000

The following is an extract from the balance sheet of Venus Hotels plc for the year ended December 31 2004:

Creditors due in more than one year

10% debenture	£500,000
Long-term loan + variable rate	£900,000

Capital and reserves

3,000,000 shares at 25p each	£750,000

The authorized share capital is 5 million shares; the current market price per share at 31 December 2004 is 145p ex-dividend. The dividend growth factor (*g*) is estimated to be 8%. The current market price of debentures is £75 (ex-interest) and interest is payable each year on 31 December.

The interest rate on the long-term loan is 18%.

The debentures are non-redeemable. Ignore taxation.

You are required to:

(a) Calculate the average weighted cost of capital for Venus Hotels plc as at 31 December 2004.

(b) Comment on why it is important to calculate the cost of capital with care.

(c) Explain the distinction between business and financial risk.

3 Forest Caterers plc is a major hospitality company wishing to expand. Currently, the company has £500 million of long-term capital and proposes to raise a further £100 million to finance the expansion.

At present, 60% of Forest Caterers' finance comes from equity and the rest from loan stock. However, one of the directors feels that more loan stocks could be introduced as these are a cheaper form of finance than equity, and suggests introducing additional loan finance so that only 50% of funds are classified as equity after the additional finance has been raised.

However, a second director argues that the best way to finance the project would be to use retained profit as this represents a 'free' source of finance to the business. Currently, the shares, which have a nominal value of £0.50, are being traded at a market price of £1.25. The dividend at present is £0.05 per share and recently has been increasing at a compound rate of 10% per annum.

The average cost of the loan stock after taxation is 10%.

(a) Calculate the weighted average cost of capital for Forest Caterers plc for each of the scenarios described and comment on the remarks made by each of the directors.

(b) Calculate the amount of finance the directors wish to raise and comment on the business plan to increase the gearing of the business.

(c) Explain the term 'cost of capital' and discuss why a company should calculate its cost of capital with care.

Further reading

Pike, R. and Neale, B. (2003) *Corporate Finance and Investment: Decisions and Strategies*, London: Prentice Hall.

Useful websites

www.cimaglobal.com
www.cimasem.com
www.cimaglobal.com/main/resources/developments/enterprise/
www.valuebasedmanagement.net/
www.vbmresources.com
www.sternstewart.com/
www.shareholdervalue.com/indexIE.htm

References

Davies, R., Unni, S., Draper, P. and Pavdyal. K. (1999) *Cost of Equity Capital*, London: CIMA.

Miller, M. and Modigliani, F. (1958) The cost of capital, corporation finance and the theory of investment. *American Economic Review* 48(3): 261–97.

V Strategic implementation and evaluation

The speed of change in the hospitality industry during the past decade or more has proven that it is essential for hospitality and tourism businesses continually to monitor market trends and adapt internally to meet each new challenge.

Structural changes in the industry have led to the emergence of a range of international players with a geographically dispersed portfolio, often as a consequence of extensive merger and acquisition activity and the increasing influence of Pacific Rim developers. The traditional patterns of ownership have been replaced with a complex arrangement of franchising, management contracts, joint ventures and strategic alliances aimed at reducing the cost and risks associated with development.

Technological developments in systems, processing capability and connectivity will revolutionize marketing, management information systems and customer expectations. Pressures from the external environment will compel hospitality and tourism organizations to review their internal structures. Teare and Ingram (1993) forecasted over a decade ago that structural changes were likely to include:

- flatter organizational structures with fewer levels of management, improved responsiveness and information processing capability
- managers who co-ordinate expert operatives rather than control subordinates
- more decentralized operations which promote involvement through responsibility, participation

and commitment from a better educated workforce.

Evidence suggests that many of these forecasts are emerging in practice, with information technology providing the capability and opportunity for managers at all levels to operate with increased levels of data about their business and the competition. The provision of monthly reporting of business performance, for example, is now available in some hospitality businesses just 3 days after the month end, whereas this activity would have taken at least 2 weeks just a decade ago. As a consequence, managers in the hospitality, tourism and leisure industries are now required to play an active role in budgeting and forecasting performance and to use business data for decision making and evaluation of business performance.

In 1991 Olsen reported that structural change in the hospitality industry was starting to affect greatly the range of tasks that operational managers undertake:

... with head office staff reduced in number to the minimum possible and growth no longer the overriding strategy of most firms, unit managers are now being asked to perform differently. They are being asked to compete effectively on the local level, where conditions are extremely competitive, to scan the environment for threats and opportunities, and to build a strategic plan for their units based on this

type of analysis. This leaves the unit manager with the need to become a much more independent decision maker and one who is much more aware of the forces in the environment and how they affect the future of the unit (Olsen, 1991).

This final section of the book considers the impact of strategic decisions on the overall value of the business. Chapter 13 reviews the problems associated with valuing a business and focuses in particular on issues associated with the hospitality and tourism industries. Chapter 14 considers the implications of global expansion for business accounting and also for risk management, and Chapter 15 reviews some of the forecasts and predictions currently being proposed for the future of management accounting in the hospitality, tourism and leisure industries.

References

Olsen, M. D. (1991) Structural changes: the international hospitality industry and firm. *International Journal of Contemporary Hospitality Management* 3(4): 23.

Teare, R. and Ingram, H. (1993) *Strategic Management: A Resource-based Approach for the Hospitality and Tourism Industries*, London: Cassell.

13 | Measuring the value of a business

About this chapter

The principal aim of business activity is often stated as being to maximize shareholder value. Several factors drive the value of a business and in this chapter these factors will be considered with an evaluation of the alternative approaches for attempting to arrive at an estimate of business value. For businesses with a market listing, valuation is derived by calculating the market capitalization value, which is the current share price multiplied by the number of shares in issue. However, as was reported earlier, a large proportion of the sector is made up of private organizations. For these organizations in particular alternative approaches for determining business value are relevant.

Case study: QMH puts nine of its UK hotels up for sale (by Dominic Walsh)

Queens Moat Houses, which was acquired by Goldman Sach's Whitehall Street property arm last year, has put nine of its UK hotels up for sale for an estimated £100 million to £110 million, *The Times* has learnt.

The company, which is managed under the auspices of Texas-based Westmont Hospitality Group, has appointed Christie & Co., the property agent, to handle the disposal of the properties, which collectively have about 1,200 rooms.

The disposal would be the first significant move by Whitehall Street since it acquired QMH's 80 hotels in the UK, the Netherlands and Germany for £544 million at the end of last summer. It recently appointed Erwin Rieck, a former Ramada executive, as chief executive.

The nine hotels, which all carry the Moat House brand, are in Bedford, West Bromwich, Cardiff, Harlow, Dartford, Northampton, Nottingham, Telford and Watford. The biggest hotel, with 172 rooms, is the Nottingham Moat House.

Analysts expect the hotels to appeal to property investment firms with exposure to the hotel sector, including WJB Mondiale, REIT Asset Management and London & Regional Properties.

QMH was brought to the brink of collapse 12 years ago by an accounting scandal that was the subject of a Department of Trade and Industry inquiry. New management was brought in to turn around its fortunes, although the sale to Whitehall failed to cover its debt of about £670 million.

Separately, it is understood that a package of 31 mainly regional hotels managed by Thistle Hotels are being prepared for eventual sale with an estimated price tag of £400 million. The properties were part of a package of 37 hotels sold by Thistle three years ago for £600 million to Orb Estates, the property firm.

▶

◀
> In 2003 financial troubles resulted in a sale to Atlantic Hotels. In December continued problems prompted a fresh restructuring of the remaining 31 hotels, with Atlantic, Thistle and Morgan Stanley each taking a third of the equity.
>
> Source: *The Times*, 29 April 2005.

Learning objectives On completion of this chapter you should be able to:

- understand the factors that drive business value
- use a range of methods to determine an estimate of business value
- appreciate the difficulties experienced by the hospitality, tourism and leisure industries when attempting to estimate the value of a business

Introduction

The principal aim for measuring the value of a business is to provide a monetary measure that accurately reflects the true worth of that business. In general terms research has indicated that a number of factors determine business value and these include:

- rate of revenue growth
- investment in fixed assets and working capital
- perceived value of intellectual capital
- brand value
- profit margins, achieved and predicted
- tax rate on profits
- forecast future cash flows.

The issue of business valuations and the choice of appropriate methodology is somewhat controversial in accounting circles and the UK hospitality industry has been particularly troubled in this area. In the early 1990s, for example, it was reported that the value of London hotels fell by up to 22% for three-star operations, 19% for four-star and 13% for five-star properties. One company to be devastated by the impact of revaluation was Queens Moat Houses plc.

Case study: QMH case

The Queens Moat House group of hotels was founded in 1968 when John Bairstow, formerly the founder of the company Bairstow Eve, which he later sold to Hambros Bank for £77 m, bought a Moat House in Essex and opened it as a hotel. There followed over the next 20 years a programme of rapid expansion both in the UK and abroad, financed by high levels of debt and several rights issues.

In 1982 26 hotels were purchased from GrandMet and by 1983 the group was confirmed as being UK's largest provincial hotel chain. By 1987, following four rights issues in as many years, the group had purchased 24 hotels in Europe plus the Dutch Bilderberg Hotels. In 1991 a further 15 hotels were purchased following the eighth rights issue.

The group continued to appear to be trading as a healthy concern right up to January 1993, when distinguished brokers such as Robert Fleming Securities were still urging investors to buy shares in the company with the encouragement that 'the rating on the (Queens Moat) shares is still absurdly low'.

By 31 March 1993 shares were suspended from trading at a price of 47.5 p. This followed the announcement of the 1992 year-end trading results with a pretax loss of £1.04 billion, the second largest loss in UK corporate history.

Much of this loss is attributed to the write-down of property values, and considerable controversy has surrounded the size and background to this write-down. In December 1991 (QMH year end) the valuers Wetherall, Green and Smith (WGS) valued the assets at £2 billion. A year later the assets were revalued at £1.35 billion, while a second valuer, Jones, Lang Wootten (JLW), valued the same assets at December 1992 as being worth £861 million. Both valuations were prepared on an open market, willing seller basis, following guidelines laid down by the Royal Institution of Chartered Surveyors (RICS). QMH directors chose to accept the lower valuation; hence the write-down of almost £1.2 billion on the group's hotels portfolio.

There are many valuation techniques available and often the most appropriate method will depend on the subsequent use of the valuation. These potential uses include providing a balance-sheet figure for accounts preparation purposes as well as setting a value for acquisition purposes, for insurance assessment, for investment monitoring purposes such as return on capital employed measures, and also possibly to provide a figure to banks as the basis of collateral valuations when raising a loan. The most appropriate method depends not only on the end purpose of the value but also on the size and type of business. This chapter will consider the application of a variety of approaches to business valuation, namely:

- dividend yield basis
- price/earnings basis
- net assets basis
- comparable transactions
- earnings multiple
- replacement value
- net present value using discounted cash flows.

Finally, the issue of hotel valuations will be considered in light of the recommendations offered by the British Association of Hospitality Accountants (BAHA).

Measuring security value

The larger sized business, which has shares trading on an apparently efficient stockmarket, can be evaluated by simply multiplying the shares in issue by the current share price. This provides an estimate for the value of the entire company and the figure is known as market capitalization. However, in many cases such an approach is not possible because the company does not have public shares trading and hence no current market price per share is available. In other cases it is not the total value of the company that is sought, but instead a value is required for a particular asset or group of similar assets. In these cases other approaches are required.

Dividend yield basis

This approach to valuation is based on the principle of estimating the value of the total equity within a business and uses the dividend yield ratio introduced in Chapter 8 as its basis. The methodology assumes that the ordinary shares of two different businesses should have a similar dividend yield ratio provided that they are similar in size, activity, capital gearing and proportion of profit paid in dividend. If the shares of one of these businesses is quoted then this will enable the price to be set for the unquoted business. The value of the business in question can then be found by applying the following ratio:

$$\text{Gross dividend yield} = \frac{\text{Dividend paid}}{\text{Current market price per share}}$$

where

$$\text{Current market price} = \frac{\text{Dividend paid}}{\text{Gross dividend yield}}$$

The following example demonstrates the method in practice.

Example

Z Ltd is a small business which at the end of the last financial year paid out a dividend of £120,000 gross. The dividend yield value for a similar listed business is 8% gross. Using this, a market price for the business can be estimated.

$$\text{Estimated market price} = \frac{120,000}{8\%}$$

$$= £1,500,000$$

There are inherent difficulties in using this approach in practice. It may be difficult if not impossible to find a similar business for comparison purposes and even if this were possible the approach assumes that the dividend paid always reflects the level of the market price for the share, which may not be valid.

Price/earnings basis

This approach is based on the ratio between current market share price and the earnings of the business. The ratio is as follows:

$$\text{P/E} = \frac{\text{Current market price per share}}{\text{Post-tax earnings per share}}$$

where

$$\text{Current market price} = \text{P/E} \times \text{earnings per share}$$

The method assumes that the P/E ratio will be the same for similar firms and therefore can be applied to calculate a share price that can be used to estimate a value for market capitalization. The following example demonstrates the method in practice.

Example

A plc and B Ltd are two businesses of similar size, activity and capital structure. A is quoted on the stock exchange, whereas B is not. The P/E ratio for A is 10 and the annual earnings after tax for B have been a static £0.40 per share. B has 1 million shares in issue. Using the formula, then,

$$10 = \frac{\text{Current market price per share}}{£0.40}$$

The market capitalization of the business is estimated to be £4 million.

The choice of P/E ratio to be used is often dependent on one or more of the following factors:

- economic conditions
- type of industry

- size of operation
- marketability of shares
- reliability of forecasted profits
- levels of gearing.

As a result, it can be difficult to establish an appropriate value to use and it is not uncommon for a specific sector to have a wide range of values.

Net assets basis

This approach is based on the book value of the assets as stated in the balance sheet and the valuation is based on the net assets less outstanding long-term loans.

The approaches described so far are fairly theoretical and do not provide the solution to finding the value to specific assets. The following section will consider this particular problem.

The practice of valuing assets

The Companies Act allows UK companies to adopt accounting policies other than purely historical cost accounting when preparing their financial statements. As a result, tangible fixed assets, such as property, may be stated either at market value on the date they were last valued or at current cost. Where market values are used the valuations should be kept up to date, but the difficulty occurs in establishing what this market value should actually be. An accounting policy peculiar to the UK until the introduction of FRS 15 was that properties such as hotels need not be depreciated on an annual basis as it was assumed that with sufficient ongoing maintenance expenditure they would at least hold their value. However, it is estimated that approximately 10–15% of total revenues should be spent on maintenance activities for this assumption to hold true.

FRS 15 has given specific rules for the revaluation policy. Previously, it was possible for a business to choose which assets were to be revalued (usually those that had increased in value) and which assets were to be ignored (often those that had decreased in value). The new standard dictates that once a revaluation policy has been selected, it must be adhered to with all assets in the class. It also describes how the revaluations should be performed. In the event of a fall in the value of the asset, previously such an occurrence was termed a 'diminution in value'. This was classified as either 'permanent' and impacted on the profit and loss account, or 'temporary' and was dealt with through the revaluation reserve in the balance sheet, bypassing the profit and loss account.

Establishing a true value for the assets of a business is required for a variety of purposes. In general, the shareholders and investors expect to see the assets stated at current value so that profit performance can be assessed in relation to the capital investment via the return on capital employed ratio. The shareholder will also want to make comparisons with the performance of other companies in the sector and with companies in other industries, and it is therefore essential that the bases used for valuation are realistic and adequately disclosed.

The responsibility for ensuring that the valuation of assets has been correctly stated is solely that of directors of the company, specifically the finance director, and this is monitored by the auditors of the company, whose job it is to ensure that the prepared financial statements give a true and fair view. On a practical level, within the accounting system the various fixed asset accounts identified should be backed by detail of the physical holdings of assets. For all assets there should be a separately maintained plant register to show:

- the organization's internal reference number
- the manufacturer's serial number
- description of the asset
- location of the asset
- the department that 'owns' the asset
- purchase date
- cost
- depreciation method and estimated useful life
- net book value.

Normally the fixed asset register is not integrated with the nominal ledger; it is not part of the double entry, but is there instead for memorandum and control purposes. Consequently, the fixed asset register needs to be reconciled to the nominal ledger to make sure that all additions, disposals and depreciation provisions and charges have been posted. It is also essential that the company inspects all the items in the fixed asset register and keeps it up to date.

In the past, UK hotel companies tended to revalue one-third of their properties each year, ensuring that all assets were revalued at least every 3 years. However, FRS 15 requires hotel companies to ensure that:

- Consistent principles are applied to the initial measurement of all tangible fixed assets.
- Where an entity chooses to revalue tangible fixed assets, the valuation is performed on a consistent basis and kept up to date, and gains and losses on revaluation are recognized on a consistent basis.
- Depreciation of tangible fixed assets is calculated in a consistent manner and recognized as the economic benefits are consumed over the assets' useful economic lives.
- Sufficient information is disclosed in the financial statements to enable users to understand the impact of the entity's accounting policies regarding initial measurement, valuation and depreciation of tangible fixed assets on the financial position and performance of the entity.

The Ladbroke case

In 1993, Ladbroke, owner of Hilton International, undertook to reduce the book value of its assets by £195.6 million. The loss was deducted from the revaluation reserve in the balance sheet, creating a £146.7 million loss in the profit and loss account.

In the UK, guidelines for revaluation are provided by RICS. BAHA has also produced guidelines for recommended practice for the valuation of hotels, published in 1993, and recommends working with RICS to establish a common approach.

The following methods offer a more practical approach to the problem, with the final approach, that of discounted cash flows, being the approach recommended by the BAHA guidelines.

Comparable transactions

This approach is based on the market value for the business if it is sold for its existing use. An existing hotel operation, for example, might typically include the land and buildings, and items such as fixtures, furniture, equipment, computers, stock, goodwill and brand value. All of these assets are classified as being tangible, excluding goodwill and brand value, which are intangible assets and can be identified as being derived from the location, the operational strengths of the site, the personal flair of the existing management team and the value of the brand name. An estimate for all of these should be included in the valuation, although in practice this can be difficult to achieve. The total value of the site can be set by simply considering similar and comparable transactions where competitive operations have already been sold for what is considered to be a fair value using a measure such as the price per room achieved. It may be necessary to increase or decrease the measure used depending on how the strengths of the operation compare with the competitive operation.

This approach is often more practical for the smaller operation, where there may be many similar businesses on which to make a comparison. However, for the larger, possibly more individual, operation in a unique position it may simply not be possible to determine the value by considering similar transactions. In this case it may be necessary to use an alternative approach.

Earnings multiple

This approach is based on simply applying a multiple to maintainable earnings, which are defined as the adjusted net cash flows in present value terms that can be sustained over an extended period. The resultant estimate of stabilized earnings will be capitalized at the appropriate multiplier, reflecting all appropriate considerations. While the maintainable earnings can be estimated fairly easily, the determination of the multiplier must reflect the perceived risk or security associated with the investment.

Net present value

The value of an asset or a business in total can be estimated by predicting the future cash flows and then discounting these with an appropriate cost of capital. The particular elements that need to be considered in the valuation process are:

- sales growth rate and operating profit margins
- the timings associated with the projected earnings
- the working capital requirements
- the hotel's residual capital value
- the magnitude of recurring levels of maintenance, capital expenditure and any additional investment required
- the cost of capital.

Theoretically, this approach is the soundest in that it takes into account the timing and value of future earnings. However, it is dependent on an accurate forecast for the future cash flows and the correct estimation of the appropriate discount rate.

The following is an example to demonstrate the methods in practice.

Example

Your colleague is considering purchasing a chain of 21 public houses, the summarized accounts of which appear below.

Balance Sheet at 31 December

	2004		2005	
	(£m)	(£m)	(£m)	(£m)
Fixed assets (net of depreciation)		8.0		8.5
Current assets				
Stocks	3.3		5.6	
Debtors	0.5		0.8	
Bank balances	0.3		0.1	
		4.1		6.5
		12.1		15.0
Current liabilities (amounts falling due within 1 year)				
Creditors	3.8		3.3	
Bank overdraft	0.3		1.5	
Dividends	0.7		0.9	
Taxation	0.7		1.0	
		5.5		6.7

Total assets less current liabilities	6.6	8.3

Long-term liabilities (amounts falling due after more than 1 year)

Long-term loan at 10% p.a.	1.4	1.4
	5.2	6.9

Financed by

Called up share capital		
4 million ordinary shares at £1	4.0	4.0
Share premium	0.2	0.2
Reserves	1.0	2.7
	5.2	6.9

The financial record for the business for the last 2 years is summarized below.

Profit and loss account, year ended 31 December

	2004 (£m)	2005 (£m)
Revenue	15.40	17.50
Profit before interest	2.34	3.74
Profit before taxation	2.20	3.60
Taxation on profit	0.70	1.00
Profit after taxation	1.50	2.60
Dividends	0.70	0.90
Retained profit	0.80	1.70

Industry analysts advise that quoted companies in similar industries have an average P/E ratio of 5, a dividend yield of 15% and a cost of capital of 12%.

You estimate the net cash flows to be achieved following the purchase to be:

Year 1–5	£800,000 per year
Year 6	£1,200,000 per year

A value for the business can be calculated using a range of approaches.

The dividend yield valuation can be worked out as follows:

$$\text{Market price} = \frac{0.9}{15\%}$$

$$= \text{£6 million}$$

The price/earnings valuation is as follows:

$$2.6 \times 5 = \text{£13 million}$$

The net assets as quoted at book value amount to:

$$£8.3 \text{ million} - £1.4 \text{ million} = £6.9 \text{ million}$$

allowing for repayment of the long-term loan.
The calculation for NPV is as follows:

Year	Cash flows (£000)	Discount factor	NPV (£000)
1	800	0.893	714.4
2	800	0.797	637.6
3	800	0.712	569.6
4	800	0.636	508.8
5	800	0.567	453.6
6	1,200	0.507	608.4
			3,492.4

The purchase price is approximately £3.5 million.

Intangible value

It is now widely recognized that for many successful enterprises there is no correlation between the value of the net assets figure shown in the balance sheet and the market capitalization of the business. In the business world today there is a growing number of operations whose market value is heavily underpinned by a range of intangible assets, including:

- intellectual capital: the value of the knowledge held by the staff and management teams within the business
- brand value: the value of the recognized brand values communicating expected levels of quality and style of service
- goodwill: arising from the location of the business, forward bookings and reputation.

The value of these intangibles can be defined as the difference between net book value of assets and the market capitalization of the business.

To summarize, Knight (1999) believes that four factors combine in an organization to increase market value. These are:

- human capital: this manifests itself as the expertise and skills of people

- structural capital: consisting of the organization's strategies, internal networks, systems, databases and legal rights to inventions, processes, brands and trademarks
- external capital: defined by the organization's external relationships with customers, suppliers, strategic partners and levels of competitor intelligence
- financial performance: involving the level of profitability and growth that an organization achieves.

Summary Considerable difficulties face the hospitality industry in setting asset values. This is particularly true in an economic environment where asset values are more likely to go down than up. Case histories indicate that the current methods are far from satisfactory and in response to this the British Association of Hospitality Accountants has gone so far as to offer guidance as to the most satisfactory approach based on discounted cash flows. Academically, this approach is superior because it is based on forecast cash flows and a discount rate that should be calculated using the cost of capital, anticipated risk and predicted inflation.

Questions 1 You are considering the purchase of a chain of restaurants, the summarized accounts of which appear below:

Balance sheet as at 31 December 2005

	£000
Fixed assets	
Cost	16,000
Accumulated depreciation	3,000
Net book value	13,000
Current assets	
Stock	4,000
Debtors	5,500
Cash	500
	10,000
Less creditors: amounts falling due within 1 year	
Trade creditors and taxation	4,500
Bank overdrafts	7,800
Dividends payable	900
	13,200

Total assets, less current liabilities	9,800
Less: Long-term loans	5,000
	4,800

Capital and reserves	
6 million ordinary shares of 50 p	3,000
Reserves	1,800
	4,800

Profit and loss account as at 31 December 2005

	£000
Turnover	38,000
Profit before interest and taxation	3,400
Interest payable	2,300
Profit before taxation	1,100
Taxation	275
Profit after taxation	825
Dividends (net)	400
Retained profit	425

Additional information

- Similar companies have a price/earnings ratio of 15.
- Forecast cash flows for the first 5 years of trading are estimated to be £900,000 per year. An appropriate discount rate will be 12%.

(a) Estimate the value of the business using:

    (i) assets valuation

    (ii) price/earnings ratio

    (iii) forecast cash flows.

(b) Comment on the merits of each valuation technique.

2   Research the latest annual report and accounts for a company operating in the hospitality, tourism and leisure industry. (Most large companies post their accounts to their website, where you can freely download the information.) Using the published profit and loss account and balance sheet:

(a) Review the proportion of fixed assets to current assets.

(b) Review the proportion of tangible fixed assets to intangible fixed assets. Use the notes to the accounts to determine what the intangible assets represent.

(c) What are the components of the current assets?

(d) Can you find any notes on the company asset revaluation policy?

Research the financial press to find the share price and the market capitalization of your chosen business. Do you think the share price is overvalued or undervalued?

Further reading

British Association of Hospitality Accountants. *Guidance Notes for the Hotel Industry on Tangible Fixed Assets*, BAHA (www.baha-uk.org)

Copeland, T. *et al.* (2000) *Valuation: Measuring and Managing the Value of Companies*, New York: John Wiley.

Useful websites

www.baha-uk.org/summary.asp   These guidance notes have been prepared in response to FRS 15

www.hvsinternational.com/staticcontent/library/NYU2005/journal6-05.htm

References

British Association of Hospitality Accountants. *Recommended Practice for the Valuation of Hotels*, BAHA (www.baha-uk.org)

Knight, D. (1999) Performance measures for increasing intellectual capital, *Strategy and Leadership* 27(2).

14 | The globalization and internationalization issues

About this chapter

This chapter considers some of the issues impacting on businesses that choose to expand their operations in overseas markets. According to Knabe *et al.* (2000) of Dresdner Kleinwort Benson Research, the hospitality and tourism industries are some of the fastest growing industries in terms of international growth. Several are driving the growth of the industry, including growth in hotel demand and brand penetration. This chapter will consider some of the financial aspects of the following:

- the nature of international involvement
- forms of international development
- accounting issues facing multinationals
- risk assessment.

Learning objectives On completion of this chapter you should be able to:

- appreciate the factors that drive international expansion
- appreciate the accounting issues that impact on businesses operating in more than one country
- understand some of the tools and models used for assessing risk.

Introduction

A feature of the past two decades or more in hospitality and tourism industries has been the rapid acceleration in overseas expansion demonstrated by firms on a worldwide basis. Early examples in the growth of multinationals, that is firms operating in more than one country, were initially confined to US-based companies who expanded their operations into Europe through acquisition and a range of other non-acquisition approaches such as franchising and management contracts.

Analysts' reports suggest that Europe still has a key role in the expansion strategies of international hospitality groups because the region accounts for eight of the world's top 12 international tourist destinations and it represents approximately 60% of all international arrivals in the world. However, global expansion strategies now dominate the growth patterns for more and more companies from around the world. This has been clearly demonstrated by the continued growth of US firms in Europe, while recently more and more Asian and European companies have established subsidiaries internationally and have even successfully penetrated the highly competitive US markets. Leading analysts project that the hospitality and tourism industries will continue to be a key sector for developing international expansion. The purpose of this chapter is to consider some of the issues facing the organizations that have chosen to pursue strategies of expansion overseas.

According to a recent editorial report in *Strategic Direction* (2004), commenting on the growth of Bass in European markets, any company taking the decision to expand into foreign markets must consider the following:

- differences between the markets at home and abroad
- the level of political and economical risk involved
- policies of local governments with regard to foreign investors
- the business culture of the target market
- any significant financial issues/practices in the host country
- size of the market and potential for growth
- the possible need to broaden outlook and adapt or change strategies, where necessary.

According to Dunning (1981), the extent, pattern and growth of value-added activities undertaken by multinational organizations outside their national boundaries are dependent on the value of and interaction between three main variables: ownership-specific advantages of multinational organizations, location-specific advantages of countries, and market internalization or co-ordinating advantages. This theory has been used by many researchers in the hospitality and tourism industries to explain the motives for overseas expansion.

The nature of international involvement

In general, business wishes to expand overseas to increase sales by penetrating new markets and to improve shareholder returns. For manufacturing companies, expansion may mean gaining access to raw materials and other factors of production that may not be available in the home country or are available overseas for considerably less cost. This pursuit of resources may also extend to gaining access to up-to-date knowledge and new technology. The prime reason for the growth of hospitality and tourism businesses overseas seems to be derived as a response to the extent of the local competition, although additional incentives exist when the demand from overseas markets allows a larger unit profit margin to be made, while at the same time increasing the worldwide presence of the group. This is true for McDonalds, the world's largest restaurant chain, which has witnessed a decline in its American trade while international operations have continued to thrive and expand, with profitability in Europe being quoted as higher than in comparable operations in the USA. In those locations of the world where operations are very much at the growth stage of the product life cycle, a premium selling price can ensure that profitability is maintained despite local resource servicing issues.

The United Nations Centre on Transnational Corporations (UNCTC) produced a general study to investigate the trends in foreign investment that occurred in the 1980s in comparison to those of the 1970s. A significant increase in foreign direct investment was identified as having taken place in the mid-1980s and in the following period. The reasons for this surge in growth were identified in the study as being:

- strong economic growth rates in developed and developing countries
- the improved economic performance of several developing countries
- the emergence of several newly industrializing economies
- the growth in cross-border mergers and acquisitions (particularly in the European Community)
- the increasing importance of the service sector.

In general, the five major investor companies during the 1980s were identified as being France, Germany, Japan, the USA and the UK, with the host countries including Europe, the USA, Japan and a range of developing countries in South America, Asia and the Pacific Rim. This trend has continued into the late 1990s and beyond with brand names such as Hilton, InterContinental and Méridien familiar in major destinations throughout the world.

Forms of international involvement

The expansion of hospitality operations overseas requires a greater commitment than, say, for manufacturing businesses, where the approach to international involvement is often characterized by the simple importing and exporting of goods and services. For hospitality and tourism businesses a tangible presence is required in the importing country. This may take the form of a management contract where the exporting hospitality operation receives a fee in return for managing a facility owned by local investors. Alternatively, a concept or a production process may be licensed to an overseas location and the owner receives a royalty in return for the use of this intangible asset. This agreement may be formalized in the form of a franchise contract where the franchisor allows the franchisee to use the name and expertise of the franchisor to sell a certain product. The agreement may extend to bulk purchasing and central administration arrangements. Finally, a firm may become involved in direct investment in an overseas operation that may take the form of an acquisition of existing operations, a joint investment with an overseas partner or the development of new 'greenfield' investment.

The trend in recent years has been to build and operate larger properties that require larger investments. As a result, ownership and management are often separated and while owners continue to provide the investment, the management of the operation may be approached in a variety ways. Hotel companies such as Four Seasons, Hyatt Corporation, Ladbroke, Marriott Hotels and Resorts and Saison rely primarily on management contracts for their expansion, whereas others such as Accor and Choice Hotels rely on franchising. Alternatively, a combination of approaches may be appropriate, as demonstrated by the Sheraton Corporation, which has a mixed portfolio of both management contracts and franchise-operated properties. Expansion through a non-investment approach offers a range of advantages to the operator, including:

- economies of scale
- international image and presence
- utilization of common marketing programmes
- common staff training
- bulk purchasing contracts.

Direct investment in the form of complete ownership or equity participation tends to be limited to developed economies where the risk is perceived to be less than for the developing countries. Service-driven operations such as those typified by the hospitality industry face certain issues when pursuing a strategy of global development. These include decisions about the product itself, whether to offer a highly internationally standardized product or whether to recognize local differentiation, as well as management and control issues. International operations may require a different organizational structure to co-ordinate operations globally with reliable networks and systems. One of the key issues in managing international operations is deciding what types of decisions should be made at the corporate level and what responsibility should be retained at the local level.

Accounting issues facing multinational enterprises

A range of issues needs to be considered when a firm decides to pursue a strategy of expansion through investment overseas. These include:

- financing of overseas subsidiaries
- foreign financial statement analysis
- national differences in accounting principles
- management and translation of foreign currency
- management control of global operations
- performance evaluation systems
- the development of effective performance evaluation
- international taxation issues.

Each of these aspects will now be considered in more detail.

Financing overseas subsidiaries

The decision to finance an investment overseas involves considerable research for the feasibility study, including considering the nature and size of the initial investment, as well as decisions regarding the policies for the reinvestment of retained profits and the local management of debt and working capital. Many international hospitality and tourism organizations deploy international development directors whose responsibility it is to investigate new development opportunities.

The method of financing the development will be reliant on the size of the investment and the location. A sizeable equity investment or long-term loan would indicate a long-term commitment on the behalf of the parent company, whereas funding from debt capital and short-term credit would indicate a short-term policy. A multinational company has the same sources of finance available as the 'domestic' company, as described in Chapter 9. However, it is also possible to make use of sources of finance derived from foreign sources.

Eurocurrency loans are short- or medium-term loans raised in a foreign currency, and the term 'Eurocurrency markets' refers to financial centres such as London where the funds are available. 'Eurobonds' are short- or long-term loans raised from domestic and foreign investors and are similar in nature to debentures. The advantages of borrowing in a foreign currency to finance overseas operations in the same currency are that the assets and liabilities in the same currency can be matched, thereby avoiding exchange losses on conversion in the group's annual accounts, and the revenues in the foreign currency can be used to repay borrowings in the same currency, thus eliminating the problem of losses due to variable foreign exchange rates. There is a range of factors to consider when appraising overseas investments, which include:

- The method and ease for obtaining the return from the overseas operation: a combination of methods such as dividends, interest and management fees may be preferable in case restrictions are placed on dividend payments by the country's government.
- The level of political interference in overseas operations in the form of employee legislation, local taxes, etc., may serve to reduce the profitability of the investment and should be anticipated in the forecasting process.

Taxation and accounting differences may also significantly affect the resulting profit and these should also be considered to ensure that local accounting requirements are met and that these do not serve to undermine the measurement of operational performance. Increasingly, global companies are using alternative approaches for achieving an overseas presence, including franchising and management contracts. These approaches to expansion strategies are discussed in more detail in Chapter 9.

Foreign financial statement analysis

The ability to analyse international statements is the key to successful investment overseas for investors wishing to purchase the whole company or a share in existing companies. To undertake such an analysis, potential investors need to have access to data, but the extent and the availability of data vary from country to country. The timelags between the year end and regulatory publication of the auditor's report vary considerably, as shown in Table 14.1, and it may be even longer before the information is translated for foreign audiences.

Information barriers commonly associated with foreign financial statement analysis include language and terminology; although many countries now offer English language translations of all or a portion of the accounts as a norm, differences in terminology may be more difficult to overcome. However, it is possible to use published accounting lexicons to translate titles and key headings. Differences in statement format can also prove to be awkward when attempting to interpret foreign statements but, although different layouts may be used for say the balance sheet, the double-entry book-keeping system is the same, ensuring that the underlying structure of statements is similar. The extent of disclosure varies considerably, with companies in countries such as the USA and the UK being required to produce far greater detail than is required in many other areas. Differences in accounting principles exist from country to country despite attempts to harmonize accounting practice. Fortunately, there are many published information sources that provide insights into a country's accounting practices.

Table 14.1 Timelags between the year end and regulatory publication of the auditor's report

Number of days	Countries
31–60	Brazil Canada USA
61–90	Australia Denmark Finland Netherlands Norway Sweden
91–120	Belgium France West Germany India Malaysia South Africa Switzerland UK
121 and over	Austria Italy

Experience and research has indicated that business is conducted differently from one country to another and these differences arise from economic, educational, sociocultural, legal and political factors. The environmental influences on accounting practice in particular arise from a variety of factors, and these include:

- the nature of enterprise ownership
- the enterprise business activities
- the sources of finance and nature of capital markets
- the taxation system
- the sophistication of the accounting bodies and professions
- the nature of the political systems and social climate
- the rate of inflation
- the legal system and the nature of accounting regulation.

National differences in accounting principles

There is a significant number of major areas of difference in accounting principles from country to country and this can seriously impact on reported earnings and financial position. For example, research has indicated that UK earnings calculated in accordance with UK accounting principles could be up to 25% higher than earnings calculated under US accounting principles. Although US accounting policies are significantly more conservative than in the UK, they are significantly less conservative than those in other areas in Europe and in Japan. The cultural influences in a country will also influence how the financial performance is actually evaluated, with the UK and US focusing on stockmarket measures such as earning per share and dividend yield, while Europe and Japan focus on the reduction of taxation payments and meeting the needs of creditors and loan finance providers, rather than maximizing return to the shareholder. The principal differences in the increased flexibility of the UK accounting system in comparison to the more conservative US approach are summarized in Table 14.2.

Simmonds and Azieres carried out a simulation exercise using the simplified accounts of a multinational company to establish the effect of the differences in accounting policy on stated earnings by making a comparative analysis of the impact of accounting measurement differences on a range of European countries, as illustrated in Table 14.3. The overall results indicate that the highest, most likely profit and return on assets occurs in the case of the UK, whereas Spain comes out as the lowest.

The Japanese experience

Cultural differences in Japan ensure that, despite an increasing internationalization of accounting practice, the interpretation of performance and the accounting procedure in preparing the statements differ from other key areas in the world such as the UK, Europe and the USA. In Japan, for example, higher levels of gearing and short-term creditors are acceptable because of longer term and improved relationships with banks and suppliers. A longer term view of profitability is taken and emphasis is placed instead on sales growth and market share. Japanese accounts often demonstrate low interest coverage ratios, low current ratios, longer debt collection periods and examples of short-term debt to finance long-term investments.

Table 14.2 Principal differences in the increased flexibility of the UK accounting system in comparison to the more conservative US approach

	US more conservative	UK more conservative
Asset valuations	X	
Business combinations	X	
Consolidated financial statements	X	
Accounting for goodwill	X	
Foreign currency translation	X	
Inventory valuation	X	
Investment properties	X	
Capitalization of interest costs		X
Research and development expenditure	X	
Intangible assets including brands	X	
Taxation accounting	X	

Table 14.3 Comparative analysis of the impact of accounting measurement differences on a range of European countries

	Net profit	Net assets	Return (%)
	(millions of European currency units)		
Belgium	135	726	18.6
Germany	133	649	20.5
Spain	131	722	18.2
France	149	710	21.0
Italy	174	751	23.2
Netherlands	140	704	19.9
UK	192	712	27.0

Source: Simmonds and Azieres (1989) *Accounting for Europe: Success by 2000 AD?*, p. 42.

Foreign currency management

A multinational company with overseas operations, each maintaining its own accounts in the local currency, will need to convert the accounts to the holding company currency to allow for the group accounts to be consolidated at the end of each accounting year. The effect of translating the assets and liabilities into the holding company's local currency may give rise to a gain or loss. The risk of heavy losses being incurred from this process can be minimized by matching foreign currency assets with foreign currency liabilities. The *Financial Times* provides information about the exchange rates for sterling against other currencies, the exchange rate being defined as the amount of one currency that must be given to acquire one unit of another currency. The rates quoted are the 'spread', that is the highest and lowest rates from the previous day, and the closing value at the end of the previous day's trading. The 'spot rate' is the rate quoted for current currency transactions up to 2 days later and represents the current exchange rate.

Exchange rates can also impact on the repatriation of cash to the investing company. Pike and Neale (2003) suggest that possible ways of minimizing this impact include:

- paying royalty or licence fees to the parent company
- utilizing transfer pricing policies, which involve charging overseas units high prices for products and services provided
- applying a management charge for services provided from central office.

Translation of foreign currency statements

The translation of foreign statements involves two key issues, the exchange rate to be used for the actual conversion and the treatment of the subsequent gains and losses arising from the translation. In the process of translation all foreign currency balance-sheet and trading statements need to be restated in terms of the reporting currency by multiplying the foreign currency amount by an appropriate exchange rate factor. There are essentially two recognized techniques for setting the exchange rate, although variations on these methods exist around the world. The first is the closing rate (or current rate) method, where the amounts in the balance sheet and profit and loss account are translated into the reporting currency of the investing company using the rate of exchange ruling at the balance sheet date. The advantages of this method are that the business does not need to refer back to historical rates and, perhaps more significantly, the relationships between the values, such as return on net assets, remain the same as in the original accounts.

Alternatively, the temporal method dictates that each transaction should be translated into the company's local currency using the exchange rate in operation on the date that the transaction occurred, although if the rates do not fluctuate significantly an average rate may be used. Current assets and liabilities may be translated at the current rate, while fixed assets can be translated at the rate at the time when they were purchased. The temporal method is more suited to the operation whose affairs are very closely linked to the investing company and whose trading environment is heavily dependent on that of the investing company. Details regarding these methods are contained in SSAP 20, 'Foreign Currency

Translation'. The arising gains and losses accrued as a result of translation should be shown in the profit and loss account and in the reserves.

Management control of global operations

The challenge facing an expanding organization is how to control and manage that operation effectively as the parts become more and more widely dispersed. It may be appropriate to pursue a 'multidomestic' strategy, where the individual parts of the organization operate relatively independently of each other. Alternatively, it may be more suitable to pursue a global strategy, where there is a significantly greater degree of co-ordination. The process of control will depend on the extent of both formal and informal mechanisms present in the organization. Formal structural mechanisms include:

- the nature of the groupings of the activities of the organization
- the extent of centralization or decentralization of activities
- the formalization of procedures and standards
- the extent of strategic planning and operational budgeting.

Informal and subtle methods include the extent of meetings and communications encouraged across the formal boundaries and the nature of the organizational culture. The nature of the management information system will obviously change as the organization expands and the successful development of a good information system will ensure that strategic decisions are made based on high-quality information. The information needs of a multinational organization are similar to those of a domestic operation in that data need to be assembled and presented as information to a variety of users. The additional burden is that the multinational organization needs to analyse the financial position of each operation in terms of its geographical position, where there may be different internal and external factors influencing the nature of trading. Generally speaking, however, the finance and accounting functions in a multinational organization tend to be more centralized than other functions such as personnel or marketing, to achieve a means of comparability on a worldwide basis. This is often supported by a system of internal audit, whereby procedures are monitored to ensure that company policies are being followed correctly and the assets of the organization are being safeguarded.

Budgeting

The strategic planning process provides the organization with a set of financial plans reflecting the key strategic moves to be made in the long-term future of the organization. As explained in previous chapters, these then need to be translated into detailed operational plans for the immediate future in the form of the budget. The key advantages of the budgeting process are centred on the benefits to be derived from communicating the plans for the organization downwards to operational managers and by then encouraging those managers to plan for the effective use of resources. These benefits apply equally to the multinational organization. However, certain additional issues need to be considered. At a practical level it is necessary to establish in which currency the budget should be prepared and how the foreign currency element should be dealt with when translating the budget from one currency to another. This will have implications for subsequently monitoring performance. On a wider scale the budgeting process is affected by cultural differences, national differences in budget perceptions and the attitude towards performance evaluation. Research based on US and Japanese managers indicates that there can be significant differences in the way the budgeting process is used. Finally, the budgeting process for a multinational organization will be significantly more affected by unstable economic environments, creating difficulties in achieving effective forecasts. The crucial factors in making sales and profit forecasts are normally competition, size, market share, facilities and service levels. However, other factors such as inflation and erratic exchange rates will also need to be considered and this can mean that accurate sales forecasts are impossible to complete.

Performance evaluation systems

Many of the problems relating to performance evaluation apply to multinational operations as they do to domestic operations. With any system it is difficult to establish a single measure that is appropriate to all types of operation and yet there are further difficulties associated with assessing performance with a multiple set of criteria. Research has indicated that the most commonly used measures of financial performance used in foreign subsidiaries include measures similar to those used in domestic subsidiaries, and that return on investment is the most widely used. This is most commonly used in the form of profit before interest and tax or profit after interest but before tax. However, owing to the inherent problems in using this measure, as described in Chapter 8, supplementary measures are nearly always used and this is often comparison to budget. The most commonly used budgets are capital budgets, operating budgets, cash flows and balance sheets. Other important ratios include return on sales, return on assets, return on equity and return on investment. In addition to these, the measurement of cash flows has become increasingly important, focusing on long-term cash flows discounted in the same way as with capital budgeting. The extent of the use of these performance criteria varies from culture to culture, and research has indicated that there are significant differences between cultures in the importance of performance criteria. Shields *et al.* (1991) researched this area by undertaking an extensive survey of the performance evaluation practices used by a variety of general US and Japanese multinational organizations. The results shown in Table 14.4 indicate the performance criteria considered to be the most important when evaluating divisional managers.

Finally, it is important to separate performance evaluation of the manager from that of the operation because a profitable unit can exist independent of good management and a good manager can work in a difficult and unprofitable environment.

International taxation issues

Systems for implementing taxation vary from country to country, but it is commonly accepted that each country has the right to tax profits earned within its borders. This implies that foreign source profit should be taxed where earned and not mixed with domestic profit, and that earnings from foreign subsidiaries are not taxed in the parent company until remitted as a dividend to shareholders.

The complexity regarding taxation means that a multinational organization must consider a range of factors based on the type and location of the operation.

Table 14.4 Performance criteria considered to be the most important when evaluating divisional managers

	Japan (%)	USA (%)
Sales	69	19
Sales growth	28	28
Market share	12	19
Asset turnover	7	13
Return on sales	30	26
Return on investment	7	75
Controllable profit	28	49
Residual income	20	13
Profit minus corporate costs	44	38
Manufacturing costs	28	13
Other	8	17

The nature of the operation, whether it be based on export, licensing, branches or subsidiaries, will affect the assessment for taxation, and the location of the operation may mean that benefits can be derived from local tax incentives, tax rates and tax treaties. As an example, tax laws in some countries encourage investment through capital allowances and 'tax holidays', whereby tax payments are cancelled for a given period. Consequently, international tax planning forms an essential part of the management of multinational operations.

Risk management

Increasingly, an assessment of risk forms part of the job role of the hospitality and tourism accountant. Expansion overseas brings with it a range of risks classified as pure risk and speculative risk. Pure risks are associated with hazards such as health, safety, environment and security, whereas speculative risks are associated with business, finance, investment human resources, information technology strategy and politics. The risk of expanding overseas is dependent on the region, but Table 14.5 summarizes some of the risks arising.

Some periodicals such as *Euromoney* produce country risk ratings for subscribers on a regular basis. The scoring system is based on an assessment of the following weighted criteria:

- political risk
- economic performance

- debt indicators
- debt in default
- credit ratings
- access to bank finance
- access to short-term finance
- access to capital markets
- discount on forfeiting.

Source: Pike and Neale (2003).

Table 14.5 Risks associated with expanding overseas

	Examples
Pure risk	
Security	Fraud, corruption, embezzlement, theft, terrorism
Environment	Local legislation, public liability, local hazards
Health and safety	Health hazards, transport hazards
Quality assurance	Poor quality control standards
Speculative risk	
Investment/finance	Local laws with regard to profit repatriation, taxation, nationalization
Commercial	Price controls, inflations, prices of local labour and commodities
Competition	Other foreign companies, national companies
Political	Instability, foreign trade policy, diplomatic relations
Cultural	Attitudes, behaviours, social expectations

Adapted from Waring and Glendon (2002) *Managing Risk*.

Summary This chapter has reviewed some of the strategic reasons for the development of overseas investments. The global hospitality industry is continuing to expand, with opportunities for further expansion arising in several areas of the world including Europe. In practice, a range of factors needs to be considered before a decision to invest is made. Often there are many unquantifiable aspects as well as the more obvious tangible risks, and a full assessment is needed before the final investment decision is made.

Questions

1 Prepare a presentation analysing the risk features likely to impact on the global hospitality industry in the twenty-first century using the methodologies for risk management and risk assessment.

2 Your hotel company is an international player looking to expand its presence in Asia and is considering the suitability of an investment in the

Islamic Republic of Iran. You have been asked to prepare a presentation outlining the full range of risks to which the investing company is likely to be exposed with this investment. Use an appropriate range of risk management models to structure your analysis.

3 Review the annual published accounts of a company operating in the hospitality and tourism sector and examine the extent of the international activities. Review the Chairman's statement to find information about the overseas development strategy. Write a short report to the Chairman outlining the issues to be considered before investing in an overseas operation.

4 Review the published accounts of an international operator in the hospitality sector and determine its policy with regard to managing foreign exchange.

Further reading

Altinay, L. and Altinay, M. (2003) How will growth be financed by the international hotel companies? *International Journal of Contemporary Hospitality Management* 15(4/5).

Go, F., Sung Soo, P., Uysal, M. and Mihalik, B. (1990) Decision criteria for transnational hotel expansion, *Tourism Management*, Oxford: Butterworth Heinemann.

Mathe, H. and Perras, C. (1994) Successful global strategies for service companies, *Long Range Planning* 27(1): 36–49.

Radebaugh, L. and Gray, S. (1993) *International Accounting and Multinational Enterprises* (3rd edn), New York: John Wiley.

Shimell, P. (2001) *The Universe of Risk: How Top Business Leaders Control Risk and Achieve Success*, London: FT Prentice Hall.

Useful website

www.hvsinternational.com/emails/rushletter/2004-11-02.htm

References

Dunning, J. H. (1981) *International Production and the Multinational Enterprise*, London: Allen and Unwin.

Knabe, R., Cumming, R., Hargreaves, E. and Purdy, M. (2000) Hot on the heels of the brewing disposal? *Dresdner Kleinwort Benson Research*, 10 August.

Pike, R. and Neale, B. (2003) *Corporate Finance and Investment: Decisions and Strategies*, London: Prentice Hall.

Shields, M., Chow, C., Kato, Y. and Nakagawa, Y. (1991) Management accounting practices in the US and Japan: comparative survey findings and research implications, *Journal of International Financial Management and Accounting* 3(1).

Simmonds, A. and Azieres, O. (1989) *Accounting for Europe: Success by 2000 AD?* Touche Ross Europe.

Waring, A. and Glendon, A. (2002) *Managing Risk: Critical Issues for Survival and Success into the 21st Century*, London: Thomson Learning.

15 | The way forward

About this chapter

The role of the accountant in the hospitality, tourism and leisure industries has changed considerably over the past decade. Advances in integrated technology have enabled the management accountants' role to be more dynamic in the business, while restructuring with flatter structures has meant that many organizations are no longer reliant on a full accounting team located at every unit. It is widely recognized in management literature that knowledge management and information sharing is the key to organizational success and competitive advantage. Clearly, the finance role has a significant part to play in ensuring that useful information is gathered and shared across the organization. This final chapter will explore some of the current models used in the hospitality, tourism and leisure industry for ensuring the effective control and use of business assets in the sector.

Learning objectives On completion of this chapter you should be able to:

- appreciate the changing role of the finance function in the hospitality, tourism and leisure industries
- appreciate the current factors impacting on the provision and use of information for business control and planning
- understand the factors that have driven the nature of change in the hospitality, tourism and leisure sectors.

Introduction

It is widely reported that during the past 30 years the international hospitality industry has witnessed a period of tremendous change which, in turn, must surely have implications for all of the functional activities in the business, and the finance function is no exception. The growth in multinational operations with diversified interests highlights the growing need for accurate and timely information for performance measurement and control. Research undertaken by Burgess (1995) focusing on the changing role of the hotel financial controller confirmed this, as has subsequent research commissioned by the British Association of Hospitality Accountants. The research highlights the fact that the modern controller is increasingly faced with the challenge of harnessing the tremendous potential to be derived from the continuing application of information technology to the systems for measurement and control to ensure that optimum benefit is being provided. Increasingly, hierarchical structures are perceived as no longer relevant and instead a team-based approach is more appropriate.

The role of the manager in the hospitality industry is also changing, with more emphasis being placed on commercial skills and entrepreneurship in many of the larger organizations. This can mean that the unit manager and departmental heads are increasingly required to take a more active role in strategic planning, forecasting and budgeting, and monetary control. The provision and management of 'business intelligence' is crucial.

The purpose of this book has been to highlight weaknesses in the traditional approaches to management accounting in the hospitality and tourism industries, although it is widely recognized that management accounting in many industry sectors has failed to keep up with advances in other aspects of business practice and strategy. It has already been noted in Chapter 1 that there are several specific issues currently impacting on the hospitality and tourism industry that will have a far-reaching effect on the future nature of hospitality finance systems.

Changing roles

Traditionally, the role of the accounting function has been heavily biased towards the comparison of costs with revenues, while focusing on the internal operations of the business. Accounts are by definition historical and inward looking, and accounting practice is governed by the underlying principle of prudence. In many hospitality and tourism operations the accountant is still traditionally viewed as the 'bean counter', focusing on historical results. Although there is still some relevance in this role, in most modern organizations it has become essential to produce accounting information with a strategic perspective. In practice this means reviewing not just internal operations but also the external environment and the role of the competition. From generic research by the Hackett Group (2005), the allocation of finance staff time across a range of business sectors is illustrated in Figure 15.1.

Despite advances in information technology, transaction analysis still accounts for two-thirds of finance staff time; however, decision support and risk management are viewed with increasing importance.

The results of an extensive study by Collier and Gregory in 1994, focusing on the practice of strategic management in hotel groups in particular, concluded that strategic management accounting was being increasingly used for planning, evaluating market conditions and competitor analysis. The research identified two main strategic management accounting areas, these being the provision of information for assisting in the development of strategic plans, and the monitoring of

Figure 15.1 Allocation of finance staff time

Source: Hackett Group (2005) (https://portal.thehackettgroup.com).

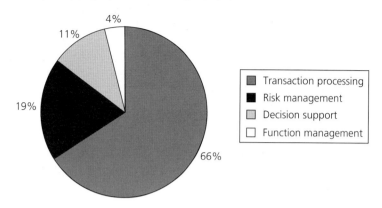

the market, competitors' price structures and competitors' costs. The development of strategic plans included the preparation of long-range plans up to 5 years in advance, including profit and loss account, balance sheet and cash flow, using spreadsheet technology for modelling. The monitoring of the market is made easier owing to the open nature of the industry and the availability of some revenue and cost data, and as a result the research indicates that regular monitoring of the competition is often included in the remit of the accounting function. Consequently, the accountant's role in the hospitality and tourism sector is to be viewed increasingly as a member of the management team bringing specific expertise to the decision-making process.

The role of the operational manager in the hospitality and tourism industry has also changed dramatically in response to the increasingly competitive environment where decisions need to be made locally and quickly. Failure to make the right business decision can lead to loss of profitability or even business demise. As a result, to make quick, frequent and correct decisions the available supporting information needs to be timely and of the necessary quality. Consequently, the role of the finance function is to deliver high-quality decision support services to its customers. The finance function needs to consider the following questions carefully:

- Who are our customers?
- Do we need to clarify the information produced to assist managers to make decisions based on this information?
- What services do other functions in the business need from us?
- What is our strategy for the production and delivery of information?
- How do we monitor whether we have met our customers' needs?

Gould and Stathis (2005) suggest that the finance function in any organization has both internal and external customers, as illustrated in Table 15.1. They further

Table 15.1 Internal and external customers of a finance function

Internal	External
Human resources	Banks, capital markets
Purchasing	Industry regulators
Brand managers	Customers
Sales and distribution departments	Suppliers
Research and development	Other stakeholders
Operations managers and departmental heads	

Source: Adapted from Gould and Stathis (2005) The future of finance, *Financial Management*, July/August.

suggest that the finance function can operate best as a commercial support device when the following conditions exist:

- a relatively stable business model
- reliable data
- well-established processes
- competence in using key financial tools such as investment appraisal and managing for value
- a decentralized organization with a culture of employee empowerment.

Critical success factors for the industry

Management accounting in the hospitality and tourism industry is governed by the operational features of an industry that is characterized by a fixed supply of certain resources such as rooms and covers, perishability and seasonality of the product, and high fixed costs, in particular, labour and maintenance. Research published by the Centre for Hospitality Performance at Surrey University and discussed in more detail in Chapter 1 concludes that there are seven core elements of best practice, which include a range of both internal and external factors.

Assuming that the fundamental criteria for location, market and quality have been met, monitoring and controlling the business is a fundamental factor in ensuring business success. Effective cost control throughout the business requires applying well-known techniques such as process engineering consistently and thoroughly in every aspect of the operation. Payroll is the largest single controllable cost in most hospitality and tourism operations and savings in this area will have a dramatic effect on profitability. Several businesses, particularly those in the contract catering sector, are now employing sophisticated labour scheduling tools to ensure that payroll costs are strategically managed. For catering operations the cost of materials is a significant cost and the larger companies are developing partnership arrangements with suppliers to reduce unit costs. The impact of this has been a marked reduction in standard cost of sales ratios over the past decade. However, public interest in the quality of ingredients used in catering operations may serve to drive these ratios upwards again. In hotels and resorts fixed costs are clearly the most significant cost, with each sale providing a contribution towards covering these costs. Ongoing site maintenance can be as much as 20% of revenues to maintain the quality of five-star operations, and many organizations in the hospitality and tourism industries have outsourced some of these activities to specialist organizations in a bid to reduce costs strategically, but maintain or indeed improve these areas.

Competitor analysis provides the opportunity not only to monitor how well a company has performed but also to track the performance of the competition in terms of revenues and market share.

Historically, medium- and long-term planning is often an activity that the hospitality industry in particular has failed to address adequately and as a result a traditional incremental approach is often adopted. However, evidence suggests that operational mangers at unit levels are increasingly being actively encouraged to improve their financial awareness skills and deploy these in producing regular budgets and forecasts for planning future performance and the effective use of resources.

Knowledge sharing

In recent years the concept of knowledge management has been the subject of considerable interest in management literature. All organizations can be considered as 'constellations of interacted practice' or 'communities of practice' (Wenger, 1998), but typically organizations tend to be classified on the basis of formal structures with communication and reporting based on lines of command. In a seminal article published in 1991, Seely Brown and Duguid suggested that organizations are typically structured on the basis of responsibility, enhancing internal competition and creating boundaries for secrecy and privacy. They suggest that to create synergistic collaboration among workers, learners and innovators, a conceptual reorganization is required. The notion of competitive advantage through effective use of information and communications technology is widely recognized (Senge, 1990; Castells, 1996). Castells suggests that the overall aim must be to create competitive advantage by leveraging economies of scale from all of the business assets, including intellectual capacity and knowledge about suppliers and markets. Senge uses the term learning organization with the objective of developing collective intelligence. Much has been written about the success that the social capital resident in communities of practice has had in improving business performance. In their research, Lesser and Storck (2001) highlight four areas of organizational performance that have been affected by the ongoing activities of communities of practice. These include:

- decreasing the learning curve of new employees
- more rapid response to customer needs and enquiries
- reducing rework and preventing 'reinvention of the wheel'
- spawning new ideas for products and services.

Clearly, fostering knowledge-sharing practices and opening up communication channels in the hospitality, tourism and leisure industries is not only the responsibility of the accounting function, but requires a strategic approach across all functional areas in the business.

The role of information technology

Tremendous advances in technology are now capable of providing the potential for developing information systems that can meet the needs of the current business environment. Information can be processed more quickly, with a wider range of applications providing vast quantities of detail. To harness the benefits to be derived from this, it is essential that the information system is linked to the critical success factors or the key drivers of the business. This includes not just looking backwards at historical performance, but also forecasting into the future to anticipate competitor strategy.

The way in which the business manages its information is crucial to its success, and the integration of the following activities enables business information to be captured and applied as business knowledge:

- electronic point of sale
- stock control and purchasing
- staff scheduling
- forecasting
- financial reporting
- accounting.

Electronic data interchange (EDI) is the process of electronically exchanging business data between organizations. Although slow to be implemented in the UK hospitality and tourism industry, EDI has been used in other industries for several years and finally has now started to be used extensively in the hospitality and tourism sector, particularly in large-scale multiunit operations, as found in the contract catering sector.

EDI is most commonly applied to the purchasing cycle and the subsequent savings in labour costs alone are potentially substantial, leading ultimately to a lower cost of sales. The implementation of EDI systems is still fairly expensive and as yet not a viable option for groups without large buying power. However, as the nature of ownership changes with more UK hotels being owned, managed or represented by larger groups or consortia, the introduction of EDI is potentially more likely.

Assessing profitability by market segment

Traditionally, the hospitality sector has structured its accounts based on regulatory guidelines and the recommendations of the Uniform Accounting System, which was first developed by the Hotel and Catering Economic Development Council in 1969, followed by the US system, the Uniform System for Accounts in Hotels, first published by the Hotel Association of New York City in 1926. The Uniform System may be defined as a manual of instructions for preparing standard financial statements and schedules for the various operating and productive units that make up an operation. The purpose of this manual is to provide a simple formula for the classification of accounts, which can then be adopted by any hotel regardless of size or type. In practice, most of the major hospitality companies use the system or an abridged version. The Uniform System is based on departmental accounting using product and service type as the basis for monitoring revenues and profitability. However, there is increasing interest in customer and market profitability. This includes gaining a better understanding of what drives customers to use the business services, what value the customer receives and what value each customer grouping adds to the business.

Risk management

Increasingly, organizations are being required to develop a co-ordinated strategy with regard to managing risks. The Enterprise Risk Management paper published in 2005 by the International Federation of Risk and Insurance Management Associations suggests that enterprise risk management programmes be established for organizations, which include:

- identifying and assessing the significant risks facing the organization, including the development of risk registers and mapping
- developing risk mitigation strategies
- managing residual risk through techniques such as insurance, hedging and other alternative techniques
- risk reporting to senior management and the board
- monitoring the effectiveness and relevance of risk management policies and procedures.

International accounting

In Chapter 3 the impact of the introduction of international reporting standards was discussed, although the full impact of the international requirements for reporting is still to be fully understood with regard to the hospitality, tourism and leisure industries. Management accounting practices generally do not differ across different countries. Businesses across the world are adopting similar integrated data packages, resulting in the standardization of information and reporting formats. Granlund and Lukka (1998) assert that the differences occur not so much in the preparation of internal accounting information, but in the interpretation, where cultural differences come into play. This aspect was considered in more detail in Chapter 14.

Summary   Preparing future managers in the hospitality, tourism and leisure industries with the skills to manage business resources effectively includes enabling them to understand the developments currently impacting on the long-term future of the industry and to be able to harness these changes to drive the industry forward. This is certainly true in the teaching of the finance function, where the education provided should be relevant and specific to the individual needs of the industry to provide the graduate general manager of the future with the multiple skills required to manage the business effectively. This is particularly relevant in the light of research that has indicated (Burgess, 1995) that approximately one-third of graduates specialize in finance as their careers progress. Effective education needs to be supported by research and yet historically the application of research effort to the field of hospitality and tourism finance has been sadly undersubscribed. Therefore, it is exciting to note the emergence of some new projects focusing on specific issues relating to the accounting and information systems. There is clear evidence that effective performance measurement systems are of paramount importance for the future, with a range of specific areas that still merit further investigation, including property valuations, revenue management and market segment accounting, and the financial implications of strategic alliances such as management contracts and franchising. It is hoped that these aspects will be researched in the not too distant future.

Questions   1   What factors do you think are reshaping the role of the financial controller and the finance function in the hospitality, tourism and leisure industries?

2   To what extent does the finance function have involvement in measuring and managing quality and customer value?

3   What type of role do you see the financial controller taking in 10 years' time?

Practical   1   Research the following terms:
activity
(a) Business process engineering

(b) Benchmarking

(c) Environmental cost management

(d) Learning organizations

(e) Knowledge management.

Further
reading   Nahapiet, J. and Ghoshal, S. (1998) Social capital, intellectual capital and the organizational advantage, *Academy of Management Review* 23(2): 242–66.

References   Burgess, C. (1995) Five years on, survey of hotel financial controllers, *Financial Management Beyond 2000*, Conference, Malta.
Castells, M. (1996), *The Rise of the Network Society*, Boston, MA: Blackwell.
Collier, P. and Gregory, A. (1994) Strategic management accounting: a UK hotel sector case study, *International Journal of Contemporary Hospitality Management* 7(1): 18–23.

Gould, S. and Stathis, M. (2005) The future of finance, *Financial Management* July/August.

Granlund, M. and Lukka, K. (1998) It's a small world of management accounting practices, *Journal of Management Accounting Research* 10: 151–79.

Lesser, E.L. and Storck, J. (2001) Communities of practice and organizational performance, *IBM Systems Journal* 40(4): 831–42.

Seely Brown, J. and Duguid, P. (1991) Organisational learning and communities of practice: toward a unified view of working, learning and innovation, *Institute of Management Sciences*.

Senge, P. (1990) *The Fifth Discipline: The Art and Practice of the Learning Organisation*, New York: Doubleday.

Wenger, E. (1998) *Communities of Practice; Learning, Meaning and Identity*, Cambridge: Cambridge University Press.

Appendix 1: Present value table

Present value of £1 in *n* years at discount rate *r*.

	Discount rate (*r*)										
Periods (*n*)	1%	2%	3%	4%	5%	6%	7%	8%	9%	10%	
1	0.990	0.980	0.971	0.962	0.952	0.943	0.935	0.926	0.917	0.909	1
2	0.980	0.961	0.943	0.925	0.907	0.890	0.873	0.857	0.842	0.826	2
3	0.971	0.942	0.915	0.889	0.864	0.840	0.816	0.794	0.772	0.751	3
4	0.961	0.924	0.888	0.855	0.823	0.792	0.763	0.735	0.708	0.683	4
5	0.951	0.906	0.863	0.822	0.784	0.747	0.713	0.681	0.650	0.621	5
6	0.942	0.888	0.837	0.790	0.746	0.705	0.666	0.630	0.596	0.564	6
7	0.933	0.871	0.813	0.760	0.711	0.665	0.623	0.583	0.547	0.513	7
8	0.923	0.853	0.789	0.731	0.677	0.627	0.582	0.540	0.502	0.467	8
9	0.914	0.837	0.766	0.703	0.645	0.592	0.544	0.500	0.460	0.424	9
10	0.905	0.820	0.744	0.676	0.614	0.558	0.508	0.463	0.422	0.386	10
11	0.896	0.804	0.722	0.650	0.585	0.527	0.475	0.429	0.388	0.350	11
12	0.887	0.788	0.701	0.625	0.557	0.497	0.444	0.397	0.356	0.319	12
13	0.879	0.773	0.681	0.601	0.530	0.469	0.415	0.368	0.326	0.290	13
14	0.870	0.758	0.661	0.577	0.505	0.442	0.388	0.340	0.299	0.263	14
15	0.861	0.743	0.642	0.555	0.481	0.417	0.362	0.315	0.275	0.239	15
	11%	12%	13%	14%	15%	16%	17%	18%	19%	20%	
1	0.901	0.893	0.885	0.877	0.870	0.862	0.855	0.847	0.840	0.833	1
2	0.812	0.797	0.783	0.769	0.756	0.743	0.731	0.718	0.706	0.694	2
3	0.731	0.712	0.693	0.675	0.658	0.641	0.624	0.609	0.593	0.579	3
4	0.659	0.636	0.613	0.592	0.572	0.552	0.534	0.516	0.499	0.482	4
5	0.593	0.567	0.543	0.519	0.497	0.476	0.456	0.437	0.419	0.402	5
6	0.535	0.507	0.480	0.456	0.432	0.410	0.390	0.370	0.352	0.335	6
7	0.482	0.452	0.425	0.400	0.376	0.354	0.333	0.314	0.296	0.279	7
8	0.434	0.404	0.376	0.351	0.327	0.305	0.285	0.266	0.249	0.233	8
9	0.391	0.361	0.333	0.308	0.284	0.263	0.243	0.225	0.209	0.194	9
10	0.352	0.322	0.295	0.270	0.247	0.227	0.208	0.191	0.176	0.162	10
11	0.317	0.287	0.261	0.237	0.215	0.195	0.178	0.162	0.148	0.135	11
12	0.286	0.257	0.231	0.208	0.187	0.168	0.152	0.137	0.124	0.112	12
13	0.258	0.229	0.204	0.182	0.163	0.145	0.130	0.116	0.104	0.093	13
14	0.232	0.205	0.181	0.160	0.141	0.125	0.111	0.099	0.088	0.078	14
15	0.209	0.183	0.160	0.140	0.123	0.108	0.095	0.084	0.074	0.065	15

Appendix 2: Annuity table

Present value of £1 receivable at the end of each year for *n* years at discount rate *r*.

					Discount rate (r)						
Years (*n*)	1%	2%	3%	4%	5%	6%	7%	8%	9%	10%	
1	0.990	0.980	0.971	0.962	0.952	0.943	0.935	0.926	0.917	0.909	1
2	1.970	1.942	1.913	1.886	1.859	1.833	1.808	1.783	1.759	1.736	2
3	2.941	2.884	2.829	2.775	2.723	2.673	2.624	2.577	2.531	2.487	3
4	3.902	3.808	3.717	3.630	3.546	3.465	3.387	3.312	3.240	3.170	4
5	4.853	4.713	4.580	4.452	4.329	4.212	4.100	3.993	3.890	3.791	5
6	5.795	5.601	5.417	5.242	5.076	4.917	4.767	4.623	4.486	4.355	6
7	6.728	6.472	6.230	6.002	5.786	5.582	5.389	5.206	5.033	4.868	7
8	7.652	7.325	7.020	6.733	6.463	6.210	5.971	5.747	5.535	5.335	8
9	8.566	8.162	7.786	7.435	7.108	6.802	6.515	6.247	5.995	5.759	9
10	9.471	8.983	8.530	8.111	7.722	7.360	7.024	6.710	6.418	6.145	10
11	10.37	9.787	9.253	8.760	8.306	7.887	7.499	7.139	6.805	6.495	11
12	11.26	10.58	9.954	9.385	8.863	8.384	7.943	7.536	7.161	6.814	12
13	12.13	11.35	10.63	9.986	9.394	8.853	8.358	7.904	7.487	7.103	13
14	13.00	12.11	11.30	10.56	9.899	9.295	8.745	8.244	7.786	7.367	14
15	13.87	12.85	11.94	11.12	10.38	9.712	9.108	8.559	8.061	7.606	15
	11%	12%	13%	14%	15%	16%	17%	18%	19%	20%	
1	0.901	0.893	0.885	0.887	0.870	0.862	0.855	0.847	0.840	0.833	1
2	1.713	1.690	1.668	1.647	1.626	1.605	1.585	1.566	1.547	1.528	2
3	2.444	2.402	2.361	2.322	2.283	2.246	2.210	2.174	2.140	2.106	3
4	3.102	3.037	2.974	2.914	2.855	2.798	2.743	2.690	2.639	2.589	4
5	3.696	3.605	3.517	3.433	3.352	3.274	3.199	3.127	3.058	2.991	5
6	4.231	4.111	3.998	3.889	3.784	3.685	3.589	3.498	3.410	3.326	6
7	4.712	4.564	4.423	4.288	4.160	4.039	3.922	3.812	3.706	3.605	7
8	5.146	4.968	4.799	4.639	4.487	4.344	4.207	4.078	3.954	3.837	8
9	5.537	5.328	5.132	4.946	4.772	4.607	4.451	4.303	4.163	4.031	9
10	5.889	5.650	5.426	5.216	5.019	4.833	4.659	4.494	4.339	4.192	10
11	6.207	5.938	5.687	5.453	5.234	5.029	4.836	4.656	4.486	4.327	11
12	6.492	6.194	5.918	5.660	5.421	5.197	4.988	4.793	4.611	4.439	12
13	6.750	6.424	6.122	5.842	5.583	5.342	5.118	4.910	4.715	4.533	13
14	6.982	6.628	6.302	6.002	5.724	5.468	5.229	5.008	4.802	4.611	14
15	7.191	6.811	6.462	6.142	5.847	5.575	5.324	5.092	4.876	4.675	15

Index